With Best Wis...
Diana Gyrm.

D0742799

Beyond the Chilcotin

Ken and Pan on a cattle drive, 1956. PHOTO: RICHARD HARRINGTON

BEYOND THE CHILCOTIN

On the Home Ranch with Pan Phillips

Diana Phillips

HARBOUR PUBLISHING

Harbour Publishing Co. Ltd.
P.O. Box 219, Madeira Park, BC, V0N 2H0
www.harbourpublishing.com

Dust jacket photographs by Richard Harrington. All Harrington images courtesy
the Stephen Bulger Gallery, with permission from the Harrington estate. Addi-
tional photographs courtesy of the author unless otherwise stated.
Edited by Meg Taylor
Cartography by Bernie Neary
Digital mapping from the National Topographic Database, Natural Resources
Canada
Cover design by Anna Comfort
Printed in Canada on chlorine-free, FSC certified paper made with 30% post-
consumer fibre.

Harbour Publishing acknowledges financial support from the Government
of Canada through the Book Publishing Industry Development Program and
the Canada Council for the Arts, and from the Province of British Columbia
through the BC Arts Council and the Book Publishing Tax Credit.

Library and Archives Canada Cataloguing in Publication

Phillips, Diana, 1945–
     Beyond the Chilcotin : on the home ranch with Pan Phillips / Diana
Phillips.

Includes index.
ISBN 978-1-55017-447-2

     1. Phillips, Diana, 1945–. 2. Ranch life–British Columbia–Chilcotin
River Region. 3. Phillips, Pan, 1910–1983. 4. Chilcotin River Region (B.C.)–
Biography. I. Title.
FC3845.C445Z49 2008   971.1'75   C2008-904851-2

To Elaine Scott

And to my family: my sons, Jon, James and Wesley; my daughters-in-law, Dawn, Tammy and Katie; my grandchildren, Amanda and Jared, Teagan and Logan, and Reagen, Tanner and Rayen; and my great-grandchildren, Kaylie, Nathan and Araya.

Here's hoping your trail is a long one
Plain and easy to ride
May your dry camps be few
And health ride with you
To the pass on the Big Divide

—Charles M. Russell

Contents

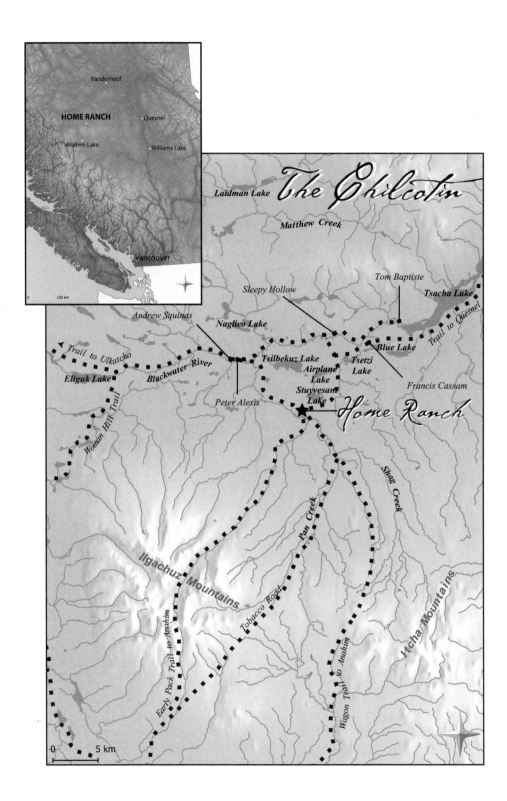

Vanderhoof

HOME RANCH

Anahim Lake

Quesnel

Williams Lake

Vancouver

0   100 km

Laidman Lake

The Chilcotin

Matthew Creek

Sleepy Hollow

Tom Baptiste

Tsacha Lake

Andrew Squinas

Naglico Lake

Trail to Quesnel

Trail to Ulkatcho

Blue Lake

Tsilbekuz Lake

Tsetzi Lake

Eliguk Lake

Blackwater River

Airplane Lake

Stuyvesant Lake

Francis Cassam

Woman Hill Trail

Peter Alexis

Home Ranch

Shag Creek

Pan Creek

Ilgachuz Mountains

Tobacco Road

Itcha Mountains

Early Pack Trail to Anahim

Wagon Trail to Anahim

0   5 km

Home Ranch, as seen from the northwest, 1960. PHOTO: RICHARD HARRINGTON

Preface

In the summer of 2006 I was able to visit the Home Ranch, where I grew up. Riding a saddle horse from Anahim Lake, I followed the original trail my father cut in 1941 over the pass between the Ilgachuz and the Itcha Mountains.

My father, Pan Phillips, and his partner, Rich Hobson, arrived in this wild, unsettled country in 1935. Here, they formed the Frontier Cattle Company and raised large herds of Hereford cattle and many horses as well. The cattle company was liquidated in 1944. My father, with my mother, then ranched here till 1970 when they sold the Home Ranch. Within five years, the place was abandoned.

Visiting the cairn that we had built for our parents after their passing, I sat for a long time with both sad and happy memories of the twenty-five years I had spent in this beautiful, peaceful setting. The Itcha and Ilgachuz Mountains rise up against the sky. Large stands of spruce and pines, dotted with poplar and willow, surround the wild meadows that now, after thirty-one years of being deserted, have almost completely returned to the way they must have looked when my father arrived so many years before.

At the time the ranch was sold, from this pine-covered ridge on the north side of the meadow, one could see the ranch house, barn and outbuildings. Fences ran in all directions. The meadows were covered with stands of hay. Horses and cows stood in the pastures.

Today, years later, the only thing I could see from the ridge was the roof of the barn. The brush and willow have returned, covering a great deal of the meadow. The log fences have long ago fallen and rotted in the thick grasses that grow in the area. When the barn falls, as it soon will after seventy years of rain, wind and snow, there will be nothing man-made visible from this spot. Once the hub of Blackwater activities, where herds of cattle and horses grazed, the Home Ranch has returned to nature.

My love of the country keeps my memory alive to recall things that meant so much to me. The pleasant smell of wood smoke and freshly mowed hay. The wonderful silence that the bush is capable of. The cries of the spring birds, the sounds the creek water makes as it flows over the gravel bottoms, and the far-off tinkling of horse bells accompanying the sounds of children's laughter.

This book is the story of my life on the Home Ranch. I have relied on my mother's diaries, my own diaries and most of all, my memory.

I would like to thank the people who told me stories, some of which ended up in this book. I relied on the following books for research: *Our Story* by Mickey Dorsey, Rich Hobson's books, *Grass Beyond the Mountains* and *Nothing Too Good for a Cowboy*, *The Cowboy at Work* by Fay E. Ward, and the *Encyclopedia of British Columbia*. My thanks to Fran and Butch Page and Christine Peters, who read the rough draft and helped with corrections and comments and words of encouragement. Elaine Scott spent hours on the computer helping me put all this together. Her constant encouragement with the words "It will happen!" kept me going. Thank you, Elaine, for all you did! Margaret Harrington kindly allowed me the use of so many of Richard's wonderful photos. My thanks also go to my editor, Meg Taylor, my copy editor, Ruth Gaskill, my publisher, Howard White, and everyone at Harbour Publishing for putting this book together and making a lifelong dream into a reality. To all of you, thank you!

CHAPTER 1

The Beginning

When my father, Pan Phillips, left Wyoming in the fall of 1934, it was with a dream to start a cattle ranch. He had met Rich Hobson earlier that year in Dubois, Wyoming. The two had become friends, and when Dad figured there had to be cattle country in British Columbia and decided he'd travel north to find it, he asked Rich to go with him. They set forth in a Ford panel truck, which they nicknamed "the Bloater."

They crossed the Canadian border on October 15, 1934, and by the time they reached Anahim Lake, a small ranching and trapping community two hundred miles west of Williams Lake, the weather had turned bitterly cold. They quickly built a small log cabin, planning to spend the winter there. Cyrus Bryant, a rancher in the area, had already spent a number of winters on the frigid Anahim Lake plateau and knew the greenhorns from Wyoming would freeze. With his wife and daughters wintering in the town of Williams Lake, there was room for the two newcomers in the Bryants' cozy little cabin. So Dad and Rich were invited to spend the winter with Cyrus and his son, Alfred, learning about the country and its inhabitants and buying a string of good horses.

In the spring when the days warmed and the snow melted, they gathered their supplies. With Andy Holte, a local frontiersman and rancher, and his son, Tommy, as their guides, they crossed the Ilgachuz Mountains. From the summit they looked north and for the first time

Rich Hobson and Pan Phillips with "the Bloater" at Anahim Lake, British Columbia, mid-1930s. PHILLIPS FAMILY PHOTO

saw the open grassland that would later become the Home Ranch. It would be the only home I'd know for the first nineteen years of my life.

The wild meadowland that Dad and Rich settled on in the spring of 1935 ran from what was later named Pan Creek (after my dad) east for a mile, then turned north for another mile. There was an abundance of wild grasses—blue-joint, brome grass and Kentucky bluegrass. The higher ground produced a great variety of highland grass. Later, reed canary grass was planted and grew up to six feet high in the wetter areas. Pine and spruce trees surrounded the meadow. Pockets of poplar and large willows grew along the sloughs. A steep, pine-covered hill rose at the south end of the meadow; the Pan and Shag creeks met at the base of this hill. From there the water flowed westward for some distance through a thick growth of large spruce to join up with Carnlick Creek. This was the spot that Dad and Rich chose for their first cabin. The ground was high and dry, close to water and sheltered by the spruce.

While Dad travelled with a string of pack horses to Bella Coola on the coast to buy supplies, Rich and Tommy Holte built the first log cabin on the banks of Pan Creek. The cabin was about fourteen by eighteen feet with three windows, a plank floor and a sod roof. Once

Pan in Anahim Lake, mid-1930s. PHILLIPS FAMILY PHOTO

The first cabin at Home Ranch, built in 1935. PHOTO: UTE MOHR

the cabin was complete, they built corrals from the standing pine and a pasture to hold the horses.

Hay had to be put up for the horses, but first they had to get a Massey-Harris mower and McCormick rake hauled in from Bella Coola. This was no easy feat. The little Norwegian settlement of Bella Coola was about 140 miles away at the head of a saltwater channel. There was a Hudson's Bay Company trading post there, and the Union Steamship visited Bella Coola weekly, hauling passengers and freight from Vancouver.

With a string of fourteen pack horses, Dad crossed the Ilgachuz Mountains, blazing trail as he went so that he'd have some idea on his return with heavily loaded horses where the best going was. Even on the best route, he encountered muskeg, rock and windfall. They had a steep climb out of the south end of the Carnlick valley. This climb was hard on the horses, and most of them became sore and galled. High in the mountain pass, he made his way across a glacier. Then he had to find a reasonably dry and passable trail down the south side of the mountain to the Christensen ranch at Behind Meadows. Nearly a week later he reached Anahim Lake. From Anahim Lake, he took the Lunaas Pack Trail down its steep drop to Precipice Valley, then the Sugar Camp Trail with a much steeper and narrower descent into the Bella Coola valley. (These were well-travelled trails, used by the Anahim Lake packers.) Forty miles farther he reached the settlement of Bella Coola, where he could purchase equipment and supplies. Everything had to be packed in to the Home Ranch.

In the 1930s, a fellow by the name of Maxie Hickman lived in Stuie at the head of the Bella Coola valley, and he provided one of Dad's stopovers when he was taking the pack string to and from Bella Coola. Even today, the trip down to the village is an adventure; the highway is extremely steep, with grades of up to eighteen percent.

In Bella Coola, Dad met up with Alfred Bryant, who joined him for the return trip. They were two weeks late in returning with the equipment needed for haying. Alfred stayed to help, and was there for the first stack of hay ever put up in Blackwater country, then left to do his own haying. Tommy helped Dad and Rich stack enough hay to winter the horses. Then he went home to help Andy finish the haying at their ranch, returning to the Blackwater in late September.

Later that fall, Dad travelled to Vancouver to have his appendix removed, and Rich returned to Wyoming to talk to George Pennoyer in Dubois about financing the Blackwater cattle operation. George had told them when they left Wyoming that if they managed to find good cattle country, he would give them financial backing. Getting control over a vast amount of land, raising money for the enterprise and forming the cattle company took the next eighteen months. In the spring of 1937, George finally sent a wire with permission to purchase some cattle.

Dad and Rich bought seventy-five pairs of Hereford cattle and bulls that spring for a total of thirteen hundred dollars. These animals then had to be driven from the Chilcotin to pasture in the Blackwater. Dad, Alfred Bryant and Mac MacEwen, who was from the Anahim Lake area, went with the cattle. It was a very slow drive because of the young calves, and it was early July before the herd was pushed over the summit, across the glacier and into the Carnlick valley in the Ilgachuz Mountains. This wide valley was filled with good grass. It was there the cattle were to spend the summer. A fence was built across the lower end of the valley to keep them from drifting down Carnlick Creek.

In spite of the fence, the cattle had scattered by fall. It took Rich and Charlie Forrester, a hired hand, some time to round them up. They were then driven in the cold and snow some eighty miles to Batnuni, where there was enough hay to winter them.

The first two years were a busy time for Dad and Rich. They cleared the land as best they could, building fences and hauling in equipment together. They had to learn about the country so that they and their cattle could get through the first winters.

At this time Kluskus and Ulkatcho Indians were scattered through-out the Blackwater country. Only one white man, Jack Day, trapped in the area. In winter, the Kluskus lived in cabins; in summer, they lived in tents or lean-tos. Very few spoke English, only some of the men. They travelled about in summer, hunting and fishing, the women drying the meat and tanning the hides. They had horses and dogs. Because very few of them had big rifles, they used the dogs to run game till the animal holed up, usually in water, and then they were able to shoot it with a .22-calibre rifle.

When they first arrived in Blackwater country, Dad and Rich could not believe the number of moose. They were everywhere! The Indians told Dad that the moose had arrived in the area only a few years before. Prior to that, the area had been an elk habitat. As a young girl I often picked up elk antlers partially buried in the moss of the forest floor or half-sunk into the soft soil of some swamp.

In the summer of 1936, Lester Dorsey and his wife, Mickey, their two small sons and Ole Nucloe Localo arrived at the Home Ranch to begin construction on the ranch house. They built it with a crosscut saw and an axe, for sixty dollars. This was a fairly large undertaking as the building was about thirty by forty feet. It had a long narrow kitchen on the north side, which originally was two rooms. The story goes that Shorty, Dad's second wife (Mom was his third), cut the partition out for firewood! The living room was the largest room and the least used, except for sleeping—a lot of bedding could be put down on that floor. Most of the socializing was done around the kitchen table. There were two small bedrooms and an office. Some years later, my mother made a bigger bedroom by tearing down a partition and eliminating the office.

The logs were unpeeled and hewn on the inside to give the walls a flat appearance. The chinking was moss covered with mud, both inside and out. There was a front door and back door, and all the windows were four or six panes with wooden frames. The floor was made of rough-cut planks, which leaked cold air in the winter. Little treasures would disappear forever if they fell through the cracks in the floor. With Mom scrubbing it weekly with bleach water, over the years the floor was worn smooth and became almost white. The roof was sod but was later covered with shakes cut from straight-grained pine. When Mom arrived from the coast, she covered the walls with cardboard and then papered over them with wallpaper; it brightened the place up and kept the dried mud chinking from falling into the house.

Lester also built a large log barn with a hayloft. The inside of the barn had four double horse stalls and two single horse stalls with mangers. The stalls were planked. Later, one of the double stalls was eliminated and a double cow stanchion for milking was added, complete with a manure trough. Many years later the barn was converted into pens for cow and calf pairs during calving.

A tack shed close to the barn was used to store saddles, pack equipment, shoeing supplies and an anvil and forge. This building also had a sod roof. Near the barn and tack shed was a hayshed built of logs with a shake roof. It had large gaps between the logs to allow for airflow, and two large openings to fork hay into or remove it for feeding.

Near the front of the main ranch house, a small bunkhouse was built for extra hired hands. Towards the river, Dad built a long, low log building where he operated a store in the late 1940s and early '50s. There was a woodshed beside the store; this had only a roof and was open on all four sides.

A cache for staples was built to store perishables, which were brought in only two or three times a year. Great care was taken to keep these staples dry and safe from rodents such as rats, mice, squirrels and chipmunks. It was built on six posts, five or six feet off the ground, and tin was nailed around each post so that the little animals could not crawl up and get into the building. A set of steps got you to the door, and these were removed each time you came out. Trappers had developed this method for the safekeeping of supplies and furs.

Down by the river, close to where the first cabin was built, was a small log building, about ten by ten feet, with dovetailed corners and two large screened windows. This was where we kept our meat. The windows were screened to allow the air to circulate, and it was built in amongst thick spruce so that the sun never reached it.

With the exception of the barn, hayshed and woodshed, all the buildings had sod roofs. A sod roof was constructed as follows: first, a

A buck fence could be built by one man working alone. PHOTO: RICHARD HARRINGTON

*Rich Hobson (in top hat) and Pan Phillips (holding gun) with two ranch hands,
late 1930s.* PHILLIPS FAMILY PHOTO

"punching" was cut, which consisted of smaller logs split in half to make
reasonably flat surfaces and then laid flat-side down on the stringers, side
by side. Hay was then laid on the punching, followed by a foot or more
of sod, and next a pole frame and shakes. The shakes used were cut from
large pine trees with a straight grain.

All corrals and fences were built of log; there were no wire fences in
those days. The corrals were mostly post and log. Around the headquarters
were snake fences, which zigzagged seven feet in each direction to give the
logs an angle so they could be notched and laid one on top of the other;
they were usually built five logs high. For pasture and range fences, a Russell or buck fence was built (also referred to as a stake-and-rider fence).
These fences, made from rails, could be built by one man working alone.

Dad met his second wife, Adelia Brewster (who was better known as
"Shorty"), in Bella Coola on one of his frequent pack trips to the valley.
They were married in Quesnel in 1937. A daughter, Gayle, was born in
February 1939. The marriage did not last long and they soon went their
separate ways.

During this time, the Home Ranch was built up and the Batnuni Ranch, eighty miles to the east, was purchased. Dad and Rich formed the Frontier Cattle Company. While Dad ran the Home Ranch, Rich operated the Batnuni Ranch. Wild meadows were scattered around the country where wild hay was put up in summer to feed the growing herd of Hereford cattle. The horse herd was expanding as well. Saddle horses and teams were needed as well as pack horses. There was also a herd of thoroughbred mares brought up from Vancouver for breeding.

In 1939, cattle prices hit rock bottom. With the outbreak of war, many of the men enlisted, leaving the ranch without enough able-bodied men to look after the large operation. Working the area covered by the Home Ranch and outlying meadows required many hired hands. Even basics, like putting up enough hay for the winter, took a lot of labour. By 1944, Dad and Rich decided it was best to liquidate the Frontier Cattle Company. Dad stayed at the Home Ranch. Rich sold Batnuni Ranch and moved on to Vanderhoof.

CHAPTER 2

My Dad

My father was born on Friday, March 13, 1910, in Pike County, Illinois, and named Floyd. His parents, Loren and Sarah Phillips, were farmers. Dad was the oldest, followed by seven sisters and three brothers.

As a child he always dreamed of living out west, with horses and guns and the freedom of wide-open spaces, mountains and grasslands, ready for whatever might appear over the next mountain. Imagine a cross between a mountain man and a cowboy, and that would have been Dad.

There was hardly enough excitement for him growing up on the family farm. He told us only a few stories from his childhood, mostly he talked about his dream of the cowboy's life. His choice of riding animals was limited to the docile draft horses, milk cows or a few mules. For Christmas one year, Dad received a pair of spurs. These were not the spurs designed for cowboys, but toy spurs, to be used for dress-up in a child's make-believe cowboy world. They were extremely sharp. Dad strapped the spurs on and mounted one of the draft horses. He drove the sharp rowels into the horse's shoulders, which put the horse in a bucking mode, throwing Dad over an apple tree and breaking his wrist.

One day, Granddad and Grandma were going visiting with the horse and buggy. Dad begged to be taken along but was told to stay home. Dad always did pretty much as he pleased, and I'm sure he had that same trait in his childhood. Now I'm not familiar with buggies, but apparently there was a small space under the seat where a child could hide, and that is what Dad did. As horse and buggy trotted down the country road, they met a car. In those days cars were rare, and the horse, never having seen one before, became excited and backed up till the buggy went off the road into a shallow ditch. At that angle, the space under the seat where Dad was hiding suddenly became pinched and he started yelling. Once he was discovered, he was made to walk back home.

Granddad soon purchased a car. Dad's dream then turned to driving this car, which he was not supposed to touch. The opportunity came one day while his parents were away and the car was parked in the barn. He got the car started and into forward gear, but had no idea how to stop it. In fact, he didn't stop till he drove it through the back of the barn!

In 1926, at the age of sixteen, Dad left for Kansas with a friend to work on the threshing crews. When the work ended, Dad didn't return home but went on to Wyoming and worked on ranches from Hudson to Dubois. He was given the name "Wildhorse," later he was nicknamed "Panhandle" and then that got shortened to "Pan," which is what he was called for the rest of his life.

In Wyoming he chased wild horses, catching and breaking them to be sold to the local ranches and for his own use. The best way to catch these horses was at a water hole, which he would fence off. He'd leave the gate open to the unsuspecting horses, and then close it when they went in. He'd have mules with him, and when he roped a horse he'd choke it down and halter it, then tie the horse's halter to the mules and turn them loose. A mule is stubborn and much smarter than a horse. The horse learned to lead, it ate, drank and rested only when the mule did, and in the end the mule took the horse home.

He told us that when he was out camping in the sand country where there were rattlesnakes, it was a common practice to pack a rope braided from horsehair. At night the hair rope was put on the ground in a circle around the laid-out bedroll. Snakes would not cross the hair rope. It saved you the surprise of waking in the morning in the company of a snake that had sought warmth from the cool desert night.

On rare occasions, Dad would write short letters home and he would enclose photos, but he always neglected to tell who was in them! Still, his mother was thrilled to receive anything from her oldest son.

Pan Phillips loved to play tricks on people and was often grinning even when he argued, 1956. PHOTO: RICHARD HARRINGTON

In 1929, when Dad was nineteen, he married seventeen-year-old Caroline Hurtado, a Shoshone girl from Wind River. In the fall of that year they moved to the Phillips family farm in Illinois and spent the winter with Dad's folks. By the spring, however, they had returned to Wyoming as Caroline was homesick and Dad missed the wide-open spaces. Their first son, Homer, was born that spring, and sixteen months later a second son, Melvin, was born. Sometime before 1934 the marriage ended.

Dad returned to Illinois in 1939, his first visit home since settling in BC. All of the siblings were together for the first time, as his sister Hazel and brother John had been born after he left home. A family photo was taken while he was there. He had left Shorty (to whom he was married by then) and their baby daughter at the Home Ranch, but he did bring a silver spoon home for Gayle.

Dad was under six feet in height, had a medium build and very blue eyes. I never knew him when his hair wasn't white but it must

Pan with Whitey at the Quesnel stockyards, 1952. PHOTO: *CARIBOO OBSERVER*

have once been blond. His most striking feature was his nose, which was large and had been referred to as a "hawk nose." (I object since I have the same nose!) He was also called bowlegged and narrow-faced, but that wasn't true either. He was fairly quick-tempered, but I know of only two real fights—one was over his dog and the other over Mom. It seems he thought someone was paying her too much attention! He loved to play tricks on people but didn't like it when the tables were turned. He liked to be the centre of attention and liked to have the last word in an argument. He was very superstitious about Friday the thirteenth, as his mother had been. I have seen him with his horse saddled or a team hooked up to go somewhere before realizing it was Friday the thirteenth, at which point he would turn the horses loose. Once when he was duck hunting, waiting for the flock to come in, he counted the shotgun shells inside his pocket by feel. Discovering thirteen, he threw one away, only to find out later he had thrown his bullet lighter over his shoulder into the bushes.

Dad always kept his hair short and I don't remember him ever having a beard. Often he'd have several days' worth of whiskers, but he would shave as soon as time allowed. No moustaches or sideburns either, even when they were in fashion. He was a good storyteller and would spend hours with company, telling tales and looking at pictures and books.

Dad had a weakness for ice cream and desserts. He also loved moose fat fried along with the red meat. He called it "white meat." If others left the fat on their plates, he'd reach over and take it. Dad loved peanut butter and would sit reading in the evenings with a five-gallon bucket of it beside him, scooping out big spoonfuls and slowly eating it. One time when he finished the bucket of peanut butter, he saw an enormous beetle in the bottom. He swore, "Jesus Christ!" over and over as he stomped through every room in the house. Jesus never did appear despite his repeated calling! He also loved puffed wheat and would buy it in huge cotton bags that stood as high as we did. He'd fill a big serving bowl with the cereal, add milk and sugar, and eat it in the rocking chair while he continued with his reading, milk dribbling down his chin. He constantly overate, especially as he got older.

Short messages were sent out on the radio twice daily for people living in remote areas. During message time we had to be quiet so Dad could hear every word of every message. If we weren't quiet, we were told to shut up—even guests were told to shut up if they'd been there for a day or two. (If they'd just arrived, they would more than likely be excused.) In later years Dad mellowed; he spoiled his horses and showed a great deal more kindness to family members. He truly enjoyed my three boys, whom he called "the mice." I never once heard him tell me he loved me, but I know in my heart that he did, and I like to think I was his favourite child. I was probably the one child most like him, although the other siblings have traits of his. Dad and I would have terrible quarrels. He would be grinning while we argued, but I think he was as mad as I was. I remember once after the evening meal we were arguing about something and fortunately Mom had nearly finished clearing off the table. One of the hired hands was still eating his pie. I was so angry I threw everything that was left on the table at Dad and reached for the pie the poor guy was eating; he grabbed it with both hands and told me to leave his pie alone!

My dad was a very strong, determined and confident person, although somewhat selfish. It was said that Dad made a better friend than he did a husband, but that can be said of a great many men. Though some people said Dad never had an enemy, he was no saint. He did have a lot of friends, including some influential men such as Alex Fraser who, after serving many years as Quesnel's mayor, went on to become the MLA for the Cariboo–Chilcotin Region. Alex helped Dad with any government business he had. Dr. Alec Holley, who was a well-known Quesnel surgeon and good friend, took care of all his medical needs.

Back in the 1960s there was a lot of commotion over Sasquatch or Bigfoot, and whether it really existed or not. It was one of Dad's favourite topics of conversation at that time, as different stories surfaced about Bigfoot. Late one fall while Dad was in the Ilgachuz Mountains with caribou hunters, he claimed to have seen one. I don't know if he wanted his own personal story to tell or if it was true. He said that while he was glassing high up on the snowy mountainside for caribou, he saw what he first believed to be a bear. But then he realized the hairy animal was sitting with its elbows on its knees in front of the snowy entrance to a cave. This is not a position bears use!

In the springtime, the long-legged snipe was one of the first water birds to arrive in the area. It was a very noisy bird. It sounded as though it was saying, "riglar! riglar! riglar!" Dad called them the "Carolina birds" after Caroline Bryant, because he said she never stopped talking (like the birds), and it hurt his ears. We kids called them the "riglar birds."

The Cassam family was on their way to Anahim Lake one day and had stopped at our place for tea. Dad was bragging in Mary Cassam's presence of how he loved beaver tail—it was truly a delicacy, he said. Hearing this, Mary trotted over to the wagon and began digging. She moved bedding, blacked pots, half a dozen mongrel puppies (whose eyes weren't even open yet) and she came up with a large, half-dried beaver tail. The smile on Dad's face diminished a bit, but he thanked her (he fully intended to throw it away as soon as she left). The look changed to horror when she insisted on cooking it for him. She cut a willow pole, sharpened one end and then pushed the point into the end of the beaver tail and proceeded to roast the tail over a bed of coals at their campfire. The skin popped and hissed and rose into pockets of steam between skin and the gristle-like flesh. Taking it from the fire and removing the skin, she presented the beaver tail to Dad, still on the willow pole. I'll say this much for Dad, he did eat some! To me it held about as much appeal as a boiled moose nose, at one time an Indian delicacy.

We had a small flock of sheep, and of course they had to be sheared. At that time, wool fetched a pretty good price. The woollen mills, which bought the fleece, would send us the bags to ship the wool in, along with the dissolving twine. We'd tie up each fleece and cram it into the bags. We had sheared all the sheep and had come in for supper, which Mom was still cooking. Dad was in his favourite chair, reading a magazine, when he let out a yell that was more like a scream. He threw the magazine over his head and started ripping at his shirt. A tick from the sheep had gotten on Dad's clothing and finally made its way down to where it could bite him. I'm not sure they bite as hard as he claims it did, but then I don't want to be bitten by one to find out, either.

When I got to be a teenager and started having male friends around, Dad didn't like it. Most of the time he was downright rude to them. He usually gave them names, like "the kid with the golf ball head" or "that guy with the yeller riding boots." There was the odd time he liked one of them. At an Anahim rodeo once, my date arrived at the camp with a box of candy for Mom and a bottle of good whisky for Dad—now that was a man well liked! By the time I finished dressing for our date, he and Dad had their arms around each other and were doing the two-step by the campfire.

Generally, any men that showed up at the ranch were put to work; the women were teased nearly to death till they either ignored Dad or got even. If they got even they were left alone, but if they got mad Dad was really happy. When the men went riding, Dad usually made sure they were mounted on green horses. Later in his life, he had to avoid those that would buck, so his guests got these half-broken horses. How no one was ever seriously hurt is beyond me, but there were plenty of bruises, scrapes, cuts, torn clothing and sprained ankles. I heard a lot of things like, "Your goddamn old man " or "That old son of a bitch" as they limped down the trail leading some wild-eyed horse that was stepping on their heels or would barely lead. If I liked the guy he got my sympathy; if he wasn't special, I usually laughed too! Then I'd get comments like, "You're as bad as that old bastard." By the time they got back to the ranch they'd settled down some, enough to be civil to Dad, who would be snickering at them. If they really knew horses, they usually wouldn't get on the horses Dad provided; then he'd give them something better. But a lot of our guests got along with these unbroken horses. Others brought their own or rode mine.

Hay was often put up at Sleepy Hollow, the old Jack Thompson place, after Ed Adams bought it in about 1960. If the winter was bad we'd feed horses there; if not, the yearlings and dry cows would be taken there towards spring and fed.

One evening after dinner the hay crew was sitting around the wooden table in the dark cabin with only the light of the kerosene lamp flickering. Dad was there along with five or six others. One of the young guys pulled a handgun and fired it into the ceiling. The hot shell-casing ejected, hitting Dad on the neck, and at the same time the concussion of the blast blew out the light. Dad, holding his neck, started to yell that he'd been shot before he realized what had happened.

Another time at the ranch, we had company and Dad was showing off his handgun. He was standing in the kitchen with one foot up on a chair, talking. (He never seemed to stop talking when we had company.) He had his handgun pointed towards the ceiling and was slowly pulling the trigger as he talked, intent on the story he was telling, when suddenly there was a loud explosion and splinters flew from the ceiling. There was dead silence and everyone was looking at Dad, whose mouth hung open in total shock. He had not known there was a bullet in the chamber. He did recover fast and said, "Scared you boys, eh?" I think he scared himself the worst!

When Dad bought his first tractor, which was an International 250 (from his friend Alex Fraser, the International dealer), he drove it as though it might buck him off. He looked much more relaxed on his saddle horse or up on a wagon seat. He did eventually get used to the tractor, but in the beginning when he wanted to stop he would holler, "Whoa!" and then he would realize that it wasn't a team of horses.

CHAPTER 3

My Mom

My mother, Elizabeth Rosemary Kushner (called Bessie or Betsy when she was young, before she settled on Betty), was born on November 26, 1919, on the family farm. The farm was located south of Cultus Lake and a little north of the US border—so close to the border, in fact, that they received their mail at Maple Falls, Washington. She was the youngest, with three older sisters and three older brothers. Her parents, George and Susan Kushner, had emigrated from Czechoslovakia in the early 1900s. On the small farm they milked cows, raised chickens, and had a large vegetable garden and fruit trees. How they made a living is a mystery to me, but things were different then. I know they sold milk, fruit and vegetables.

Mom was tall—five feet nine inches—and large-boned with dark hair and eyes. Her skin was beautiful till the day she died. Being raised with a religious background she rarely swore and seldom drank, and she frowned on dirty jokes. She had a beautiful voice, and when I was young she sang often. She could even yodel quite well.

She'd dreamed of being a nurse someday, but she never got the education to become one, and she always regretted this. The little community where she grew up had only a grade school and there was no money to go further, and also she was needed at home. Her life on the farm was not easy as her father was an alcoholic and abused her mother. But he never harmed Mom. He would take a one-horse cart down to

Betty on the ferry to Victoria, 1940s. PHILLIPS FAMILY PHOTO

the nearest watering hole on occasion and drink till he passed out. Then one of his drinking buddies would dump him back in the cart and turn the horse loose. The horse would find its way home to the farm, stop at the gate and whinny till someone came out and opened it. Pa was home, drunk again!

During what was called the Hungry Thirties a lot of men stopped by the farm asking for food. They would work for their meal and then move on. A letter written to Uncle Paul in 1935 from a girl named Lillian who lived in Star, Alberta, tells of the hard times: "It's really hard to express just how bad it is. There is nothing left of the crop. Most people cut it down with mowers and burned it. Others tried to sell it as low as one dollar to the acre, and no one will buy it. I am not worried any more now that Social Credit came into power. I guess you have read all about the Social Credit in the papers. Now don't you wish you lived in Alberta?!"

One day when Mom and one of her brothers gathered the cows for milking, the Jersey bull charged them. This was not an uncommon occurrence—he was a mean bull—but this time Mom hit the bull on the head with a large rock and knocked him out. They were afraid to go home because of Grandfather's temper, but soon the bull staggered to his feet, much to their relief.

Mom and her brothers and sisters attended a country school at Lindell Beach, a three-mile walk there and back every day. When Mom was fourteen she went on the bus to Vancouver to help her married sister who had given birth to her second son. This was the first time Mom had left the farm and she was terrified. Later when the war started she went to work in the fish canneries in Vancouver. My uncle George stayed on the farm with my grandparents. Grandfather by then was blind from an accident that happened when he was blasting stumps. From the fish canneries, Mom went up the coast to Ocean Falls and worked in the pulp and paper mills.

In 1944 my grandmother Kushner was in the Sisters of St. Ann Hospital in Victoria (where she spent a long time and, I believe, died). In September of that year my mother received a letter written by Sister Mary Paul at the hospital, thanking Mom for her letter and the two dollars she had sent asking that a present be bought for my grandmother's birthday, which was August 28. Sister Mary Paul wrote that with the two dollars, she had purchased a nice cup and saucer and some toilet soap, a pretty plant, and a birthday card. My grandmother barely spoke English and was unable to read, but a Miss Garonsky, who spoke my grandmother's language, read my mother's letter to her.

It was in Ocean Falls that Mom met Alfred Bryant, who was Dad's friend from Anahim Lake. Alfred talked Mom into going to the Home Ranch as a cook. Mom had a young son, Ken, and she liked the idea of starting a new life far away from the mills. They took the train from Vancouver to Quesnel. She said the train was slow. Another lady on the train asked the conductor how soon they would reach Quesnel, as she was expecting a baby. The conductor told her she should never have gotten on the train in her condition, to which she replied she wasn't in this condition when she got on!

I believe it was on this train that my mom met Marguerite Gunson, who befriended her. When they reached Quesnel, there was no one there to meet Mom, so Marguerite took her home. My parents did meet up soon after that—after all, Quesnel was only a small village then. They left a few days later with a team and wagon. Mom was riding a saddle horse and Ken rode in the wagon. The journey was about 180 miles of wilderness that Dad knew well, but Mom was lost as soon as the last

house disappeared from view. She was saddle sore and the flies ate her alive. Dad travelled from early morning till late at night. One day Mom fell asleep in the saddle, exhausted, but her horse kept up with the wagon even with its rider sleeping, swaying from side to side. A willow tree bent over the trail and Dad grabbed and held a branch as long as he could before letting it go. It struck Mom on the

Betty working at the pulp and paper mill in Ocean Falls, west of Bella Coola, 1943. PHILLIPS FAMILY PHOTO

face, waking her abruptly and nearly knocking her from the saddle. Dad told her it was a good thing he had held onto the branch for so long because it could have hurt her, and then he laughed his head off.

On reaching the Home Ranch six or seven days later, Mom was in for a rude awakening. The house was rough-built with no running water and was in need of a thorough cleaning. There were piles of dirty laundry and Dad had three or four hired hands who needed three meals a day. Fortunately, Mom was no stranger to hard work and she made the best of the situation.

Dad wanted Mom to bake some pies so he brought in dried apples. Mom had never seen dried apples before. She packed a large pot with the dried fruit and proceeded to cook it. One pot led to two pots, and two pots to three pots! There were apple pies and applesauce and laughs from the men.

Soon after Mom's arrival it was branding time. The guys gathered all the testicles from the castrated calves in a bloody pail and brought them to the house to be prepared with the evening meal. Mom gagged at the sight. One of the men took pity on her and showed her how to clean and prepare them for cooking, but I'm sure that she didn't partake of the feast.

Life was not only hard, but also very lonely for a lady from the Lower Mainland now stuck miles from nowhere, and Mom always was a very social person. The only women she saw for some time were the Indian women, who spoke broken English or no English at all. They were very shy of the first white woman most of them had ever seen. Over time trust developed and friendships began.

Over time a close relationship also developed between my parents, and it was not long before I was on the way. Towards the end of her pregnancy the following spring, my mom returned to Quesnel with Ken to await my birth. They stayed with Marguerite Gunson.

On a very hot day in July 1945, I was born in the old hospital in Quesnel, weighing seven pounds ten ounces. I gave my mom a hard time during labour—this should have been some indication of what was to come in the future! Marguerite wrote a letter to Dad saying that Dr. Avery came to the house at 4:45 p.m. and told her I'd been born. She wanted to go see Mom, but first she went to the Indian camps on the banks of the Fraser River to see who was there from the Blackwater area to take a letter to Dad. Even then it would take weeks to reach him.

I was christened Diana Lynne on July 26, 1945, at the United Church. My dad had not yet seen me and may not have even known then that I was born. My godmother, I never knew. My godfather was a very colourful and well-known pioneer in the area, Paul Krestenuk. I can't really picture him cleaning up for the ordeal, but apparently he did. Mom said he arrived at the church in a suit and tie, shaven and shiny. I can't remember him ever wearing anything but greasy coveralls and woollen shirts, beard stubble and a shaven head. I was dressed in the traditional white baptismal gown that I found later in my mom's trunk, all yellow with age.

I don't know exactly how old I was when I was placed in a cardboard Pacific Milk box, which became my cradle for the journey, placed on top of the rubber-tired wagon behind a team of horses, and headed west 180 miles through the plateaus and valleys, across creeks and rivers, to my future home at the Home Ranch. I'm not even sure Dad came to get us; it could have been one of the hired hands. My dad was not known for his dedication to family life! He more than likely had other, more important things to do. A hired hand could easily deliver the woman and kids home. The trip to the ranch would have probably taken seven to eight days at least. It was a rough and rocky road, very hard miles for a team of horses pulling a wagon, which was no doubt loaded down with supplies.

My brother Ken—Dad nicknamed him "Willie" since he thought Ken was a sissy name—was eighteen months old when I was born. He was along on the trip, so Mom had to contend with a toddler, a new baby, diapers to change, wash and dry at night in camp, plus cook meals, wash dishes and make up our beds in the canvas tent when it was pitched each night for shelter. At least the weather was warm, although we may have had rain, and the mosquitoes would have been a problem as well. When the day's heat began to cool, they would have come out in swarms. The constant buzzing is nearly as bad as the mosquito bites.

We didn't cross any mountain ranges but the trail crossed several rivers, streams and small creeks. Most of the trail was rocky, and what wasn't rocky was muskeg, which was corduroyed with logs to enable the horses to cross without bogging down. Most of the corduroys were put in by Paul Krestenuk when he travelled west, loaded with supplies for his trading posts at Nazko, Kluskus and Ulkatcho.

Trails criss-crossed the countryside. Some were wide enough for a team and wagon, but others were fit only for saddle horse or foot traffic. Some of these were the Indian trails that had been there before Alexander Mackenzie passed through in 1793. Along lakeshores the soil was sandy, and if you were riding in a team-drawn, rubber-tired wagon it was a relief from the constant bouncing and slamming about on the rocky trails. Soon after passing Kluskus Lake and Squirrel Lake, through the openings in the pine, spruce and poplar, you begin to catch sight of the Ilgachuz Mountains to the west. To the southeast are the Itcha Mountains, to the northwest the Fawnies, which are seldom visible, but Mount Davidson rises up high enough to be seen from some places. Tsacha Mountain is one of the highest points. On the north side of the Blackwater River the Naglico Hills provide a backdrop for the Blackwater River valley. The Home Ranch is on a plateau below these mountains but above the river.

Mom was a good cook considering what she had to cook with. Dad provided quite well for us. We always had meat—wild, of course, because game was plentiful—moose, deer, grouse, ducks and geese. We

had milk cows and fresh eggs from the hens. Mom always planted a huge garden but the growing season was limited by the high elevation of the ranch. We did grow a great deal of turnips, carrots, beets and parsnips. The odd year, cabbage grew well, and we also grew spinach, head lettuce, radishes and green onions—great salad stuff, but available only in summer. Dad liked to have a green

Diana sitting on the front step of the porch at Home Ranch, summer 1946.
PHILLIPS FAMILY PHOTO

salad with lunch and supper. If Mom didn't serve salad at both meals when the garden was producing, Dad was irked and he'd give her a hard time about it.

Every year Mom planted cabbage seeds in wooden trays on the windowsills inside to get them started. Some years it paid off, and she would grow beautiful cabbages, but not always. She always planted a few potatoes as well and every year they froze. We got frost every month of the year at the ranch, which killed off the less hardy plants in the garden.

Root vegetables were stored in the root cellar through the winter. Potatoes, onions and cabbage were brought from town in fifty-pound bags. Mom's family also delivered boxes of apples to Anahim Lake that we'd store in the root cellar.

We had three meals a day, and meat was served at almost every meal. Dad was a meat eater. In the summer, Mom would go to the meat house with a knife and a dish and cut off whatever meat she wanted for the meal. In winter the quarters of meat were frozen solid. So the meat was laid in the snow and chopped into smaller portions with an axe, then brought to the house and thawed. If hamburger was on the menu, it had to be ground with a meat grinder, which was bolted to the table or countertop.

Mom baked bread once or twice a week, depending on the amount of company we had. She made delicious homemade soups for lunch, which she'd serve with fresh-baked bread or baking powder biscuits with grated cheddar cheese in them. Soups were made from moose bones with lots of marrow, or from the older hens that had stopped laying and had gotten fat. She scalded the feet from the chickens, peeled them and added these to the soup, making a rich yellow broth.

Dad bought cheese by the block, which was covered with waxed cheesecloth. Since Dad did most of the grocery shopping, whatever was on the shopping list that he figured we didn't need, we didn't get. If he liked it, he bought it.

For most breakfasts Dad insisted that we have Red River Cereal, moose steaks and pancakes. That would be our breakfast eighty percent of the time. We used Rogers Golden Syrup (purchased in the big tin cans) on our pancakes, and Mom would always heat it on the back of the stove until it was hot and runny. No one should use that syrup cold! Mom made pancakes from scratch; there were no mixes in those days. Some mornings instead of moose steak we would have eggs, but not often. When Dad was away, we often had waffles, which Mom made on a waffle iron that was heated on the wood cookstove. She also used to make a lot of Czechoslovakian foods: dumplings and soups with home-made pasta. She would make a small egg dumpling and put it in the stews.

Most evenings we had dessert. Dad always asked as he loaded his dinner plate, "What's for dessert?" This would make Mom mad. We didn't have a lot of pies but homemade puddings, cakes and cookies were plentiful. There was always stewed fruit made from dried fruit such as figs, prunes, apricots, raisins and pears.

There were no prayers in our house at mealtimes, not that my parents did not believe in the Bible. We just never said grace at the table.

To make clothes for Ken and me, Mom cut the backs out of the legs of the men's worn-out jeans and sewed coveralls for us. She was also given clothes for us kids, which helped. Aunt Margaret, my mother's sister, sent a lot of cousin Linda's clothes that she had outgrown. I really liked her clothes but they were dressy, so they weren't really practical for a tomboy climbing trees and falling into manure. But when we went to Anahim Lake or Quesnel, I had some decent clothes to wear.

In the evenings my mom would sit by the kerosene lamp, and in later years by the gaslight, darning stockings or mending jeans or embroidering. Mom did beautiful embroidery work; she was taught by her mother. Mom tried to teach me but my needle skills weren't too good. I still have two dresser scarves my grandmother bought from Czechoslovakia; they are handwoven and beautifully embroidered.

Mom had a great love of flowers and, in spite of her huge workload, she still managed a flower garden. She had fenced an area around the house and put in boardwalks from the front and back doors to the gates. She planted pansies, lupines, sweet peas, tulips and Sweet Williams along these walkways. These were pretty much the only flowers that would grow at that elevation, but they came up year after year. Every window in the house had ledges, and she had houseplants at every window—mostly geraniums.

One day two red foxes were spotted out back of the woodshed where the slop pail was dumped. This was when long-haired fur was in fashion, and fox coats and capes and collars were all the rage. Mom was really excited—she was going to get herself one! She had a single-shot .22 and a full box of shells. We stayed on the porch while Ma went a-hunting! She shot and shot but never did hit one.

Sometime in the late 1940s my mom talked Dad into giving her a heifer. It was a long-legged brindle thing and, as I remember, it had frozen its ears off as a calf. She wasn't pretty, but she was a cow! The first calf she produced was a bull calf, and when Mom sold it as a yearling, she bought herself a gas wringer washing machine, which she ordered out of the Simpsons-Sears catalogue. The washing machine was brought in from Anahim Lake with a team and sleigh. It made life so much easier for Mom and she got rid of the scrub board.

A couple of months after Mom got the washing machine, something got in the wash and ended up under the agitator. (It was probably a bolt or a big-headed screw.) It wore a hole in the tub of the washing machine. Mom was "Mrs. Fix-it" around the house so she drilled holes in the bottom of the tub, put down felt from an old hat and part of an inner tube, and then she bolted it down snug. She used that machine for many years after that.

In 1950 Mom got her own brand for her cattle, "S lazy P." As her little herd increased, she was able to buy things for the house: better lights, curtains for the windows and a decent kitchen table and chairs. She also bought a treadle Singer sewing machine for all the sewing she did, and that speeded up the pile of mending.

The mail was her only contact with the outside world, and Mom wrote and received a lot of letters. She would sit up late writing letters or writing in her diary after she had finished her other work. On November 26, 1951, Mom wrote in her diary that on this day she turned thirty-two, but felt so terribly old! She wasn't well that winter and often complained in her diary about chest pains. She feared she might have contracted TB, which was very common amongst the Indian people in those days. (There was a hospital in Mission where they were sent to recover.) After that winter there was no more mention of chest pains. She did smoke quite heavily, as did Dad and everyone else back then. In one of her diary entries, Mom wrote that she was happy because Dad had made her new sawhorses, which made it easier for her to saw the wood for the stoves with the swede saw.

Dad gave Mom a black gelding, part thoroughbred and, as I recall, a rather showy horse. As far as I know it was the only horse my mom really loved, and after he was gone she never did get attached to another horse. She named him Dick. One day Dick ran a stick into his foot above the hoof and was lame and not expected to recover. But Mom found the time in her busy schedule to soak his foot daily and put poultices on it, and slowly over the weeks the poultices drew all of the stick out, and he did recover. Mom used to ride a lot but a fall from a horse caused injuries to her lower back and made horseback riding painful for her, so she rode less and less.

Rhubarb grew in abundance at the elevation of the ranch and Mom used to can quarts and quarts of stewed rhubarb. It was a nice treat to have in winter when our diet didn't vary much. She also canned a lot of moose meat for us to eat in spring when the moose were thin after the long winter.

One time Mom told Dad we needed more milk than we had been getting for cooking and drinking. They ended up having a heated discussion over it. The next time Dad brought in the milk, he had added an equal amount of water to it. Banging the pail on the counter, he smirked and left. Mom cried. What was she to do with two gallons of watered-down milk?

Another time, Mom was on her hands and knees scrubbing the kitchen floor when Dad came in for something or other. He had muddy boots on and he walked the full length of the kitchen. He never believed in removing his boots at the door. Mom snapped at him, and on his way out he kicked over the pail of soapy water and as it spread over the floor, he said, "At least you can tell which way the house slopes." He then went out the door laughing and slammed the door behind him.

When Dad was away, all the responsibilities fell on Mom. He tried to be home during calving season, but sometimes he wasn't. One of these times a calf was born a bit short on brains and it wouldn't suck its mother no matter what Mom tried. Mom put the pair in a small corral, she roped the cow and tied it to the fence, and then she would struggle with the cow to get milk into a bottle and pour it down the calf's throat. This went on for three days and Mom's patience was wearing thin. On the third day, after she had gone through all the trouble of milking the cow, the calf went to the cow and began to suck. Mom was so mad that she kicked and swore—and Mom didn't swear often!

Mom was cleaning one day when she looked inside a shoebox and found a live mouse. She was a bit queasy around mice, as many women are. They can face a mad cow or a bear in the garbage, but a *mouse*! She must have asked Dad to get rid of it. Dad grabbed his handgun and shot through the shoebox while Mom was still holding it! As luck would have it, he killed the mouse. I'm sure my mom stood with her mouth hanging open, and my dad probably spun the handgun on his finger, Clint Eastwood–style and strutted away.

In the summer when the house became hot, the flies crawled out of the moss chinking and buzzed around the house. If you are familiar with old log houses, you know that they are notorious for flies. They would congregate by the hundreds on the windows, and their endless buzzing got to Mom one day. She complained to Dad about it. He got out his handgun and shot through the windowpane, shattering the glass. He then turned to Mom and said, "There, got rid of one fly!"

Mom's diary for New Year's Eve, 1949, records that it was thirty-five degrees below zero. January was even colder. My parents spent the first day of 1950 quietly enjoying the warm fires and the radio. They made homemade ice cream and ate it with us kids by the fire. The second day of January was thirty-eight below, the third day it warmed some and snowed hard, clearing off by dark and dropping to thirty-two below by bedtime. It slowly warmed the next day, and Dad went out to the meadow and shot a dry cow moose. The whole family gathered for the dressing out of the meat, which was then loaded into the team-drawn sleigh and taken to the meat house. The hide, head and innards were left to fast-freeze on the blood-soaked snow. Everything left would be taken by the coyotes, wolves, ravens and eagles in a short time, leaving behind only traces of hair. Even the blood-soaked snow would be eaten.

Dad left a few days later for a freight trip to Anahim Lake. Mom had been busy for a couple days getting mail ready and packing a grub box for Dad to take with him. He left late, and the first day got only as far as Peter Alexis's place, seven miles northwest of the ranch. His plan was to reach the Ulkatcho Reserve the following day and stay with one of the Indian families there, and then be at Andy Holte's place the next night. The temperature was rapidly dropping as evening approached on the third day. The following day it snowed most of the day and cleared as darkness fell. At night the temperature dropped to thirty-four below. The trees popped and cracked with the frost. The owls called out their throaty hoots to whoever might be listening in the silent forest and snow-covered meadows.

When Mom arose the next morning it was thirty-eight below, warmed up to ten below, then with darkness it quickly dipped to forty below by bedtime. The sixth day after Dad left it was fifty below at 7 a.m. It was cold all day and by 7 p.m. it was back at fifty below. Mom wrote, "It's getting kinda cold, I reckon." On January 13, it was fifty-two below and cold all day. By bedtime it reached fifty-four below. On the eighth day it warmed slightly. Mom was kept very busy with the chores. The next day it was only forty-four below. Mom turned all the animals but the milk cows into the meadow. (She had probably run out of hay at the barn and didn't have time to replenish the supply.) She wrote, "Pan has been gone ten days. It is at fifty-five below at 7 a.m. My arms are causing a great deal of pain." — no doubt from all the heavy work of sawing and chopping wood, opening the water holes, pitching hay and throwing the heavy harness on the team.

While my dad was away, my mom would have been up several times during the night adding wood to the heater, trying to keep the house warm. When daylight came she would have started the kitchen stove with shavings she had made the night before. She would make coffee, feed us kids breakfast and do chores at the corral while we were left alone in the house with repeated warnings to leave the fire alone. At the corral she would milk the cow, feed the few animals at the barn and chop the water hole open for them to drink and then feed the chickens and gather the eggs. There was water to pack to the house with two large pails. The wood had to be sawed, split and packed to the house for both stoves. Then there was a certain amount of work to do in the house. She would have to catch and harness the team, hitch them to the sleigh, then go down the meadow to a haystack. She would load a large pile of loose hay into the big hayrack, and then pitch it to the herd of cattle as the team walked along. A second load went to the stock closer to the barn. By then it would be nearly dark. She'd have to do the chores at the corral and chop the water holes again as by now they were frozen solid. Then she had two lively children to contend with and the evening meal to prepare. The temperature stayed between thirty-six and sixty degrees below. There was no mention of wind. She did this for thirteen days in January of 1950, and it was not the first time. Tom Baptiste, Peter Alexis, Andrew Squinas and the Thompsons, our closest neighbours, took turns checking on her when she was alone, but everyone had their own cattle to care for, chores to do and traplines to run.

On January 17, it was even colder—sixty below. Mom wrote in her diary that she wishes Dad would get home or it would warm up. She is tiring out. The temperatures vary little day by day. The next day it warmed a bit and began snowing. Dad arrived home late that day. He had been gone thirteen days altogether. It had been too cold to travel, so he had holed up in some cabin along the way. It was on one of these trips that several travellers were huddled around a heater in a small log cabin. The heater was burning wide open, and one of the travellers had set a box of apples by the heater to keep from freezing, but the apples cooked on one side and froze on the other!

On New Year's Eve the following year, we took the team and sleigh and went to Jack Thompson's place at Sleepy Hollow, seven miles north. Mom wrote in her diary that it was a nice evening, and when midnight came the team was hitched up and we drove home in the wee hours of 1951. It would have taken us a good two hours to get home.

All one winter Mom baked bread and sweets for Francis Cassam, the medicine man. In lieu of payment, Mom got either buckskin gloves or moccasins or fur. Francis would ride his skinny horse the seven miles from his place every week to pick up the baking.

One spring when we were small, Mom took us kids on the bus from Williams Lake to Chilliwack and out to her family's farm to visit with them. That was the only time that I ever saw my grandfather, and I was afraid of him. But at least I got to see him.

On that trip Mom bought tricycles for both of us. While we were on the farm, Ken ran into an apple tree that was very close to the porch.

Finding an axe in the woodshed, Ken had nearly cut the tree down before Uncle George discovered him. Our uncle was very upset as it was one of the better producing trees. Ken said it was too close to the house. I recall Uncle George taping it up; whether it survived Ken's attack, I don't know.

Mom seldom drank, but it was at one of the stampedes when I was small that she did overindulge. I remember her sitting in front of the tent and laughing and throwing her shoes away. I couldn't understand what was the matter with her. No one else seemed upset by her actions, they just teased her and laughed when she threw her shoes.

Mom loved houseplants. Someone gave her a plant called a Wandering Jew. She had a number of them and they did very well, adding a little green to the house even in winter. Alfred Bryant told Dad that these plants brought bad luck. He said that when his wife grew them, all kinds of bad things happened: cows died, wagons broke down, snowstorms swept through in haying season and on and on. Alfred was a good storyteller.

One day when nothing seemed to go right for Dad, he came storming into the house where Mom was teaching us our lessons and making lunch. He said, "Them damn Wandering Jews are bad luck!" He grabbed all the plants and went out and dumped them on the burn pile back of the cache. Mom never said a word, and they were never mentioned again.

A few years after we had met him on a cattle drive, Rex Bartlett visited us at the Home Ranch. Rex noticed how rough our kitchen was and when he returned home, he built Mom a kitchen counter complete with drawers and cupboards. There were two large lined bins that pulled out—one for sugar and one for flour. It had a double stainless steel sink as well. He must have done some measuring during his visit as everything fit as well as it could in a log house. He hauled it from Marysville, Washington, to Anahim Lake and had it stored until Dad could pick it up with the team and sleigh.

When it arrived, Mom cried with joy. I'm quite sure that she enjoyed ripping out the crude countertop and makeshift shelves to make space for the new counter and cupboards. Help was needed to pack it into the kitchen because it was very long, giving Mom as much counter space and storage as possible. It took a few months before the septic was dug and the drain put in, so at first she used a pail under the sink, but that was a minor problem. It was certainly the most beautiful thing in the house.

I believe that Mary Cassam was my mom's closest friend in the Blackwater. Mary would visit about once a month—not so often in the summer. She would arrive at the ranch on her skinny horse with her bedding tied behind her on the saddle. For the first few years, her daughter, Lisa, would be perched on the bundle. Buckskin bags hung from the saddle horn and these contained her sewing and beadwork. She would be dressed in a long handsewn skirt with cotton stockings; her skirt would be pulled up some when she straddled the horse, but no skin showed. Mom would make tea when she arrived and they would make small talk, then Mary would get out her buckskin beadwork and Mom would have her darning or mending and they would pass the afternoons with their sewing. Most of the time there was very little conversation—just two women from two different worlds seeking each other's company. This continued for many years, and I think they felt a great deal of respect for each other and developed a friendship that most people wouldn't understand. Mary would spend two or three days with us and then she would ride off home, her legs kicking the worn-out old horse to keep it moving. As Lisa got older she didn't come as often—mainly on day trips—but Mary continued to come regularly till we sold the ranch.

Our outdoor toilet was some distance from the house. I don't know if this was the men's idea or what. One night my mom went outside in the dark, and she was just about ready to sit down when she heard a rustling noise. Lighting a match, she looked down and discovered a porcupine on the toilet seat!

One winter a young moose lay down right against the house under one of the living room windows. When Mom got up in the morning and began adding wood to the heater, she startled the moose. It stood up, blocking the window, which in turn startled Mom, causing her to screech and wake the household.

Another morning in winter, Mom was listening to music on the radio while she made coffee. A moose passing close by the house came up to the yard fence and stood with its head over the fence, ears forward, apparently enjoying the music. It stood there for some time till the dog discovered it and ran it off.

CHAPTER 4

Early Events

In the winter of 1948, I was three years old. Dad used to trap through the winter months and run down coyotes on his horse. Part of trapping was chasing coyotes in the deep snow—that is, if you could catch them crossing a meadow or a lake and run them down with a saddle horse and shoot them. If the snow was crusted, the coyotes could run faster than a horse, so it was a sport only for powder snow. One time an Anahim Lake trapper was shooting a coyote with a handgun, and his horse threw up his head and he shot his horse—it was a long walk home through the deep snow! Trapping and chasing coyotes was also a good chance to break horses. One day Dad was riding a thoroughbred that he had gelded that fall. It was a huge bay horse, well muscled from running as a range stud for several years. He was a descendant of the thoroughbreds brought from Sea Island, as described in Rich Hobson's book, *Nothing Too Good for a Cowboy*, in the chapter "Big City Wild Horse Drive." (My dad and Rich drove the horses through the city of Vancouver to the stockyards to be put in railroad cars and hauled to Vanderhoof, about 1940.)

When Dad saddled up that day, Mom had a premonition that something was about to happen. Jack "Happy" and Alan "Shag" Thompson were both working for us at the time and Mom insisted that he take one of them with him. Usually Dad never listened to anything that my mom asked him, but this time he did listen and it saved his life.

Betty, Pan, Diana and Ken in front of the ranch house, 1947. PHILLIPS FAMILY PHOTO

It was fairly cold with deep snow and most of the morning went well. Dad had pulled a number of traps and had them tied behind him on his saddle. For some reason Dad's horse started to buck. Dad was an excellent rider but this was a powerful horse and hard to ride. He always said that horses buck harder in snow than on bare ground, because in the snow they stayed in one spot.

One of the traps came loose from the back of the saddle and landed right in the saddle. Now Dad was not only dealing with a horse bucking but also an iron trap between him and the saddle. He came down hard on the trap and separated his pelvic bones. He then lost control and was thrown into the snow, where he drifted in and out of consciousness from the pain and the cold! Whichever one of the Thompson brothers was with him rode home as fast as he could. The team was quickly hooked up to the freight sleigh and some hay was loaded on. They were then driven as fast as they could go, breaking trail in the deep snow to where my dad lay. They put him into the sleigh and made a fast trip back to the ranch. I remember my dad lying on a cot in the living room for a number of days. He refused to let anyone go for help as he felt he would be okay, but after a while he decided that he needed medical attention, and Shag was sent to Anahim Lake to phone for a plane.

Shag left the next day for Anahim via the Ulkatcho Indian village. It was over a hundred miles by saddle horse to the nearest phone. I'm sure it took him several days to reach Anahim Lake, what with the snow and cold. He had to count on horse feed and shelter at night from the Indians scattered throughout the countryside who always opened their homes to the white people and offered the best that they had.

Upon reaching Anahim there

Diana in Pan's top hat, in front of Betty's flower garden at Home Ranch, 1948. PHILLIPS FAMILY PHOTO

remained the task of finding a plane to fly in to the Home Ranch. It would have to be a ski plane, and the pilot would have to have some idea where he was going. After several days, a plane piloted by Russ Baker was able to land, pick up Dad and fly him to the hospital in Prince George, where he was X-rayed and put in traction for some weeks. His recovery took a fairly long time but he returned home, flown in by Tom Corless, another bush pilot. He spent the last part of his recovery at the ranch, being cared for by Mom.

This was probably the real end to Dad's bronc-busting days, as the injury bothered him for years whenever he was riding. Dad somewhere came by a sidesaddle, and he rode that for a few months or so after his accident until he was able to swing up into a regular saddle.

That was a hard winter, with deep snow and many days of extremely cold temperatures hovering at forty or even fifty degrees below zero. We kids could not see over the snow piled high along the walkway. Spring came late, hay was short and moose were scarce or too thin to rely on for meat. I can remember Shag and my dad, who was still on crutches, standing outside, watching three ducks flying about. Shag got the shotgun and when the ducks passed over the ranch house, he fired. One fell from the sky—big excitement—we had meat! One duck for four adults and two kids: it didn't go very far, but it was meat.

Early in the summer of 1949 Dad went to Anahim Lake to pick up his mother, my grandmother. She was visiting with his youngest sister, Hazel, and his two brothers, Joe and John. They all stayed with us for quite a while. My dad took Hazel, Joe and John up to the mountains accompanied by Jack Thompson, who had a crush on my young aunt. His mother stayed behind with Mom and us kids. They also did a trip to Kluskus, and still Jack stayed on! My grandmother asked my mom if "that man is ever going to go home," to which Mom replied that he would go when he was ready.

In September of 1952, Red Olson arrived in the Blackwater with Ronnie Harrington. Ronnie was leaving Anahim with two horses—one pack horse, and he was riding the other. Red had no horse, so Ronnie shared the saddle horse with Red, each taking turns walking and riding. While passing through Anahim they met Freddie Elkins, a local fellow, riding a bicycle. Freddie agreed to sell the bicycle to Ronnie.

This would solve their problem, and now they would take turns on the horse and the bike. This went well as they travelled through Clesspocket Ranch and on up the trail to the Ilgachuz Mountains. However, the further they went, the steeper it got. It was now hard work pedalling the bike, so it was tied to the tail of one of the horses. Again all was going well till the bike went on the wrong side of a tree from the horse and the front wheel got badly bent. They then had to abandon the bike and go back to riding and walking. To this day we believe that that bike is still somewhere on the mountain.

The winters of 1949–50 and 1950–51 were busy ones, with a lot of visiting from Arnie Thompson and his two sons, Jack and Shag. The Indians were back and forth to visit and buy goods at Dad's store. They bought a lot of hay one winter and were hauling it home with teams and sleighs with a hayrack. Dad charged a flat rate per load of loose hay. Those large Indian ladies could really tromp down the hay, and they got a lot of hay in a load.

In 1952, we were also feeding Jack's cattle and Shag's cattle so we must have had a real good crop of hay. Dad traded Trooper, the horse that had thrown him, to Shag for two cows. He also traded Jack a nice team of Clydesdale geldings, dark bay and blaze-faced, for some cows. Jack named the horses Pat and Mike, after the Lehman twins, no doubt. Dad broke a lot of horses in the winter and traded them to the Indians for cattle. Quite a few of the Indians had taken to raising cattle of their own. This type of trading was how Dad managed to build the cattle herd back up after the Frontier Cattle Company dissolved in 1944.

My mom told a story over the years about something that happened when I was a baby, so I have no recollection of it. For some time, if Mom left clothes on the line overnight or when they were away during the day, the odd pair of socks would disappear. The clothespins were still there, leaving a gap where the socks should have been. No big deal was made of it till a shirt and a pair of jeans disappeared. This caused a lot of speculation for a few weeks, but was eventually forgotten. But then there was the mystery of the can of tobacco, which was always on the table in the kitchen and was sometimes found empty with no explanation. There never seemed to be any other things missing, but who knows if very small quantities or items were taken now and then.

One evening towards fall, the days were getting shorter so darkness fell sooner. Mom had finished the supper dishes and gone out to get some clothes off the line. As she stepped off the walkway to start towards the clothesline she got the feeling she was not alone. People who spend a lot of time in the bush seem to develop this sense. She stopped, and she felt the hair on the back of her neck begin to prickle. When her eyes adjusted to the dark, she saw the outline of a person standing in the corner of the yard against the fence. A cigarette glowed red in one hand. She whirled and raced into the house, saying there was someone out there. My dad replied, "Well, ask him in." Dad went out and looked around, then came back and told Mom her imagination was running wild.

Dad was leaving for Anahim a few days later and Mom and we kids were to stay home, but suddenly Dad decided we were all to go with him, that maybe there was someone around. I don't know what changed his mind. After that summer there was no evidence that anyone was ever around again. But if the subject came up in conversation he was always referred to as the "wild man."

Dad smoked a pipe when we were young. Ken was walking and talking a little, and I was still a baby. Dad hunted squirrels with a .22 rifle and used .22 shorts (I don't think they are available nowadays). Somehow Ken got hold of a .22 shell and put it into the bowl of Dad's pipe. After the evening meal, Dad lit up his pipe, leaned back in his favourite chair and calmly puffed away. Well, the gunpowder exploded with a rather large bang! Mom said that Dad sat perfectly still with the stem of the pipe clutched in his teeth, his face all black except for the whites of his eyes. Ken jumped up and down squealing, "Big bang!" The bowl of the pipe was never found and luckily no one was hurt.

One winter when we were young my mom had the opportunity to accompany some Indians who had found a bear den and were going to dig the bear out. I'm not sure what the purpose of doing this was, as most of the time the Indians did not like to kill bears. My dad was to babysit, a job my mom didn't often ask him to do.

In those days we had a slop pail under the kitchen counter for dirty water, cold coffee and other liquids. Also under the kitchen counter were two bins—one for sugar and one for flour. When Mom left, Dad

settled down in his rocking chair by the heater with his book and probably a bag of dried prunes or figs. He may have dozed a bit.

Well, we kids got right busy. We couldn't pass up an opportunity
to play a little in the dirty water. Maybe a little flour should be added?
Why not some sugar? Perhaps some water in the flour bin or sugar in
the flour? Mom returned a couple of hours later to our kitchen in a
total shambles! Our hair was full of flour and dough, and I think I had
messed my pants to add to the melee. She strolled into the living room
and asked Dad how the babysitting had gone. He told her that we had
been good—playing the whole time—he hadn't heard a peep from us!

About this time we had a small flock of sheep to add variety to our
meat diet, I guess. My mom once brought a newborn lamb into the
house to warm up. Ken was terrified of the lamb. On our bedroom wall,
there was a framed picture of a lamb. Ken wouldn't sleep in there again
until that picture was removed.

Our mail wasn't always on time. The longest period that we went
without mail was from November of one year until the end of February
of the next. I don't remember this of course, but it was mentioned in
Mom's diary. We missed Christmas, but we were young and wouldn't
have known the difference. The freighting conditions must have been
bad as Dad always made a trip to Anahim Lake before Christmas with
the team and sleigh. He would break the trail from the ranch down to
the Blackwater River and from there on it was usually well travelled by
the Indian people. He would then travel the four or five days to Anahim
Lake via the Ulkatcho Reserve to pick up supplies and mail.

When he arrived in Anahim Lake that February there were bags
of mail! Altogether there were eight parcels, eighty-plus cards and letters, and also magazines, newspapers and miscellaneous stuff. Mom was
thrilled with all this mail. To top it all off, Dad had bought her a lovely
cowboy hat! Gifts from Dad were rare. He also brought home a bottle
of Old Navy rum.

I can well imagine the scene in the kitchen that winter evening. I
would have been put to bed, but Ken was still up. The groceries would
have been stacked on the kitchen floor to be put away in the morning
when there was light. The kerosene lamps would have been sending
off their orange glow, the flames flickering with the drafts that blew

through the place. The kettle would have been singing on the back of the kitchen range and the stove would be popping and cracking as the fire burned. Mom would have been sitting at the table with her stack of letters, reading Dad bits of news, while he'd have had his chair pulled back and turned a bit to catch the best possible light while reading a magazine or paper. Their cigarettes would have been sending a thin curl of smoke towards the ceiling. Ken must have been on the table amidst the parcels and magazines.

Dad was having a hot toddy, which consisted of hot water, rum, a dab of butter and a dash of cinnamon. Mom may have even joined him with a drink. Apparently the cap had been left off the Old Navy and Ken was sitting with the bottle between his legs and taking slugs of the bitter dark rum! Just how much he drank before he was noticed we don't know. Mom was in a panic and Dad just said he'd sleep it off. Ken began to giggle and bounce around. Mom put him on the floor. He would try to stand and then fall over. He rolled around giggling and then fell asleep. Mom held him all night, afraid that he wouldn't wake up. The next morning he slept a little later than usual but woke up with no apparent side effects.

In the 1940s and '50s, neighbours spent a lot of time visiting each other, especially in the winter. If you did not spend time with other people, the loneliness could play games with your head. Very few people had radios, and even if reading material was available, not everyone could read. The companionship of another human being was important. Evenings were spent quietly visiting or listening to the radio. Poker was the card game played around the kitchen table. It was rarely played for money; mostly, wooden matchsticks were used. It passed the long evening hours when conversation lagged and people grew restless. Later, cribbage became popular, especially amongst the Indians. Even people who could not write their name learned how to play and were very fast when adding up their scores.

No one questioned how long a visitor stayed—there was always another plate on the table and a spare bed. Feed was provided for the visitor's horse and the table scraps were shared between the dogs. The dogs knew their place; they stayed where the horse was unsaddled, guarding the saddle and using the blanket for a bed. When the visitor got ready to leave and saddled his horse, the dog was usually leaping about, happy to be on the move.

Mickey Dorsey told the story of having a party when she first came to the Anahim country. There wasn't any music but a broken gramophone, and they took turns spinning the record with their fingers while the others danced. The music could be speeded up or slowed down depending on how fast that person chose to turn the record. They danced all night.

CHAPTER 5

Early Memories

After the long winter, spring always promised new adventures. Ducks called as they passed overhead. The sun was warm. Birds sang in the trees and bushes, which sported tiny green leaves. For two young children, the world seemed exciting and beautiful again.

As the snow melted, small ponds would form, holding the water till it broke over the ground and rushed forward to form a larger body of water, then continuing on until a waterway was reached. In this memory of my childhood, a slough handled the spring runoff, carrying the water to Pan Creek.

I had my first experience of trapping in the early spring. With a Number 1 leghold trap, Ken and I set about catching a muskrat. In the large willow bushes below the slough and close to the ranch house, we found a narrow spot where the water rushed through between two hummocks. Tying our trap to a willow and then setting it in the rushing water, we left to await our fur.

Just how often we checked our trap I do not recall, but on one of those checks we caught us a trout, which was the last thing we expected. Still, we took it home and ate it. On the next visit to the trap, we had bagged us a duck, which I'm sure met the same fate as the fish. I can't recall that we ever caught a muskrat that spring.

When Pan Creek overflowed its banks, flooded meadows filled the sloughs and ran down ditches. We kids were thrilled. After our lessons,

Diana and Ken playing in the wood lot at Sleepy Hollow, 1950. PHILLIPS FAMILY PHOTO

which Mom taught around the kitchen table, away we went, building dams and digging new routes for the water to follow. We sailed our homemade boats—usually just a piece of old board with a nail driven in one end and a piece of string tied onto the nail. We sloshed through the water in our gumboots, which didn't keep us dry for very long. Water splashed into the boots, and soon we were making that squelchy sound. If it was a warm day, we went barefoot.

As we got older we built rafts to float in the really big ponds on the fields. We would push our rafts out amongst the ducks and geese. The screaming cries of killdeer and snipes echoed at the water's edge. The warm spring wind smelled fresh and clean with a hint of grass smoke in the air, as Dad would be burning meadows, pastures and range so all the grass would be fresh for the cattle and horses. The cows would be grazing near the pond on any new sprouts of grass, while the babies slept in the sun or raced around playing and butting heads with one another. The mares with their new colts passed by, grazing as they went, babies sticking close to their mothers' flanks, their fuzzy little tails bobbing up and down at the mosquitoes that were biting their tender bellies.

We'd leave our rafts at the edge of the pond when night fell and head for home. Sometimes the rafts floated away if the waters rose during the night. We'd find them the next day on some high, dry ground or lodged against a fence where the water had passed underneath. Often the rafts were forgotten till Dad found them during the haying season while he was mowing; we were then ordered to dismantle them and pack them off the field.

We built tree houses and forts and cut trails through the pines and bush, cut logs and built miniature corrals and barns. There was always lots for us kids to do. There was very little fear of bears, as most of them avoided human contact unless there was food close by. If one of our animals died, it was taken a good distance away from the ranch to avoid drawing in the bears, wolves or coyotes. One of the dogs usually stayed close to us, so we were safe to play all day, in and around the ranch.

One day we were playing in the sandpit, which was a ways out from the house. We'd filled a bucket with sand and were starting to play with various toys. Suddenly, we heard the wind coming at a real roar through the trees. The large spruce and jackpines were bending in the wind. Twigs and acorns flew skyward. Stuff was picked up off the ground, flying debris, grass and dust, as the whirlwind approached where we were. We fled towards the house and then stopped to watch the giant whirlwind cross our sandpit, picking up our toys, sand and the metal bucket full of sand. Then it swept northward where several cows stood chewing their cud and watching the scene unfold. They were not moving! It passed right over them, raising their tails straight in the air. They ran off, bawling loudly. We kids laughed because it looked so funny.

Our root cellar was dug into the side of a small hill. It was made of logs and had a roof made of punching that was covered over with about four feet of dirt for insulation. There were two doors on one end, back to back, and a vent in the top, which was stuffed full of gunnysacks during the cold winter months, and opened in the warmer weather. This was where the vegetables were kept, along with Mom's canning. The root cellar was not opened when it was very cold, but only when the temperatures were close to zero.

In the early 1950s, my mom's family would bring a lot of apples to Anahim Lake in the fall. At the Home Ranch, the apples would be stored in the root cellar. Whenever the door opened, there was always that good strong smell of sweet apples. As the years went by, the punching in the roof began to rot. A big bay mare named LD was grazing on the roof one day, as the cellar looked like a small hill from the back and the animals passed back and forth over it. Well, she fell through the roof and was held up only by her neck and tail. It was a bit of a struggle to get her out and it completely destroyed the cellar. The fall also broke LD's tail, so she never could use it the rest of her life. Dad decided that a new root cellar would be built under the floor of the living room in the ranch house. This took a bit of time too as all the dirt had to be packed outside in pails and dumped. When the cellar was finally big enough, the walls were lined with lumber, bins were built and shelves put in. A trap door in the floor could be opened and a ladder took you down to the cellar.

I was about six when the Cassam family came to our place with a team and wagon and camped down by the creek. In the wagon they had a baby colt that was maybe a week old. Its mother had died and they were giving it a small amount of canned milk, but only enough to keep it alive. Mary told us kids that we could play with it. Mom started feeding it cow's milk, and after three or four days, this little colt started to play and follow us around. We just loved it. Then one day they packed up camp, tied the colt's legs together, put it in the wagon and drove away. I cried for days! Whatever happened to that colt, I'll never know.

Sometime in the late 1940s, some of our cattle had wandered away. Dad was fairly sure that they were living in some heavy spruce swamps north of the Blackwater River. They had been in the bush for two or three winters and had often been looked for, but never located at the right time. I believe it was about February when they were brought back. The snow was still deep, so they had been easier to locate. Also, they were in a weakened condition at the end of a long winter, so they played out faster. It must have been an interesting chase. I'm sure they must have been located by the trails in the snow and the rustling grounds. Cows will learn to paw like a horse in the snow. Just how many riders on strong, conditioned horses it took to bring them in, I don't know.

I was just small, but I remember when they brought them home. Coming down the meadows nearing dusk, there was a huge cloud of steam rising off the cattle as they had been travelling fast and were very hot. They had stuck together and were nearly manageable by this time. Some of them had huge horns, and there were many with calves as well. I'm not sure how many there were to start with, but apparently there had been a bull calf in the bunch when they originally escaped, so they had reproduced.

In June of 1950, while we were at the Dorseys' place, Mom received a telegram telling her that her brother Pete had died. She went alone to Chilliwack for the funeral, leaving us kids with Mickey. That was the first time that Mom had ever left us. I don't know exactly how long she was gone—maybe a couple of weeks—but the first time being without my mom was quite an adjustment for me! At least I had Ken, who consoled me as best he could. Dad was not the type of father to understand the feelings of a five-year-old girl, and he no doubt was off somewhere doing other things. Judging by my mom's diary, she was missing us as much, but it was also "wonderful to be home! Sis [her sister Margaret] and I went to the funeral home to view the body. First time I've seen him resting comfortably," my mom wrote. (Uncle Pete had suffered from severe asthma.)

Frank Dorsey, Diana and Ken at Three Circle Ranch, about 1950. PHILLIPS FAMILY PHOTO

For quite a while Alf Lagler ran the General Store at Anahim Lake, I believe the one now owned by the Christensens. Alf used to chew his tongue when he did figures and it looked as though it hurt badly. We kids used to love to tease him about that while he slowly added up the columns of figures—his jaw worked and his tongue seemed to take an awful beating.

Alf had a wife called Lisa and she was a fairly large lady. They lived in the back of the store, and they would have some pretty loud arguments after closing hours. We often camped on a grassy knoll behind the store when we stayed in Anahim Lake. One night they were having a very loud disagreement while we were at our camp. There was a fellow with us who thought perhaps he should intervene on behalf of Lisa because he feared Alf might hurt her. My mom had no sooner said that he should worry more about Alf when there was a loud crash and Lisa screamed, "Take that, you S.O.B.!" Alf was not heard from again that night.

I think it was at this same camp where a fellow fell asleep by the fire after too much "joy juice" and celebrating the rodeo. Nearby, there was a large section of log lying on the ground, with the butt sawn flat. Now this unfortunate cowboy had somehow gotten on Dad's bad side. (He'd probably flirted with Mom). While he lay sleeping in the dirt, Dad unlaced and removed his boots and, with a hammer and a couple of six-inch spikes, nailed the boots about twelve inches off the ground onto the butt of the big log. Then Dad proceeded to drag the cowboy to his boots, put his feet back in them and lace them up. The poor fellow lay on his back in the hot sun with his feet in the air for several hours, while everyone passing through the camp made remarks and Dad laughed. By and by the cowboy awoke. He groaned and moaned for some time, twisting and turning, struggling to get to his feet. People gathered to watch. After a time he came fully awake, sat up, unlaced his boots, removed his feet and walked down the dusty road in his socks, followed by my dad's laughter. I'm sure that he never found his way to our camp again.

We were at Jack Thompson's one winter day when a group of Indians came by with teams and sleighs; they were headed for Ulkatcho for the burial of a little girl called Trudy who Francis and Mary Cassam had raised. Mary told Mom that the girl's throat had swollen shut and she had choked to death. They had the wooden coffin in the back of the sleigh, and Mary opened the lid so that Mom could view the body. I wasn't allowed to look. I hung onto my mom's leg for fear they'd put *me* in a coffin! In those days, burials in the Indian graveyards were straight-forward: no death certificates, just a hole dug in the ground, a coffin, a body buried, tears and prayers, and then generally there was a potlatch by the family of the deceased. Personal items and belongings were given away. These items could include horses, cows and, in some cases, even children! Following that was the homebrew party with lots of food as well. These parties could get quite wild and sometimes resulted in black eyes and broken relationships. More often than not, wives or husbands returned home after a few days. Kids were rounded up, horses caught, dogs sorted out and everyone would head for home.

In the fall, Dad guided big-game hunters in Anahim Lake before he got his own guiding area. We would camp at Three Circle Ranch with Mickey Dorsey while Dad was out hunting with Lester and sometimes with Alfred Bryant and Shag Thompson. We kids would play with the Dorsey kids, and Mom enjoyed her time with Mickey in between cook-ing for the American hunters.

It was one of these times that Frank Dorsey, Ken and I decided to experiment with smoking. In those days everyone smoked, so tobacco and rolling papers or tailor-mades were left lying all over. It was only a matter of taking some when no one was looking, and then we headed to the barn to practise our future bad habit. All was going well until Lester (Frank's dad) caught us. Well, if I thought my parents gave us a licking that hurt, I learned differently in a hurry! I never forgot the one Lester handed out! I can't say that I blamed him—all his harnesses hung in the barn along with collars, saddles, halters and blankets, and there we were playing with fire near a hayloft full of hay.

During one of our visits to Mickey and Lester Dorsey's place, Ken, Frank and I were allowed to ride over to Five Mile Ranch, which was five miles away, to visit with Mike and Pat Lehman, the twins who were a few years older than us. We were not allowed saddles so we rode bare-back. Why I didn't have my own horse I can't remember, but Lester let me use one of his—a very tall, raw-boned mare called Mabel. She was a gentle horse but her worst feature was her backbone, which must have been three inches high! Well, riding five miles on that was like sliding down a small jackpine pole for an hour and a half. My behind was raw when we arrived at the Lehmans' ranch.

We spent the afternoon at play, had supper and then a storm moved in along with drenching rain just as we were leaving. We hadn't taken our coats, as the day was warm when we left the Dorseys' house. Jane Lehman was the local nurse and was a very gruff lady, so no child dared say "no" to her. She bundled us up in coats and wool pants much too big for us, or at least for me. The pants she gave me kept falling down so they were tied up with rope or twine, I can't remember which, but I know the knot was well tightened. Then Jane threw us astride our mounts and told us to ride like hell for home! My poor behind was crying with pain and I was soon soaked to boot, so it was a pretty lousy ride.

About halfway home, nature called and I couldn't wait. Sliding off Mabel, I tried to remove the woollen pants but the knot was too tight! Soon I was crying. Ken dismounted and tried to untie the knot. Then Frank also hit the ground and tried to undo it as well. We didn't have a knife and we couldn't break the homemade belt. With Ken holding me and Frank pulling on the pants, they finally got them off! I rushed into the bushes, took care of nature, discarded the wool pants in the bushes, and after finding a log high enough, I crawled back onto the back of the mare, groaning with pain. We arrived back at Three Circle hours late. Mom examined my backside and said it was raw flesh. She teased Lester about his bony horses. I never heard any mention of the missing wool pants when the clothes were returned.

Around that time, a nurse in Anahim Lake was giving vaccine shots for polio or small pox or something like that. Jane rounded up every kid that she could find, paying no attention to the parents. She had us lined up like soldiers in training; we were scared to move, let alone protest or cry! Frank was ahead of me. He made the mistake of watching the kid ahead of him get the needle, and he promptly fainted. Jane just kept shoving us forward till Frank came around and then she dragged him up and told him not to be such a baby. Boy, were we ever happy to escape!

We were at Three Circle Ranch one time when Ken cut his thumb really badly. No one knew if it was broken or needed stitches, so someone was sent to fetch Jane. She arrived shortly afterwards, galloping into the yard on a black horse that was covered with white lather and blowing hard. She pulled him to a stop with such a hard rein he slid on his hindquarters to stop. Leaping from her saddle with her doctor's bag in her hand, she asked in a booming voice, "Where is the little bugger?" In the meantime, Ken had his hand wrapped up and had gone back to play. He heard her arrive, leapt to his feet, fled into the house, up the stairs and hid under Mickey's bed. Mom and Mickey had to drag him out, kicking and crying. Jane felt he didn't need stitches, thank god, so she put a splint on his thumb and bandaged it. As soon as she rode away, Ken tore off the bandage and splint. He likely has a crooked finger to this day.

When I got older I lost my fear of Jane and learned to love her. She was a very abrupt and fairly loud woman. I think every kid in Anahim Lake was terrified of her except for her own kids. It was just her nature to be abrupt and she spoke with authority. If you were her junior, you'd especially mind her. But she had a heart of gold. Many meals I ate at her table with her encouraging me to eat more—she had a very hearty appetite of her own. She was also an excellent horsewoman. I went riding one day with her when she was in her sixties and we were going to visit some neighbours. She was breaking in a new horse, a tall, long-legged, black gelding. Shortly after leaving the corral, the horse became unglued and bogged his head. Jane leaned back, toes pointed ahead and she rode this horse till he quit bucking, all the time yelling, "Whoa, Junior, whoa!"

She was the only registered nurse in the area for many years and she served the community faithfully. She received her training at Royal Inland Hospital in Kamloops and then returned to Anahim Lake and worked for the Department of Indian Affairs, riding saddle horse as far as Ulkatcho village, which was about fifty miles away. She tended the Indians and would take patients to Bella Coola (a hundred miles through the mountains). She was very modest and refused to be honoured for her work. After her death in 1983, she was awarded the Red Cross Florence Nightingale Medal.

One of my favourite foods when I was small was bologna with macaroni and cheese dinner. In those days the bologna came in huge rolls sold by the pound. When we were leaving Anahim Lake, Mom usually bought a good hunk of bologna and several packages of Kraft Dinner.

She would heat the cast-iron skillet on the campfire, add shortening and then slice the bologna about a half-inch thick. She'd fry it until it was golden brown. Meanwhile the macaroni boiled in another pot. It was considered junk food in the 1950s, but to us, this was a great treat—our junk food fix!

When Dad was away freighting in the winter, Ken and I would be very excited the day he was expected home. Because the winter days were so short, it was always dark when he arrived. We would be outside without our coats and boots, standing on the board walkway that ran from the kitchen door to the front gate, listening for the first sounds that he was coming. We would strain our ears to hear the trace chains jingling or the creak of the sleigh as it travelled over uneven ground, or maybe one of the horses blowing its nose. If it was a clear, cool night, the sounds carried a long way. The dog would stand behind us, staring off into the night and wagging its tail. If it was clear the stars sparkled like millions of diamonds in the navy blue sky, and there might be a moon or, better yet, the northern lights would dance across the sky. The world was still and silent except for the occasional hoot of a horned owl from the top of some tree as it called its hunting partner. If it was really cold, the trees and buildings "popped" as the temperatures dropped. Once in a while sounds could be heard from the cattle that were now on the bedding grounds in the spruce—either a cough or the crunch of snow as they moved about. And sometimes a loud booming sound came from the lake as the ice cracked from one end to the other. If the night was overcast or windy the sounds did not carry as far, and the team and sleigh would be nearly at the porch before we would hear it.

We would run in and out, in and out in our excitement. If it was cold, there would be a cloud of mist when we opened the door. We'd go out in our sock feet with no coat, so we would only stay a short time and then run back in by the fire. I heard this expression years later but it certainly was appropriate for the occasion: "Kids would wear out the ball bearings on a revolving door." Yes, that would have been us! When we could finally hear something that definitely meant Dad was near, the door slammed much faster.

When the frost-covered team pulling their load came out of the darkness into the pale light shining from the window and up to the yard gate, Dad would holler "Whoa!" to the team out of habit, but they knew to stop. They were tired, sweaty and very glad to be home. Dad would crawl down from the sleigh with the fur on his parka frosted up and icicles hanging from his whiskers, as he would not have shaved since he left home.

Dad always had a brown paper bag of candy bars for us, kept close at hand, so that one of the first things he did when he arrived was hand us the treats and we could race inside by the fire to share them and warm up. He would call a greeting to Mom, who by then would be standing in the doorway. He would unhitch the traces, hooking each one on the hook provided for it on the harness high up on the horses' hips. He'd then go to the front and unhook the neck yoke, dropping the sleigh tongue to the ground. He'd drop the halter shanks, do up the reins on the hames and remove the bridles, hanging them on the hames as well. Then he would go off to the barn, leading the team, where he would remove the harness and then turn them out to feed and water.

When he returned from the barn, any freezable items on the load were packed into the house. Mom would meet him at the door to take whatever box or bag he had while he went for the next one. Once our candy was consumed, we would wonder if any of the other parcels he'd brought contained a small toy or maybe a game for us. The last parcel to be packed in was the mail, which Mom always looked forward to more than anything else. The mail was her contact with family and friends. The letters would sometimes be weeks old, but Mom would read each letter over and over while drinking hot tea with the steam rising from her cup. Meanwhile, Dad's face would gradually lose its dark red colour from the cold.

Often while riding in the sleigh in the cold, he'd wrap his legs in a heavy blanket, then light a kerosene lantern and place that between his feet to keep them warm. I can't remember him ever having lined coveralls—they either didn't make them or he felt he couldn't afford them.

For some time after the Frontier Cattle Company dissolved in 1944 we could not afford to have hired help, so while Dad was gone, Mom had to leave us often while she went out to feed the animals and do chores. In summer she was able to take us with her, but in the winter it was too cold. Doing all that she had to do was pretty much an all-day job, so we were left by the fire with our toys and magazines and scissors to cut out pictures. There was an old grizzly bear hide on the floor that we played on. The fire would pop and crackle and there would be the occasional thump as the wood fell in the stove. It had been drilled into our heads not to touch the fire and we minded our mom.

As I got older I was a demanding child, and Ken was the patient one. I was also very hotheaded. Ken would always give in to my demands. Once in a while he would lose his temper and pound me on my back between the shoulder blades, and I can tell you that hurt!

One cold winter morning when Dad was away, we kids were in the house while Mom went to the barn to do chores. I had never had my hair cut and it was down to my waist. Mom would brush it and braid it every morning and she made the braids so tight I could barely close my eyes. How I hated those braids!

On that day Ken and I got into a quarrel and he grabbed a pair of scissors and cut off one of my braids, right up against my scalp. I grabbed my shorn locks, and in my bare feet, with no coat on, I raced through the snow to the barn, which was a good three hundred yards away. I darted between cows in the barnyard and, leaping cow-pies, I raced into the barn screaming, "Ken cut off my hair!" Mom was sitting on a block of wood, milking the cow. She leapt up with a look of shock and dropped the milk pail, then headed for the house with me hot on her heels. I didn't want to miss anything and besides, by now my feet were growing numb!

As my mom opened the door, she called Ken's name. Knowing he was in trouble, Ken hid under Mom's bed behind the boxes she stored there. He would not come out willingly as he knew what was in store for him. Mom got the broom and poked at him, making him pretty uncomfortable. By this time, I'd forgotten all about my hair, as I didn't like it anyhow, being the tomboy that I was. I was jumping around, happy that Ken was in trouble and not me. When Ken finally came out and got his spanking, Mom took the scissors and cut off my other braid, giving me a boy's bob, which I loved.

Some of my earliest memories are of the store at the Home Ranch where my dad traded with the Indian people for furs, cattle or work, in exchange for horses or wares he carried in the store.

The thick-planked shelves carried coffee, tea, salt, sugar, flour, dried beans, rice, dried prunes, figs, raisins, apples, macaroni, lard, jam, baking powder, Rogers syrup, margarine, chocolate bars and much more. There was also tobacco, papers, matches, plug tobacco and Copenhagen snuff. He carried some GWG jeans and jackets, moccasin rubbers and gumboots. There were horseshoes and nails, traps, axes, swede saws, various sizes of nails, fencing wire and fencing pliers. He kept ammunition for .22 and .30-30 guns, as they were the two everyone carried. There was also a good supply of black and white thread, buckskin needles (a three-sided, sharp needle used for buckskin sewing) and very thin beading needles, some colourful beads in glass tubes and embroidery thread in a variety of colours. Coloured scarves were also very popular with the Indian women as head coverings—especially for the older women. Some of them I never saw with their heads uncovered.

On the rough countertop was a set of scales where Dad weighed dried fruit from twenty-five-pound boxes or sugar from fifty-pound bags. He would stand behind the counter in the dimly lit log building, examining fur, and would calculate the value, then write it on a brown paper bag with the stub of a pencil. (The paper bag would later be used for someone's purchases, as you didn't waste anything!)

He would add up the total of the fur and if the customer already owed money, that sum would be subtracted first. Then the purchases were subtracted from the balance. Most of the Indians were honest and were allowed credit, or jawbone, as they called it. The odd one owed too much and was not allowed credit, so they would take their fur elsewhere to sell—thus avoiding repaying Dad.

Some of the Indians would get downright mad if jawbone wasn't given and the women, even with their limited English, would raise their voices, saying, "You bastard, Phillips!" Dad would stand there and laugh, which never helped the situation. Or he would lean on the counter and barter over a horse one of them wanted. Dad would want a certain amount of fence built, or a cow for the horse, and eventually a bargain would be struck. Dad would be grinning while the Indians talked amongst themselves in their language.

Dad ran the store until the mid-1950s and then the building sat idle for a number of years before it was torn down and sawn up for wood. While it sat idle it was an excellent place to play in the warmer weather.

I remember winters when the temperature dropped to the minus thirties or forties—even the minus fifties were not uncommon. When the cold came with the winds on the single-pane glass windows, the frost built up, leaving beautiful patterns almost like the leaves on ferns. As a child I really believed in Jack Frost. On the beautiful frost etching I would press my small hand, holding it there till the imprint was left amongst the frost.

I loved Christmas at home as a child. Mom would have done her Christmas shopping in Quesnel in October or ordered through the mail-order catalogues—either Eaton's or Simpsons-Sears. As I got older I did my Christmas shopping through the catalogues too.

We would have a huge tree in the living room. Well, it seemed huge to me! But that may have been because I was small and our ceilings were high, I think about eight feet. Mom had candle holders that had clips on them, almost like a clothespin. You could clip them on the ends of the branches and then light the candles. It was beautiful, but a real fire hazard! Mom would light them in the evening, but would keep a close eye to make sure they didn't cause a fire. On the radio there would be Christmas music playing: "White Christmas," "Jingle Bells" and "Silent Night." We would crack nuts and eat mandarin oranges. This was the only time of year we got these treats!

Every time I smell spruce it reminds me of our Christmases long ago. There were no presents under the tree on Christmas Eve as Santa would be coming and he delivered them. We kids were allowed to leave out a glass of milk and some cookies before going to bed. Sometimes we left a cigarette too, because maybe Santa smoked—everyone did back then.

Christmas morning we would be up bright and early before it got light. The presents would be stacked under the tree. The tinsel twinkled as it moved with the movement of air we created with our jumping around. The milk glass would be empty and the cookies gone. I was pretty sure there would be farm animals under the tree for me to add to my growing herd of animals. Ken loved machinery, while I wanted horses and cows. Dolls didn't interest me much although I did get them from faraway relatives.

Rex Bartlett and his wife used to send beautiful Christmas parcels. In one of them was a gas iron for ironing clothes. It was great and so much faster than the flat irons that used to be kept on the stove. Sometimes they sent me a doll.

One year during Christmastime we had a mongrel puppy. The puppy being in the house was unusual, as the dogs were not normally allowed inside. We kids were eating candy canes and one of us gave the puppy a piece. While the puppy was chewing the candy, it slipped from his mouth and stuck in the hair on his throat. The puppy began to yelp and, seeing the candy cane stuck in its hair, I assumed it had cut through its throat and I began to scream. Mom began chasing the yelping pup around the house and under the furniture while I ran along behind her screaming. My dad no doubt looked on with amusement.

Mom would stuff the turkey and put it in the oven. We would always have sweet potatoes, vegetables, cranberries, gravy, mince and pumpkin pies and old-fashioned carrot pudding. We would all stuff ourselves.

We had a radio in a large wooden cabinet. It ran on two square six-volt batteries. We kids were not allowed to touch it, especially if Dad was home. Dad felt that he was the only one who should operate it. We had to listen to whatever he listened to, but in the evenings we all listened to programs like *Dragnet, Yours Truly, Johnny Dollar* and *The Life of Riley,* to mention a few. For the mystery shows we would sit close to the radio and listen. Dad never turned the volume up very high; I think he thought it used more battery power. We had a chart on the wall that listed the programs, so we knew when to switch to certain radio stations. Often Mom would make popcorn or homemade ice cream in the hand-cranked ice cream maker. We would eat, listen to the radio and feel content and happy.

On one of Arnie Thompson's frequent visits—this one was probably at New Year's as the rum bottle was on the table—hot buttered rums were being served. Back then it was a rare treat, saved for when there was something to celebrate. The conversation had somehow got around to religion. One of the denominations being discussed was predicting the end of the world. Arnie pounded his fist on the table and proclaimed that the end of the world was near! For a small child, this was frightening, and till I was older it was constantly on my mind that the world could end at any time.

I wasn't much more than a toddler when I found a hatchet, which I thought was neat as it was something my size. We had always been told to stay away from the creek, but often I didn't mind. Pan Creek is a fairly large creek, certainly something a two- or three-year-old shouldn't go near. Anyway, this time I was cutting willow bushes on the creek bank when I dropped the hatchet into the water. I got down on my stomach and was trying to reach it when the next thing I knew I was headfirst in the water! My mom had come looking for me and, seeing me hanging over the bank, she had grabbed my feet and stuck me headfirst down into the water, hoping to teach me a lesson. I think the lesson worked, as I can't remember any more water escapades.

When I was about five or six, we had a big Hereford shorthorn-cross cow, bought from George Aitkens. She was having a problem at calving time and couldn't deliver her calf. Dad ran her into the round corral and roped her. Now she was a cow to be reckoned with. We kids had to stay outside the corral. I remember the cow being on the ground with Mom sitting on her head. Dad delivered the calf, removed the ropes and then ran to the fence. Now there was Mom, stuck sitting on the cow. She finally leapt off and headed for the fence. The cow, having to get up, gave Mom enough time to climb the fence, then tried to crawl up after her. Dad was leaning against the fence laughing his head off when the cow turned and charged him. The cow helped him over the fence with her nose and it was Mom's turn to laugh. The cow was so mad she kept trying to get through the fence but by the next morning she had quieted down and claimed her calf.

Wood was hauled in log-lengths to the woodshed and dumped in a pile to be sawn with a swede saw, then split and packed to the house. This was work for the women and kids. Why we ever had a woodshed was beyond me. After cutting a day's supply, chopping it and carrying it to the house, who wanted to cut extra?

We started getting wood when we were young. Ken, being older and stronger, usually chopped the wood while I watched. Once I was standing too close and the axe bounced off the block of wood and struck me in the shin. Usually those axes were dull, but this one was fairly sharp and cut my shin and hurt the bone. I still have the scar to this day. Of course I screamed bloody murder at the time, and limped about for weeks getting the best possible mileage out of it.

When I was very small there was a wooden bridge across Pan Creek upriver from the barn. This allowed access year-round to the hay in the timothy patch. Small poles were used in place of planks, as planking was unheard of in the Blackwater back then. When the bridge became rotten and dangerous to use, it was taken apart and hauled to the woodshed for firewood. My mom cut most of the firewood, and there were a few arguments about that. The swede saw blade kept sticking while cutting the soggy wood, and when it was finally in the firebox, it wouldn't burn!

Water was packed in pails from Pan Creek, which was a hundred yards away from the house. This was considered women's work. Although the hired men did pack water, I can't remember my dad packing any, unless it was to impress some lady guest! He always said Mom had running water, provided she was running with a pail in each hand.

Hot water was heated in containers on the stove for dishes, laundry, cleaning and the weekly bath. Our house had no plumbing. There was a slop pail under the counter. When the pail was full, it was packed outside and dumped behind the woodshed.

Our outhouses were sometimes pretty disgusting. You sat down gingerly for fear of splinters and in winter the waste froze and built up into a pinnacle. There was usually a pole outside to knock the build-up down every once in a while. Men urinated wherever the notion hit them, often right off the porch. Men didn't need to visit the outhouse often and for that reason, toilet tissue was a luxury not often seen. Simpsons-Sears and Eaton's catalogues were in most of the outhouses—ours being no exception.

Sugar was brought in to the ranch in fifty-pound bags, as was the flour. It came in cotton sacks, many with prints. All these bags ended up as dishtowels and curtains.

We produced very little garbage. All paper products were burned, and there were hardly any plastics back then. Any food scraps were given to the dog or the chickens. The few bottles and cans went to the dump. It seems that nowadays if something doesn't come in a box or carton, you don't eat it. I was raised on homemade bread and pastries. The farm women like my mom worked very hard. Nowadays, we're spoiled—we don't work like our moms did and we complain more.

To do the laundry, my mom had to pack the water, heat it on the kitchen stove and then put it into a washtub. She scrubbed the clothes with a scrub board and brush, not only for our family but also for whomever was working for us at the time. When she got her first gas washing machine, her life became so much easier. Still, clothes had to be hung outdoors to dry. This was fine in the warmer months because the clothes dried quickly. In winter they froze hard on the line and were then brought into the house a few at a time to be thawed and dried.

Only once can I remember my dad spanking me, and it was for something I didn't do! We had been playing in the saddle-tack shed, and later my dad discovered one of the traces on his set of harnesses had been cut in half! Dad was very angry. He had the cut-off piece of the trace in his hand and he whacked on the bottom three or four times with it. I set up a good howl. I was doing my best to notify the world that I had been spanked by my dad. This was unheard of! My mom was the one who handed out discipline in our family, but it was never harsh enough for me to remember it for very long.

My dad kept a bag of coal in the tack shed for use in the forge. Coal provided a much hotter flame than wood did. As kids we loved to turn the handle of the forge, which fanned the flames and got the coal to burn.

Our playmates on the ranch were the Indian children, whose families were often camped there for working, hunting or just visiting. The kids couldn't speak English and we couldn't speak Carrier, but we communicated without a problem and for years I understood their language although I spoke only a few words. I remember being at the home of an Indian family where one of the women did not like white people for some reason, and she voiced her opinion to the others in the Carrier language. I picked up what was being said and told her what I thought of her in her language. If she didn't like me before, she certainly didn't like me after that.

While playing with the Indian children I came in contact with lice. At the supper table one evening, I kept scratching my head and was told to stop. "But it just itches," I complained. After close examination, Mom discovered the lice! She washed my hair with some home remedy and managed to get rid of them. She then went through the camps and encouraged everyone to get rid of the lice. Eventually they got us kids cleaned up and lice-free.

I've always been a country music fan. Radio reception at home was good, so we were able to get a lot of stations, including country music ones from Nashville. My parents enjoyed country music as well. When I was eleven or so I started sharing the early morning check on cows during calving. Dad liked to sit up late and read and raid the kitchen, so he'd do the late check before going to bed. Then Mom or I would get up about daylight and have a look. I liked the quiet mornings and would turn the radio on low and listen to music. That was when Dad started letting us use the radio—when we were sharing the work. Mom also enjoyed the chance to sleep in and get up to a warm house and coffee made.

I have always enjoyed the singing of the birds, and one of my favourites is the red-winged blackbird. They used to come to the ranch in huge flocks and sit in the treetops and sing, especially after a spring storm—that really seemed to set them off. They would fly off, their wings making a roar, from one group of trees to the next, all the while chirping and singing. As time passed there were less and less of these birds, and I never knew why.

Many people think that the life we lived was hard, and it was. It was definitely harder on the women than the men and kids, but very strong friendships were made. Friends would ride for hours through the cold and snow to visit. Neighbours too would ride for hours—a neighbour could be someone who lived twenty miles away! People didn't come to visit for an hour or for lunch; they often stayed for days, sharing food, work and laughter. Nobody had fancy homes or a great deal of money, but no one seemed to care. There were a few people who didn't treat Indians well, but most of them were fair. Our home was always open to whoever came by. It didn't matter if it was someone we had never seen before who rode up to the house. They were always invited in for coffee and a meal. People were generally honest back then and could be trusted. No one locked their homes. You could leave your saddle on the hitching rack, a gun leaning against the porch and the door wide open, and that was the way you would find it when you returned home. Food was always shared with family, friends or strangers—it didn't matter. Company was always a time of sharing news, what was happening elsewhere. Since any news was always greatly appreciated, visitors were especially welcome.

CHAPTER 6

Women on the Trails

Late in the fall one year when Ken and I were still small, Mom loaded us up and left Nazko for the Home Ranch with a team and wagon. Dad had gone on to Batnuni to pick up some horses and would be following us home—so it was just the three of us heading out across ninety miles of desolate country in November!

The first few days went okay. The creeks were somewhat frozen, but Mom would force the team onto the ice, which would then break, but it was not deep so we got across without a problem. At one of the rivers she had to chop the crossing open to get the team in, and then it was a bit of a scramble to get them out on the other side, not to mention the challenge of bringing the wagon up onto the ice while the team slipped and slid. Still, we were making progress. The miles were falling behind us. We had passed Kluskus. Kushya Creek was frozen enough to hold the team and wagon. It was nearly dark when we pulled up by Antoine Baptiste's house. There was no one home. I think my mom nearly cried, as it meant the fourth night of pitching the tent and staking the team out on the frozen brown grass so they could eat. Then she had to gather dry firewood, chop a hole in the ice for water, feed us kids, make our beds and try to keep us warm. She worried that the team would escape during the night, or that we would get two feet of snow and the team would no longer be able to pull the wagon.

We awoke the next morning with the tent sagging under the weight

Betty on a trip to Quesnel, wearing chaps and Tom Baptiste's army cap and jacket, late 1940s. PHILLIPS FAMILY PHOTO

of wet snow. It had started snowing during the night, and there was a good lot of it! Mom fed us a cold breakfast and loaded the wagon. She shook the snow from the tent, folded the soggy mess as best she could then threw it on top of the load on the wagon. She then harnessed the team and hitched them to the wagon, and we pulled out into the white world of falling snow. I looked back and saw that the bare patch of ground where the tent had been was fast turning white.

Mom kept the team going at a steady pace. The horses were covered in snow, soaking wet and steaming, but they still plodded on side by side, sharing the burden of the load. Mom stopped the team for a while about noon. She didn't even unhook them, just gave them time to rest while she built a big fire for us to warm up by, as the temperature was dropping, although the snow never let up. We stretched our muscles and snacked on foodstuff from the grub box. We were about ten miles from home and, at the rate we were going, we would make it home about dark.

The horses knew we were near home and their work was nearly done, so they stamped their feet in anticipation. The snow continued to fall. There was about a foot and a half now, and the branches of the trees were weighed down with snow, making the trail harder to see. There are summer trails and winter trails—the winter trails cut across wet muskeg swamps where it is unsafe to travel before freeze-up. It was one of these winter trails that my mom took by mistake. She realized her mistake when she was well out on the swamp and the horses began breaking through and bogging down in the mud. The only thing she could do was to try and keep going!

When she was near the edge of the muskeg and was sure that she had made it across, both horses sank to their bellies in the mud. They started lunging and drawing the heavy wagon in with them! When they could no longer move forward, both horses quit pulling, their sides heaving and shoulders quivering. Mom knew that they had given all they had. She climbed off the wagon, unhooked the traces and drove the team ahead. Without the weight of the wagon they scrambled out and made it the short distance to solid ground.

Mom then tied up the horses, built a fire to keep us warm and then she began the back-breaking job of unloading the wagon and packing everything to dry ground. This job took a long time and it was nearly dark when she was finished, but she still had the wagon in the mud and it would freeze in if she left it there overnight.

Mom removed the doubletree from the wagon and then hooked the team back up to it. She then doubled the picket ropes, tied one end to the wagon tongue and the other to the doubletree. Now that the team was on solid, hard ground and the wagon was empty, they were able to pull it out of the mud. Mom was by now completely played out, wet and covered with mud. She managed to put a tarp over the supplies, pitch the tent, gather more firewood and feed us kids. She had to tie the team to a tree, as there was no place to stake them out in the snow. There was no water, but bed was all she wanted. She was so close to home and the snow was still falling.

We slept soundly and the snow on the sagging tent insulated us a bit from the cold. Mom woke at daylight and started the fire. She melted snow to make the coffee. The snow had stopped during the night but now there was about two feet! The horses nickered to her from their spot under the trees. While we stood around the fire, in the distance we could hear the jingle of traces. Our horses threw up their heads and nickered to the team that appeared on the trail with a sleigh behind and a man on the driver's seat. It was Tom Baptiste. He said, "Oh, Mrs. Pan, I knew you were in trouble. I came as quickly as I could." Mom wanted to know how he knew where we were. All he would say was, "Moccasin telegraph," as he continued loading all our gear and supplies into his sleigh.

When Tom's sleigh was loaded, we broke camp and Mom hitched her team to our wagon. With the wagon empty and with Tom's team and sleigh ahead of us breaking the trail, our team could manage the wagon quite well. Just a few miles from the Home Ranch there is a very steep hill and Tom's sleigh, along with me, as I was riding with him, slid off the trail, went over the bank and tipped over, dumping Tom, the supplies and me out. I cried my heart out because "Daddy Tom" had dumped me into the snow!

We had to unhook the sleigh, get it straightened up, and then the team was able to pull it back onto the trail. The sleigh box had to be hauled up by hand and put on the sleigh. Once everything was gathered up and the sleigh reloaded, we continued on our way—just a few more miles.

We finally arrived home, and my mom was so happy she cried. Dad arrived home a few hours later with a big grin at seeing us there. When it had started snowing, he hadn't expected my mom to make it home alone, and he expected to find her along the trail. Dad was not often known for giving out credit, but for once he told Mom it was "a job well done!"

In the spring or early summer of 1949, when the horse feed was good and the worst of the high waters had receded, Mickey Dorsey arrived at the Home Ranch along with her four sons and several pack horses. Mickey was on her way to Batnuni to see her friend Leila Smith, who had moved there from Anahim Lake with her family the year before.

It was decided that Mom and us two kids would go with Mickey and her sons—Dave, fourteen, Steve, twelve, Mike who was about eight, and Frank who would have been four. A couple more pack horses were needed. We kids were to ride bareback on Alex for eighty miles. My mom had her horse, Dick. What we packed or the exact number of horses we took, I can't remember. Mickey was a good packer and my mom must have had some experience. The two older boys could pack as well; back then, at that age kids could do just about anything around the ranch.

I am not sure of the exact date that we left for Batnuni but I recall blue skies, warm weather and the excitement of travelling along with other kids. Some of Mom's excitement no doubt rubbed off on us. After a long winter of hard work, cooped up with two rambunctious children and next to no female company, this trip with Mickey would have meant a great deal to her.

We travelled east through Francis Cassam's and Antoine Baptiste's places and then on to the Indian village of Kluskus. The feed was good, so the horses were easier to keep near the camp at night. Most of the horses were hobbled and a few were put on picket ropes. Several of them would be belled. We kids ran around in the evenings after having sat on horses all day long.

As night fell the weather cooled and the mosquitoes started buzzing around. The horses stamped their feet and shook their heads. Their tails swished back and forth and they bunched together, rubbing against one another, trying in vain to get rid of the bugs. Canvas wall tents were pitched and the campfire crackled, shooting sparks skyward when more wood was added. Supper was prepared and eaten, dishes washed and the pack boxes covered for the night. All that was left to do was to go to bed. Stars shone in the night sky, a half moon had appeared, night birds hooted and in the distance a loon called from a lake.

In the early morning the grass was wet with dew, or frost if it had turned cold during the night. The horses would be grazing quietly. Smoke rose up into the sky from the campfire that either Mickey or Mom had started. Coffee was set to boil, pots and pans rattled and slowly everyone assembled around the fire. We kids were barefoot, curling our toes away from the cold ground.

Dishes were washed, pack boxes packed, bedrolls rolled and the tents taken down. Then the horses were caught and the hobbles removed. They were brought into camp, tied to trees and saddled. Next the packs were put on the horses, canvas tarps thrown over and tucked under the packs and then the diamond hitch applied. The tent poles were propped against a tree for the next person who travelled by. All that remained were the smoking embers of the fire and the flattened grass where the tents had been pitched.

One day we were camped at the Pan Meadow crossing on the south side of the Blackwater River. There were some grassy meadows there and a good camp ground. The river crossing is fairly wide and very rocky. Years before, a pathway had been created for wagons by clearing the rocks—they'd been thrown upstream or down. Not only did this path allow wagons to cross more easily, but also saddle horses were no longer in danger of falling into the swift water along with their rider.

While camped here, we were in need of fresh meat. Dave spotted a small black bear and went after it with a .30-30 rifle. When he shot it, it began to scream almost like a human. Mickey, thinking that the bear had gotten Dave, took off running, fearing for her eldest son. Mickey was not a tall lady, quite short-legged, but she sure could run across those grassy meadows, and even leapt a creek. Fortunately the scream was that of the bear and the second shot took care of it. Now we had the chore of skinning the animal, and not one of us had a skinning knife.

The only one we had with us was a large butcher knife that was quite dull. Mom and Mickey took turns sharpening the butcher knife on a rock and then they would skin for a minute and then sharpen again.

We arrived at Batnuni and spent several days there while everyone enjoyed themselves. The horses also enjoyed the pasture and rest. Without hobbles to hinder them, they were also better able to fight off the bugs.

I recall that one day Steve took his horse and swam it across a small bay in Batnuni Lake. There were a number of large trees at the water's edge. Somehow his horse had got tangled in the roots or branches of one of the trees. For a while it appeared that Steve was in serious trouble, but then the horse managed to get loose. At four years old I was unaware of the danger he was in, but I could see that our moms were very concerned, yelling directions and gasping and moaning while standing on the shore, unable to go to him.

On our return trip we took a different route. We didn't cross at the Pan Meadow crossing but continued upriver another eight to ten miles and decided to cross at Dead Man Crossing by Jerry Boyd's place. This crossing is on the west end of Lower Euchiniko Lake. The river was deep and dark; a large raft, big enough to accommodate a wagon, was tied on the shore. There was a smaller raft there as well. One raft would always be on the opposite shore so that if the big raft was needed, a person could pole across on the small one and return with the larger one.

Everything was piled on the large raft to be poled across. The horses had their saddles and packs removed so that they could all swim across. When Mike's horse, Beaver, was swimming across he ended up downstream and got caught in an undertow. He went around and around with only his nose above water. We were all sure that the little horse would drown, but somehow he managed to get out and reach the opposite shore below the crossing. As far as I know, the rest of the trip went along without a problem. We got back to the Home Ranch, and Mickey and her boys went on home to Anahim Lake.

CHAPTER 7

A Trip to Illinois

Dad had bought an Austin in 1951 and planned to drive us to Illinois to see his family. We left at the end of May 1952, leaving our team in the care of the Dorsey family at the Three Circle Ranch near Anahim. We stopped in Chilliwack and visited Mom's relatives, then on to Sumas to more of Mom's relatives. I met my grandmother for the first time. Passing through Montana, we saw our first antelope and buffalo. It was in South Dakota where we got a hotel room with a television, the first that any of us had ever seen.

My dad would drive and drive, from early morning until late at night, and we were all exhausted and cranky. It was hot, so we drove with the windows down. We were travelling on dirt roads and dust would settle on us. Somewhere in Minnesota I was so thirsty that Mom bought me a bottle of Orange Crush in a restaurant. I drank it down fast and then proceeded to bring it right back up—all over the restaurant. I was so embarrassed! To this date, orange pop still makes me gag.

There is very little I can remember of our time in Illinois, other than the heat and a lot of people. Mom put me in dresses, which I hated. I do remember the fried chicken and potato salads and the big family picnics.

At Aunt Helen's house in Detroit, we were fascinated by the water pump at the well in the backyard. We would pump and pump, packing water to the chickens in the wire pen and anything else that needed water.

Aunt Ethel later told me that the first time she met my parents and us kids was on this visit. At the time, she was a young woman dating Uncle Joe, whom she later married. She said that she met us at a picnic held at my grandmother's house, where Dad had been born and raised. A man by the name of Paul Finley from the Pittsfield paper came to interview Dad. Aunt Ethel said that everyone was gathered on the north side of the house in the shade. She had purchased a copy of *Grass Beyond the Mountains*, Rich Hobson's first book, and Dad had autographed it for her. She said it was more like being introduced to a celebrity than meeting her future brother-in-law. Aunt Ethel said that my mom was "a delight to know," and my dad was "very gracious." Later we went to Peoria to visit Aunt Vivian and her husband, Jake. I remember the big grey squirrels in the park where we went for an evening picnic.

After we left Illinois we went to Lander, Wyoming, where I met my brother Melvin for the first time. He was home from university for the summer. My brother Homer was in the navy and was not home. We stayed with Caroline, Dad's ex-wife, and her new husband, Howard. Melvin asked to borrow Dad's car and Mom had to shame him into letting Melvin take it for a short run.

While we were in Lander the rodeo was on. Funny how certain things stick in your mind, but there was a fellow at the rodeo who was supposedly Gene Autry's or Roy Rogers' brother. He was riding a beautiful palomino horse and was supposed to put on a show of rope twirling. He stood up in the saddle in the centre of the Lander rodeo grounds and promptly fell on his head and was hauled away! The rumour was that he was drunk.

From there we went to the fair, where there were Ferris wheels and all sorts of rides, popcorn stands and cotton candy. "Hit the Rabbit" —three-shots-for-a-dime types of things. This was another first for us kids. While we wandered through the fairgrounds, we spotted a ride overhead called something like "The Jam Can." Anyway, it was swinging around and one of the riders began to throw up! The crowd scattered— women screaming and men swearing as they examined their clothing. We kids giggled loudly, finding this the highlight of the evening. From

Lander we went to Crowfoot and stayed with Dad's ex–sister-in-law. We visited with old friends of Dad's from his days in Wyoming.

From Wyoming we went to Yellowstone Park in Montana to watch Old Faithful shoot its gush of water high into the air. There was water everywhere! Our parents never slowed down for any of the bears—black or grizzly—but everything else we got to look at.

Some Americans didn't seem to know much about Canada. In Montana, a gentleman saw our licence plate and asked us what the crossing had been like. My mom said, "We're from BC," and he replied, "Yes, but you had to cross the ocean, didn't you?" And in South Dakota some lady ran up to Dad and said, "You're from BC! You must know my uncle, Tom Baird?" My parents nodded—yes, in fact they did know him! She probably thought BC was the size of a postage stamp!

We also visited the Grand Coulee dam on our way home. It was a great holiday, and we still did not go home, but went on to Vanderhoof and the Rimrock Ranch to visit with Rich and Gloria Hobson. The Hobsons' ranch was about twenty-five miles south of Vanderhoof. It is a beautiful ranch in a valley on Greer Creek.

Rich was working on his second book, *Nothing Too Good for a Cowboy*, and Gloria was busy with Cathy, who was a small baby. Their cook was a woman from England by the name of Joyce Hoppi. She had two sons our age, Richard (Rick) and Peter. This family was to become our lifelong friends. Rick spent many years with us on the ranch and to me he was a brother. Joyce later married Mack Boland, who was then working at the Kenney Dam site. Also working at the ranch at that time was Sam Goodland, and he had a daughter, Carol. She was a bit younger than we were, but we five kids had a lot of fun together.

One of the hired men was Willie Paul, an Indian fellow who seemed to be there only to entertain us kids with rides around the ranch in an open Jeep. Willie was very short—well under five feet—and he couldn't see out of the windshield. He would sit on a box to see, but after driving over some rough ground the box collapsed, sending us kids into peals of laughter. When Willie wasn't minding us it seemed that Joyce did, while my parents and the Hobsons socialized.

On the return trip through Quesnel my parents got talked into going to Baker Creek for Mary Paley and Stan Hayward's wedding. It was

July 19. I can't remember any details from that day, but early the next morning while our parents slept, Ken and I amused ourselves in the upstairs bedroom of the Paleys' log house. The windows looked out on the yard where the last of the wedding party and guests were still celebrating. A fight broke out. While they slugged it out, one gentleman's toupée was knocked off! We kids were yelling for our parents, saying the men were fighting and one had just lost all his hair!

When we got back to Anahim we had to borrow a team of horses from Lester Dorsey because Shag and Happy had taken ours back to the Blackwater and hadn't brought them back in time for our return. We met them at the Corkscrew basin on our way home, so we switched teams in the middle of the road and continued on. When we got home the grass was high all around the house. We had been gone two months to the day! All the buildings were covered with swallows' nests. There were hundreds of them, and what a racket they made as they circled and dove about.

CHAPTER 8

Dad's Methods

Dad had a dog named Gin. It seems he had traded a bottle of gin for the dog! Gin was just a mongrel, large and long-haired. He turned out to be a good squirrel dog, plus he was a fairly good stock dog. And he always enjoyed nipping at the heels of strange horses. Dad got a lot of amusement out of horses bucking and kicking around the yard. On some occasions the riders got thrown off the horses.

Gin would nip at a horse's heels, and when the horse took off or started bucking, Gin would stand back with a look of innocence while my dad would tip his hat back, peek out from under the brim, and laugh and laugh. Sometimes everyone would laugh along with him, but not always. Sometimes there would be a great deal of cursing, and one time I recall Dad getting into a fist fight. People would threaten to shoot Gin, but it never happened. He met his fate one day by eating poisoned bait that had been put out for wolves. When Gin died, it took my dad a long time to get over him. I believe he was the last dog that was ever really "Dad's dog." Dad dug a hole under a huge pine tree near the house and buried his friend there, carving "GIN" in the bark of the tree.

Before Gin's death, Andrew Squinas came to visit. He was riding a small black horse that I wanted to ride in the worst way. I was about five at the time. Andrew assured my mom that the horse was gentle and I would be safe. Well I was, until Gin came along and pulled his delightful trick of nipping at the horse, which leapt in surprise. I fell from the horse and was knocked out! My mom was so scared and Andrew was devastated—for once my dad was not laughing.

Dad's watch would start and stop at random. He never succeeded to wear a wristwatch and expect it to run. He finally gave up, threw the watch on a countertop and shot it with his handgun!

Dad believed the cure for any illness in cows was turpentine and mineral oil, in equal measure. If a cow was sick to the point that it looked hopeless, she got the treatment poured down her throat with

Duke, Judy and Buck at the salt block, Home Ranch, 1960. PHOTO: RICHARD HARRINGTON

a long-necked beer bottle. Horses that appeared wormy got boiled to-bacco juice—also poured down their unwilling throats.

Once we had a yearling steer that was fat and healthy looking, but one day he quit eating, and after a couple of days he had pretty well quit moving. There was Dad, out with the turpentine and mineral oil. The steer put up a fight while he was being "doctored" and fell onto a stump. About thirty minutes later he died. I think he hurt himself quite badly when he fell. Dad couldn't see a fat animal wasted, so it was butchered and hung for a few days. Dad wanted some nice beefsteaks so Mom cut some up and cooked them, but those good-looking steaks could not be eaten, as they tasted strongly of turpentine.

A few days later, Ernie Harris, a bush pilot from Fort St. James, and Milt Warren, who worked for the game department, flew in on a ski plane and stopped for coffee. They were working on a program to control the fast-increasing wolf population. Poisoned baits were dropped on the lakes where generally only wolves would travel, keeping the smaller fur-bearing animals from coming in contact with the poison. When Dad heard of their mission, he said he would donate a hindquarter of beef to such a worthy cause. When he brought the meat up to the plane, both Milt and Ernie asked if he was sure he wanted to give away such good-looking beef. Dad said, "Sure, sure! No problem!" After they had left, Dad laughed and said he was sure that they would take the beef home and try to it eat themselves, but we never did find out if they did or not. If they did use it for bait, I know that the wolves would have rejected it too.

At one time Dad had a little bay mare that he was trying to make into a rope horse but she kept getting spooked when the rope dragged behind her. Some of Dad's methods were different! One day, after he saddled her, he put her in the round pen. Then he tied one end of the lariat rope to the saddle horn and to the other end he tied a rotten quarter of moose meat. And then he went off to do whatever it was he had planned for the day. The mare stood for a long time watching the rope. She finally decided it wouldn't hurt her, so she moved, which moved the moose meat! I'm not exactly sure what happened next, but I saw her crash through the gate on a dead run. There were poles splintering and flying through the air as she crossed the large corral and out the second gate, which led past the house and fortunately was open.

Mom was on her way to the henhouse when she saw the horse coming at her as fast as it could run. The quarter of meat kept hitting the ground, then flying up into the air so violently the rope seemed to pop. The horse was zigzagging to try and get away from the rope, and my mom was zigzagging to try to avoid getting run over. The chickens were squawking and trying to take flight. I thought for a while that my mom was in serious trouble, but she and the horse managed to pass one another without connecting. The mare ran into a log fence and fell. It was a good thing the fence stopped her, as one could only guess where she would have ended up! I cut the rope, and then got her up. She was wringing wet and wild-eyed, her nostrils flaring, her eyes rolled back and forth. She was afraid to move. The poor thing never did make a rope horse—actually, she was pretty goofy for a long time—especially when something moved behind her!

One fall when Dad was in Quesnel, he acquired a black and white Shetland stallion. What a pain in the ass that horse was! Art Lavington hauled it to Nazko, and from there we made the trip home with this thing following the saddle horses. Mom, Ken and I were riding and Dad was driving the wagon. The Shetland would drop way back, then trot to catch up. He would dart past our horses, irritating the saddle horses. Horses have their own pecking order and he was supposed to be at the bottom, but he wasn't aware of that. Being a stud probably gave him more nerve, and ponies are gutsy!

He came loping up, passing between my mare and Prince, the gelding Mom was riding. Prince laid his ears back and Chief, the Shetland, made a grab at the gelding. Unfortunately, he missed Prince and instead got my mom on the fleshy part of her thigh and refused to let go. Prince was dancing sideways and Mom was screaming and pounding Chief on the head with her free hand, while still trying to control her saddle horse. Dad was laughing. When Chief let go, Mom shouted at Dad to "tie that damn pony of yours behind the wagon or I'll kill it!" At this point, Dad quit laughing. The pony made the rest of the trip home tied to the tailgate.

Mom had a huge, ugly bruise on her leg for weeks after. Distemper went through the country that winter and Chief was the only animal we had that died of it. Dad had planned on breeding his mares to raise some big black and white ponies, but this didn't happen. I cried as I always did whenever anything died, and Mom consoled me as best she could, and even Dad patted me on the back.

In July one summer, Barry Wilwand, a pilot and friend from Quesnel, flew three young fellows from Bella Coola in to the ranch. They were of the Baha'i faith and their motto was, "Make love, not war." They didn't appear to be in a hurry to leave and all three had hearty appetites. Dad decided that they should do some hard labour. For some reason he wanted a load of gravel hauled, so he took the tractor and wagon down to the gravel bar on Pan Creek and gave each of the fellows a shovel. Dad supervised the job and shovelled very little. As time progressed the young men began to squabble amongst themselves—none of them happy with the turn of events. As the sun beat down, tempers were lost and a shouting match began. Dad hollered, "Whoa, whoa, make love, not war!" I think they left the next day.

Dad loved company, probably more than anyone. He loved to drink coffee and tell stories. He would show his guns to anyone who was interested. Same with photos. If someone was considering buying land in the area, Dad would have maps spread out on the kitchen table, even if Mom was trying to put a meal on. He loved to be the centre of attention and begrudged anyone else who might be getting centre stage. He also hated to leave a conversation. One day it was milking time and Ed, who worked for us and usually milked, must have been away as I was told to go milk. One of the young men who was visiting at the time decided that maybe he would go observe the milking too, so everyone headed off to the barn. Dad said, "Well, if everyone is going to the barn, I might just as well do the milking myself." So in the end he milked alone, and everyone else came back to the house. Mom and I had a good laugh about that.

We had a few wild cows and one was a two-year-old heifer that was having trouble calving. We tried to run her down the alley to the round corral. There was a gap of about eight feet in the alley fence by the tack shed, and I was worried she'd get out through the gap. Just why we were chasing the damn thing on foot and without a horse, I'll never know. Dad was yelling at me to head the heifer off. I told him that she was on the fight and was going to run over me. He said if you stand still, a cow would go by you rather than over you. I stood in the space between the tack shed and the fence, and the heifer came straight for me. At the last second I jumped in the air and grabbed a stringer that stuck out from the tack shed roof. It's surprising what you can do when you're really scared! My legs dragged over the heifer's back and she started bucking. I hit the ground with a string of profanity and stomped off, after telling Dad what he could do with his heifer.

Mary Cassam had a small, skinny Hereford heifer one spring that was obviously in calf and she wanted to sell it to Dad. He was reluctant to buy it. She was persistent. Finally a bargain was struck. Dad would pay her the money they agreed on but only after the heifer calved. If she died, it was Mary's loss. The heifer was delivered a month or so before calving. She went into labour but was unable to give birth. Dad decided to perform a Caesarean on the heifer. He got her standing up and she stood through the whole operation. She kicked the first cut he made, and then he started pouring turpentine and continued slowly cutting. Turpentine will numb and disinfect. After the calf was removed, his stitching job left a lot to be desired. I had to leave as soon as he started cutting as I cannot stomach too much of that sort of thing. So I did not witness the stitching job he did inside, but the outside one was there for all to see. There were six or seven stitches on an eighteen-inch gash. For the next few weeks it was touch and go if she would die of infection or live. The turpentine treatment continued. It was probably due to the turpentine that she survived at all; it killed the flies and disinfected inside and out. By rodeo time in July the heifer went to range and Mary got paid. The heifer was shipped that fall to the cattle sale in Quesnel. She had a very thin scar that was hardly noticeable.

At one time Carnlick Creek used to join up with Pan Creek south of the barn, but then Dad got the brainwave to dig a ditch from Pan Creek behind the corrals to where both creeks passed by—a distance of a couple of hundred yards. He wanted water in the back corrals. Soon he had a small stream of water running through the corrals. That June the runoff from the mountain was unusually heavy. The creeks overflowed their banks, and the corrals and meadows flooded. The strong current turned all of Pan Creek into Dad's shallow ditch and it washed away most of the corral system, leaving behind a wide creek bed. (This is where the creek still runs today.)

Everywhere you looked, there were upturned trees lying helter-skelter with pieces of fence stuck in the branches. That wasn't all: the current started another wash, which ran through the tack shed, going in through the double doors and out one side. It was a good thing that

Pan with Beauty and Buck pulling a logjam out of Pan Creek in high water, June 1960. PHOTO: RICHARD HARRINGTON

the water dropped when it did, because in one more day the tack shed would have tipped over. It was like a miniature Grand Canyon on the dirt floor of the tack shed, from the double doors and out under the side wall, across the corral and back to the main channel. Dad was devastated, but for us kids it was a new paradise. We had small lakes where I could water my toy animal collection, and canyons and dirt banks where Ken could build roads. Oh, we had fun all right!

One year during trapping season, Dad spotted some unusual tracks in the snow going under the meat house where different animals had dug holes over the years. They resembled fisher tracks. (A fisher is a member of the weasel family.) Dad had just butchered a fat, dry cow moose, and the meat was hanging in the meat house. Dad was sure this is what had attracted the fisher.

What with the heavy trapping by the Indians in those days, the fisher was not that common and their pelts fetched a fairly good price. Dad was pretty excited. With Mom and us two kids outside guarding the three holes, he went inside with his rifle and hammer and began to remove the floor screening and the floorboards.

It seemed as though we stood over those holes forever, listening to the creaking of boards and the squealing of nails as they were pulled from the dry wood. Then we heard Dad say, "I see his eyes," and the loud pop of the .22 rifle. Then the disgusting smell of a skunk! We took off running in whatever direction gave us the fastest escape. Dad stumbled from the meat house, coughing and swearing. The skunk's strong odour ruined all the meat and nearly the meat house as well. It was months before it could be used again. I'm sure there were some strong words exchanged between our parents over that one!

Dad believed that saddles and all leathers should be greased to keep them in shape, and he greased his well with rendered mutton fat. He'd warm up the fat and then line up harnesses, saddles, bridles and reins on the fence. He'd often get me to help. I would dip a rag in the warm fat and rub it onto the leather. If the day was hot the grease soaked into the leather well. The part I didn't like was the first few rides on those greased saddles! The seat of your britches got a greasy film and the smell wasn't that pleasant, as the fat got a bit rancid.

Hired hands were paid by the day but women were paid a dollar less than the men. I thought this was totally unfair as the women worked harder then the men did, but Dad didn't think so.

Dad had many favourite sayings: Only a fool or a newcomer predicted the weather. A fool and his money were soon parted. Poor people had poor ways. (Referring to families who, the poorer they were the more dogs they had.) Every kid knows its mother but it takes a smart kid to know its father. When someone asked Dad how many cows he had on the ranch, he'd reply with the question, "How much money do you have in the bank?" This generally caused his guest some embarrassment, while Dad laughed.

CHAPTER 9

The Fifties

One morning in late May or early June, sometime in the early fifties, we woke up to prairie chickens doing their mating dance in Mom's flower garden and on the lawn. They must have stayed an hour or more, right around sun-up. They puffed themselves up and swayed to and fro with their wings on full display, almost like people square dancing and passing by each other.

Jack Thompson's place, Sleepy Hollow, was a hub of activity in the winter. The Indians travelled by his place with team and sleigh on their way to Anahim, Ulkatcho and Kluskus. They travelled a lot in those days. I suppose some of it was to attend services at the Catholic church in Anahim Lake and occasional services at Kluskus. They also travelled for funerals. If there was one at Ulkatcho, all of Kluskus and Anahim Lake went, and vice versa! It was good for the mail service because the Indians always picked up our mail at the post office in Anahim Lake and then passed it on from one to another till it reached Jack's place. Or they'd deliver it to the Home Ranch and stop in for a visit. It worked the same for taking the mail out. The mail was left at Jack's to be picked up or given to a visitor at the Home Ranch and again passed on till it reached the post office.

Eve Wilson and her son, Gordon, and daughter, Diane, came back to the ranch with us in early July 1950 and stayed for some time. My mom enjoyed their visit. When and Diane left, Gordon rode to Anahim

Diana and Ken rode bareback until they were ten, Home Ranch, 1950s. PHILLIPS
FAMILY PHOTO

with them. He rode a mare of ours that he was breaking. When he returned a few days later to help with the haying, the mare died for some unknown reason. Dad and Gordon had built a perch in a tree to hunt bears. They put the horse carcass beneath the tree and waited in the perch for bears to be attracted by the rotting flesh of the dead horse. They did get some shots, but no bear.

When the haying was done that summer and after the cattle were gathered up, George Aitkens, who once worked for the Frontier Cattle Company, and Shag Thompson came over to help Dad, Gordon and Jack Thompson move the beef and the string of horses needed for fall guiding to Anahim Lake. The cattle were sold in Anahim Lake to a field buyer who bought large quantities of cattle, then had them trailed to Williams Lake. Mom and us kids took the wagon along. My mother cooked all fall for the hunters at Three Circle Ranch and visited often with Caroline Bryant and Chris Clayton at the Bryant place while their husbands, Alfred and John, guided as well. Mickey Dorsey was away, no doubt teaching school somewhere.

In the spring of 1951 Dad went to Vancouver to get his citizenship papers. While he was there, he got all of his teeth taken out. He didn't get his citizenship papers, not until November, but he did get his new teeth. I remember being half-scared of him with his mouth full of huge white teeth when previously he'd had very few. Dave Dorsey, on his way back from Batnuni on saddle horse, stayed with Mom and us kids till it was time to go to Anahim Lake to meet Dad. That was when Dad bought the Austin car and brought my sister, Gayle (Shorty's daughter), and her friend Bernice out to the Home Ranch to visit. Bernice was a year or two older than Gayle, and she had a crush on Shag. Ken had a crush on Bernice, or this was the way it seemed to me.

Betty and Diana harvesting vegetables, 1956. PHOTO: RICHARD HARRINGTON

The four of us would take our horses and ride three miles to Sill Meadow, one of the hay meadows bounded by Tsetzi Creek. Just before it came over some gentle rapids, the creek emerged from a spruce thicket. This was where we liked to fish. We would tie our horses in the shade of the big spruce trees, cut ourselves a willow pole three to four feet long, and attach a piece of string and a bare hook. Meanwhile, the horseflies would have found the horses, and we would catch them to put on the hook. Putting several other flies in our pockets, we'd approach the creek, not making a sound in the thick green and yellow carpet of moss. Dropping the hook in the water, you were almost certain of a hit. Those were the hungry, hard-hitting little fish, about six to ten inches long—just right for the frying pan. When we had caught thirty or forty of them, we'd clean them in the creek near the rapids where the water was shallow. Then we would bag them up and race our horses for home.

Summers were a lot of fun for Ken and me, as we didn't have many responsibilities yet. We did pretty well as we pleased till we got old enough to be sent to the hayfields to work. Our chores were mostly packing wood and water, but not much wood was needed in the summer with only the kitchen range going. We spent hours in the creek playing in the deep holes, although neither of us could swim. No one seemed to worry about us drowning, and the icy waters felt good on hot summer days. We also rode a lot, although Ken was not fond of riding. During the few summers that Gayle spent with us we rode more often. The two summers that her friend Bernice was there, we rode lots and Ken did too. There were just the three of us the day we raced our horses down through the timothy patch to the gate at the lower end. Ken was leading on his horse, Brewster, and I was second on Hammerhead. Gayle was on the drag on her horse, Smokey, but was right on our heels when Hammerhead decided to lighten her load. With the abundance of green feed available, Hammerhead was fairly "loose." Gayle got most of it on her chest, but some on her face and through her long hair! Ken and I had a good laugh over that, as she looked pretty funny with the horse dung all over her.

Arnie Thompson (Jack's dad) offered to watch our dog while we were on our trip to Illinois. One day he was out riding with the dog and it spooked his horse. Arnie got bucked off and broke his leg. He eventually got gangrene in the leg and had to have it removed at the knee. My parents felt bad about it since it was our dog that had spooked the horse.

Arnie returned to the Blackwater the following year. He had built himself a peg leg, which he strapped to what remained of his leg. He still rode around the country on Popcorn, his white mare, and kept up his beloved goose hunting. One day, while he was walking up the river at Sleepy Hollow to reach a goose pond, he had to go through some thick bushes. Suddenly, a huge grizzly bear stood up right in front of him! Arnie took up his 12-gauge shotgun and blew part of the bear's head away.

In 1951 we again spent the fall at Three Circle while Dad guided. It must have been extremely dry as there was a brush fire, which was being fought by about thirty men. About the same time, a fire threatened the Home Ranch. Dad and Shag, who were both guiding hunters with Lester, had to leave to make sure that the Home Ranch wasn't in danger.

In the summer of 1952, the road to Bella Coola was being built. The people of Bella Coola had no access out of the valley other than the pack trail or by boat. This new road was to free the people of the valley and thus it was nicknamed "Freedom Road." It was built by local people with very little help from the government, which had determined that the terrain was too extreme (and therefore costly) to build a road on. We visited Bella Coola a year after the road was built, and the trip was pretty terrifying—about eight miles from start to finish. There were very steep switchbacks and drop-offs down the face of the mountain. The road was gravel-based and only one lane in most places, but there were spots where a vehicle could pull into and let another vehicle pass.

By this time Dad had gotten rid of the Austin and had acquired a Studebaker pickup. On our way down the hill we met a car driving up in the other direction. The couple in the car was from the Prairies— flatlanders, as they were called. They had come into Bella Coola by boat and were now attempting to make their way up the hill on the Freedom Road. The lady was walking ahead while her husband crept along behind her in the car, clutching the steering wheel. We pulled over against the rock wall so they could pass. The lady asked my dad if her husband could please pass on the inside, as he was so afraid of the edge. So we switched around, and they went on up the hill. I'm not sure if she walked the whole way up the hill or not, but it certainly wouldn't have surprised me in the least.

We spent a few days in the valley visiting with friends. While we were there, Louise, who was about my age, and I were allowed to attend the movie theatre. As we were going inside, we passed another girl whom we both knew. She had on a beautiful dress, and we envied her. She was a bit of a snob and pretended that she didn't know Louise or me, so we just went in and sat down. After a few minutes "Miss Snob" came sweeping in and sat in front of us, still ignoring us and talking with her friends. Before we left the theatre, Louise and I had both reached between the seats and smeared our chewing gum onto the hem of her beautiful dress.

At that time, cod liver oil was believed to be the answer to the long winters with little sunshine. Well, Bella Coola no doubt lacks sunshine in winter, with its narrow valley and tall mountains, but the Blackwater did not. However, Mom came back with several large bottles of the stuff and faithfully administered a huge spoonful to each of us every day. It is the grossest stuff imaginable. Thank god, when it was gone she bought no more.

In 1952 Elizabeth Windsor was crowned Queen of England. Funny, I'd have been seven years old, and I still remember it today. Mom's days were busier than ever, as she was home-schooling both Ken and me. The mornings were spent around the kitchen table with pencils and school books, while Mom patiently taught us reading, writing and spelling. Art was a subject that we both found hard, as we seldom had all the materials that were required for the projects, but we did the best that we could.

In the summer of 1953, Aunt Vivian and her husband, Jake, and Uncle Fred and his wife, Pauline, visited with us. They were Dad's sister and brother from Illinois. Gayle was also with us that summer. We had a great time visiting with them and did a lot of riding about the countryside. Dad took them hunting and they got a moose. Jake brought Pabst Blue Ribbon beer and T-shirts with that logo on them, as he worked at the Pabst Blue Ribbon brewery in Peoria, Illinois.

Andy Holte began raising Brahma-cross cattle at Lessard Lake and

Eldash Ranch in the early 1950s. He must have had seventy to eighty head when he decided to sell them all. He made arrangements with Dad to drive with us to Quesnel, arriving at the Home Ranch late in September with his herd. There was a real variety of colour and sizes—some were white, others grey, with a lot of striped and brindle

Diana on Hammerhead, Home Ranch, 1956. PHOTO: RICHARD HARRINGTON

animals. Some were white-faced like Herefords but had tan or grey bodies with stripes. There were tall ones, blocky ones and calves as well. The smallest was a white-faced black heifer calf with black rings around her eyes and big floppy ears. This calf was born late so she was small and was usually on the drag as she tired easily. The herd had been driven about sixty miles to reach the Home Ranch and then they were allowed to rest for five or six days and mix with our herd so that all the fighting would be over by the time we started on the 180-mile drive to Quesnel.

Every day I rode behind this little calf, and I thought she was adorable. When the drive ended three weeks later, Andy gave me the calf. I was very excited. Dad arranged for Art Lavington to haul the calf back to Nazko so that she could begin to retrace her steps back to the ranch, tied behind a wagon. She may have been a cute five-month-old calf, but to get hold of her wasn't easy—she could knock an adult down if she was given enough rope. While she was at Art's place, Dad dragged her to the creek for water; she was only on the early lessons in halter breaking. While she stood in the water, eyeing Dad with rage, a gentleman visitor walked down to the creek. This was all she needed! She came out of the creek at full charge and hit the gentleman dead centre, flattening him on the ground. Dad howled with laughter and then began dragging her back to the corral, suggesting to the flattened gentleman that he get up and push her from behind.

We did finally reach home with the calf; she was led behind the wagon all the way back to the Home Ranch. The only one who could untie her from the wagon was Dad. She was more than I could handle. She'd back up close to the wagon, giving herself some slack so that when you went near her, she would jump at you. I didn't know it then, but this Hereford-Brahma cross was to be the beginning of my future herd.

In the fall of 1956, a well-known Canadian photographer by the name of Richard Harrington travelled to the Home Ranch from Toronto to accompany us on the cattle drive. Richard was used to hardships and he had a great sense of humour. He filled us in on trips he had taken visiting every country in the world, and of spending six winters in the Arctic with the Inuit. He told us about the year the people and their dogs died from starvation when the caribou herds never came. He told of the terrible cold, the endless days of almost total darkness and the silence of the hungry people. It made us feel very fortunate to live where we did.

Richard spent about a week at home with us, shooting pictures around the ranch before we left on the drive. Some days he rode with the herd and on other days he stayed with the wagon and got shots of camp being set up and dismantled, and the team and wagon in the rivers or just trotting quietly down a tree-lined trail. I loved to tease Richard while he rode old Hammerhead, who by then was rather slow and set in her ways. I would tear around them on my younger horse. I had now graduated to a saddle and really enjoyed riding. I hated posing for pictures though, and still do to this day.

Richard's black and white photos were published in scores of magazines and newspapers. Even the little Singer magazine featured a picture of my mom sewing on her new Singer treadle machine, which she'd purchased the year before. As a result of these photos and their

Diana had pen pals from all over the world as a result of Richard Harrington's published photographs of Home Ranch, 1956. PHOTO: RICHARD HARRINGTON

publicity, we received a lot of mail. Some of it was addressed to "The Phillips Family at the foot of the Ilgachuz Mountains," some to Quesnel and some to Anahim Lake. It was the beginning of a lot of correspondence for both Mom and me. I had pen pals all over the world and I wrote many letters, exchanged photos and learned a lot about other countries.

When we returned home from the drive, we discovered there'd been a grass fire at the ranch and we'd lost a number of haystacks. This was very serious, as we lived so far from feed and it was too late in the year to move cattle or hay. We were hoping for an easy winter and an early spring, but we went into a long, hard winter, with early snow and bitter cold temperatures! This was the only winter I can remember that we were short of hay.

The cattle bawled for feed and their flesh dropped away, their hip bones and ribs showing. The worst time was when calving season hit

Milk cow Roanie with cattle at haystack, 1956. PHOTO: RICHARD HARRINGTON

and the hay was gone. The fields were bare, allowing the cattle to graze on the stubble, but this had barely enough food value to keep the cows alive, let alone produce milk for their calves. A few of the calves were shot at birth, but these were from the cows that were walking skeletons. Some of the cows abandoned their calves at birth, as they were too weak to care for them, while others lived only for their babies. Some cows seemed to thrive in spite of poor rations; it just depended on the cow. Every day we waited for the warm rains to bring green feed, and in the meantime, we cut willows and poplar trees for the cattle to feed on the branches and bark. This gave them some nourishment, although very little.

It was late spring, but finally feed grew for the cattle and they slowly gained back their lost weight. The calves perked up and started to look healthy. We had not lost many cows, but quite a few of our calves. It was a winter that no one wanted to see again and, thankfully, we never saw another one like it!

In 1959 Dad bought a portable sawmill. Lumber was hard to come by in the Blackwater, but now we could produce our own. We put a new floor in the bunkhouse by the creek (the first building ever built there), built a new outhouse, and put a porch on the ranch house. We completely rebuilt the inside of the barn and removed most of the horse stalls, as horses were rarely kept there. It was now used as a calving barn with four nice-sized pens and a smaller one for calves only.

That summer, Eileen Moore came home with us, so I had a girl-friend to do things with, and this was a real treat for me. Rick Boland was living with us too. Stan McKee, whom Dad called Sam McGee, worked for us through the summer. Maurice Tuck came by in September and worked until haying was finished.

Aunt Margaret and cousin Linda visited that summer as well. Linda was several years older than I was and very attractive. Linda seemed to be all the things that I wanted to be. She had a very tiny waist, which I envied, beautiful long nails and a stylish haircut. We were out riding one day and she got bucked off and broke one of her nails. I must admit I was absolutely thrilled!

That same summer, Warren Kerr flew over the ranch with his amphibian aircraft and dropped off a gallon of ice cream. He then went on to Tsacha Lake. While he was attempting to land, he dipped a wing into the lake and it was torn off! Warren hired Dad to haul a new wing in from Anahim Lake and I went along for the trip. Warren and his friend Vic Felton accompanied us. It was a very slow trip back with the wing tied on top of the wagon box with as much padding as possible. The wing was a lot wider than the wagon, and longer as well. The length didn't matter but the width did, as the trail was narrow in certain spots.

Diana at fifteen, in the dandelion patch, 1960. PHOTO: RICHARD HARRINGTON

Dad drove a little bay team that we called Mike and Nora. The men raved about the team—how nicely they handled the narrow spots and also how they held the load back on the very steep hills. Warren rode alongside the wagon wherever possible to watch that the wing never touched anything.

When we reached Tsacha Lake, the wing was replaced and they flew the plane out of there. Dad hauled the damaged wing back home and put it behind the woodshed, beside a very small garden plot. The reflection of the sun off the wing thawed and warmed the ground, so we had rhubarb coming up early, the winter onions had green tops early and the chives were ready to use before the snows melted. These little things were always a treat.

The summer of 1958 Wayne Escott worked for us. He and Ken had a disagreement one day and it must have been a fairly serious one, as tempers raged. One of them got a little hand scythe and the other grabbed Mom's washboard, and they were ready to do battle in the backyard when Mom intervened.

Jack "Happy" Thompson got married in the mid-fifties to Lucille Trudeau, a red-headed lady whose father, Oscar, and stepmother, Bunch, lived way up the Baezaeko River, but later moved to Euchiniko. Jack and Lucille lived at Sleepy Hollow for a number of years. They had a daughter, Gail, and two boys, Clifford and Clint. After the boys were born, they moved to Bella Coola.

We usually had a young guy helping us with haying in the summer, and sometimes two. Most of the hired hands came from Quesnel and were friends of the family. One of these young guys was Donnie Tingley. The summer he was there, Alex Logan was working for us as well. During a rainy week when the haying came to a halt, Alex and Donnie wanted to go to Anahim Lake. Dad wouldn't give them horses as he felt they were too inexperienced to take horses on their own, so they decided they'd walk. It's forty-five miles of rough terrain to Anahim Lake, and it's easy to get lost on one of the side trails. They'd been over the trail only once, and that was with us when they came in to the ranch. But they wouldn't change their minds and off they went.

It was six days before they returned. They reported that the trip over was okay. But on the way back they took a wrong turn in the Corkscrew basin and ended up at Alfred Bryant's hunting camp in the Itcha Mountains before they realized their mistake and had to retrace their steps. They were not prepared for being confused for two days. No one gets lost, only confused, my mother used to say. When they did arrive back at the ranch two days late, having walked for three days with no food, only water, they could hardly put one foot ahead of the other. Donnie's cheeks were hollow and his eyes seemed to have sunk into his head. He

Ken and Diana on a water break while fixing the hay rake, 1960. PHOTO: RICHARD HARRINGTON

looked like one of those shipwrecked men on a deserted island. Alex had fared better. The mosquitoes had been awful. Without bug dope, they'd had to tough it out. Mom prepared food for them, cautioning them to eat slowly and only a small amount. Donnie wouldn't heed her advice and overate, developing stomach pains that drove him outside to lie in the grass and moan. There was nothing anyone could do for him. But I'll bet he never did that again!

The wood for the stove was originally cut with a swede saw. Later, Dad got a buzz saw that ran off the PTO (power take-off) of our small tractor. This buzz saw made getting wood much easier. In the late 1950s, Dad bought a chainsaw, a David Bradley. These new saws made cutting rails and logs for fencing so much easier. It had all been done by hand before. I was allowed to use the heavy chainsaw, but the tractor was out of bounds.

At one time, we had to replace the ram for our small flock of sheep, and Dad purchased a truly nice-looking black-face ram from someone in the Dragon Lake area, by Quesnel. He had Art Lavington haul it to Nazko and then it walked to the Home Ranch behind the wagon, the same as my Brahma calf did. The ram was around the front yard one day when Mom went to the cache for supplies. When she came out of the cache, he was waiting by the bottom step. When Mom started down the steps, the ram backed up, ready for his flying leap. Just how long he kept Mom there, I don't recall, but I know she was furious when she was finally rescued. In the spring the ram was kept in the small pasture around the house with the bulls. Whenever the bulls started to fight, the ram would take a flying leap and hit one of them. It wasn't long before there was no fighting amongst the bulls. Then the ram turned to the horses kept in the pasture. The ram would run up to a horse, and if the horse turned away in an act of submission, it was left alone. But if it laid back its ears or kicked, the ram would hit it. One day someone came to visit and turned their horse loose in the pasture. The ram came charging up and leapt at the rear end of the horse at the same time that the horse kicked. The ram landed with his head between the horse's front legs, looking up at the horse, which was looking down till they nearly touched noses! Both had a foolish look and went their separate ways.

Everyone found the ram amusing till he went head-to-head with

Rick's new cow. Rick had bought a cow, and she was delivered to the Home Ranch with her very young calf. They were put into the very pasture the ram was in. The cow, protecting her calf from an animal that she had never seen before, met head on with the ram so hard that it popped the cow's eye out! That was the end of the ram.

One summer a pen pal from Sweden by the name of Anita Carlson came to visit me. This was pretty darn exciting! She was to arrive at Anahim Lake on a certain date, and I was to meet her there. This meant that I had to ride to Anahim Lake leading a spare horse with a saddle for her, and hope that she didn't have much luggage. She'd been told to bring just a duffle bag—no suitcases. A duffle bag could be tied behind the saddle.

I left home early in the morning, planning on going to the Lehmans' Five Mile Ranch the first day. This was about thirty-five miles. Then on to Anahim Lake the second day, about another twelve miles. Then I was to pick up Anita and return to the Lehman ranch. I took our dog, Gyp, with me in case I ran into a bear. This was to be my first trip across the mountains alone, but I wasn't afraid, as I'd ridden that many miles alone many times while out hunting for the horses.

The first ten miles were good trail—not too many stones—and although it was hilly, I trotted right along. The next miles from the foot of the mountains to the other side were rough going—a lot of mud, rock and semi-swamp. The wagon trail followed a little draw in which a small creek ran through. I think the trail crossed the creek thirteen times as it zigzagged up the draw. After crossing at the top and going down the other side, I encountered more swampy ground. Once I reached the Corkscrew basin the ground was firm, and the horse could trot right along. I had to cross Corkscrew Creek at Three Crossing before Alfred Bryant's ranch. Then, skirting along Alfred's pasture fence and going through a drift fence, I reached the Lehman ranch.

I rode into the corral and dismounted. I was getting ready to unsaddle my horse when Jane came striding out from the ranch house with her big German shepherd dog running ahead. I cringed from the dog but he paid me no heed. He took off after Gyp, who was about a quarter of his size, and soon the fur was flying. Jane grabbed the shepherd by his tail, swung him around and threw him over the fence! By this time

Diana and Ken's horse, Judy, in front of the bunkhouse, 1960. PHOTO: RICHARD
HARRINGTON

both dogs were yelping. Then, dusting off her hands she said, "Put your
saddles in the shed, dearie, your horses out that gate, and then come on
in the house as supper is nearly ready," and off she went, striding back
to the house. I put Gyp in the shed with the saddles, turned my horses
loose through the gate she had shown me and went to the house, where
I was made welcome with cups of coffee and plates full of food.

The next day, I rode on into Anahim Lake and tied the horses in the jackpines across from the general store and next to Ann Punt's little café. I then went and found Anita, introduced myself, and took her to Ann's for a sandwich. After we had eaten our sandwiches and drank our coffee, which was served on the rough pine counter, Ann came back to gather our plates and refill our coffee cups. Spying a hunk of chewing gum stuck on Anita's plate, she asked, "That yours?" Anita shook her head, "No," and said that it had been on the plate when she got her sandwich. "Oh," Ann said, "Must be mine," and popped it off the plate and into her mouth! We nearly gagged. The return trip to the ranch was uneventful, thank heaven.

We always had access to guns and at a young age we learned to handle them properly. One day, Jack Thompson rode over with another fellow, and they turned their horses loose in the pasture and went into the house for coffee. I got bored with the adult conversation and wandered outside. The stranger who had come with Jack had left his rifle leaning against the yard fence. This one was fancy: it had a scope, which was quite uncommon then. I picked it up to see what the scope was like and put the crosshairs on different targets, including the shoulder of Jack's saddle horse. Well, I squeezed the trigger and, lo and behold, the damn thing was loaded! It was a good thing that it was only a .22! The horse leapt into the air, spun around and ran off. I knew I had hit him. I tore into the house crying that Jack was going to kill me 'cause I'd just shot Bimbo. Much to my relief, Jack tore into the other fellow for leaving his rifle loaded. The horse was caught and Jack inspected the wound. It wasn't deep, and my dad said the bullet would no doubt work itself out with infection.

I learned a lesson that day that I never forgot: not everyone leaves his gun unloaded! I had been taught that you never put a shell in the barrel until you are ready to shoot it, and if you didn't shoot, you removed the shell.

The horse recovered. Whether or not the shell came out, we don't really know, but after a week or two of drainage the wound healed over and that was the end of that, thank goodness.

As a child I loved the cattle and horses and couldn't wait for spring when the calves and colts were born. I was constantly out amongst the cows, even at a very young age. I loved playing with the calves. They would lie in a group and I would curl up with them. They were my playmates. Most of the cows were used to me and tolerated me. One snowy day, a cow left her new calf under the trees, and I decided the calf should be brought back to the feed ground in the sun. I was pushing the calf down a cow trail when the mother cow came running. She knocked me down with her head and rolled me around in the snow while I screamed bloody murder.

Our dog Gyp heard my cries and Mom, who was in the house, saw Gyp leap the yard fence and race off, so she knew I was in trouble and she ran outside. By then, Gyp was bounding through the snow. He reached the calf and bit it, distracting the mother. That gave me time to scramble to my feet and run.

The only damage was a bruise and a cut on my rib cage. I was very lucky, as the cow could have stepped on me, causing serious injuries. I was wet from the snow, and the cow had slobbered all over me, which hurt my feelings, but as far as I can remember, to this day, she was the only cow who ever knocked me down.

I loved old Gyp because he had saved me. I don't know if he bit the calf because he knew it would distract the cow or just because he knew he had to do something. Whatever, it was the right thing to do.

As I got a little older, I took over the milking for Mom when Dad wasn't around, as he usually did the milking. We had a long-legged Hereford cow with a spot on one eye—not surprisingly, she was called Spotty. I was doing the milking that day and I knew Spotty was one of those fussy ones, so I put on Dad's jacket and turned the cuffs up, thinking that it would be a familiar smell for the cow and might put her at ease. I took the pail and went off to the corrals.

We always milked with the calf on the cow unless it started bunting too much. We would bring the cow in from the pasture and the calf came in from another pasture. When I appeared at the gate, the cow seemed to ask, "What's this?" with her eye. I guess she noticed I was pretty short. I opened the latch and pushed the gate open. The cow went by me and stopped when her calf reached her and started sucking. I set the pail down and took up the hobbles, sometimes called kickers, which fit over the cow's hocks with a chain between them that can be tightened, and keep the cow from moving around and kicking you. She let me put them on her. I got the pail and milk stool, sat down and started milking. Spotty turned her head and looked at me as though she knew something wasn't right, and then she decided to smell my shoulder. That was okay. Most cows would have stopped sniffing at that

Pan crossing the cattle at the end of Squirrel Lake, 1956. PHOTO: RICHARD HARRINGTON

point, but no, not this cow! She wasn't a genuine milk cow, and she was a bit goofy besides. The second look around, she went for my hair and my neck, sniffling and drooling on me. I'd had enough! I whacked her on the nose, and then all hell broke loose! She took off, kicking and bucking around the corral. The calf stood with me, watching her mom's performance. Milk foam dripped from the calf's mouth and his tail stood up in the air as if it was frozen there! The kickers broke and went flying. Spotty then leapt over the five-log fence (crapping all over it), headed down the cow trail behind the corral and vanished into the willows and spruce trees. Not one thought about her calf! The calf came out of his daze and ran around the corral making murmuring sounds: "Where did breakfast go?"

Spotty returned later in the evening but I knew better than to try to milk her again. We went short on milk till Dad came home and got her back in a routine. She never did trust me after that.

Branding was usually done at the ranch in the beginning of June or whenever the range feed was good. It would vary a bit year by year, but the water was always high in Pan Creek at the time. I felt so sorry for the baby calves as they were separated from their mama, branded and castrated. Then the calves were mothered up with the cows again and the whole herd would be driven down to the creek, which was usually brimming with dirty run-off water. The cows plunged right in, heading for range. The better mothers stuck with their calves, but many left them behind without a thought. We would leap from the back of our saddle horses and begin pushing calves into the creek. The ones that avoided the creek and went along the banks were pushed off into the running water. Some of them kept swimming along the bank and trying to climb back up. If they missed the crossing on the other side, they would try to climb out on the steep bank and would end up sliding right back in. Then they might turn and swim back across the creek to the side we were on. Once in a while one would get caught in a back eddy and swim in one spot, its head getting lower and lower. Dad would ride out into the water with his saddle horse, drop a loop over the struggling calf's head and drag it upstream underwater, fighting like a fish. Then he'd pull the calf out on the shore at the crossing and remove the rope, booting it in the rear. Some really young calves would leap into the water with the saddle horse and swim back across, totally confused. But most times the calves that were left behind would wait at the water's edge, not wanting to get in again. Sooner or later, mama cow would return for them.

Dad often traded with the Indians for weaned calves, which were delivered by team and sleigh, sometimes from as far away as Kluskus. Often they were bull calves from Anahim Lake. Getting bull calves was the easiest way to get new herd sires. They'd be about ten months old when we got them. Some of these bull calves were bought from Lasha-way Chantyman at Kluskus, who raised beautiful Hereford cattle on the sidehills of the Kluskus Lakes, where the pea vine and vetch grew up to the cows' bellies.

If the trip to the Home Ranch with a calf took longer than a day, the calf was left tied in the sleigh overnight, fed hay and watered with a bucket. The sleigh box had to be built up so that the animal had a place to stand or lie down. It had to be positioned and tied securely enough that it didn't fall out, even on a steep trail and even if the calf started bucking. The hardest part was loading the calves. The sleigh would be backed up against a bank, the tailgate removed from the sleigh box and the calf dragged onto the sleigh—usually fighting, bucking and bellowing. It was then securely tied, and the tailgate was put back in.

I was always excited when new animals arrived at the Home Ranch; they usually came either with Dad or were brought in by people of the Kluskus. When I was older and raising my own horses, I often traded for cattle as well, and some of my herd was delivered the same way. A horse that I had traded for cattle would be tied to the back of a sleigh, and would trot behind it on the way to its new home. This was a sad time for me, as I always hated to see a horse leave, but I was raised to accept it as a matter of survival.

In the 1940s, Dad ran short-horned bulls with our Hereford cattle, throwing a lot of roan colour into our cattle. One of these nearly roan, white cows was to be one of the best milk cows we ever had on the ranch. She had her first calf as a three-year-old and had seventeen more calves over the years. We milked her every year and she never seemed to age, but when she was nineteen, Dad felt that she should be sold. I cried for days. She was a family pet and a good milk provider, but she was old.

I think that after driving her all the way to Nazko and then Quesnel, Dad got about sixty dollars for her!

About this same time, a lady showed up at the ranch by the name of Hannah Weber. She was originally from Zurich, Switzerland, but for some years had been working as a teacher in BC, mostly in schools on the reserves. She loved the bush, and when school let out for the summer, she made her way to the Three Circle Ranch, where her horse was kept. Then she'd set off into the mountains with her buckskin horse, her dog, a bag of rice and a sleeping bag. She would live all summer on what she carried on her horse. She usually came to visit once a summer and she became good friends with Mom and Mickey Dorsey. Dad loved to tease her, as he did most of the gals.

During the haying season one year, Joseph Jimmie showed up, wanting a horse that was out on the range. Joseph was John Jimmie's oldest son; they were Kluskus people Dad traded with. Dad was busy haying so I was allowed to go running horses with Joseph and his three

Diana holding a lynx she trapped, with Snip the dog, about 1959. PHILLIPS FAMILY PHOTO

big dogs. We rode most of the day without any sign of horses, but about mid-afternoon we ran into a big tom cougar. Joseph's dogs took after it and so did we. For a twelve-year-old who had never done anything like this before, it was exciting! We pounded our horses through muskeg, windfalls and over rock piles, up hills and down hills with the dogs howling ahead. After about an hour and a half, Joseph gave up and said that the cougar wouldn't tree, so we may as well go home. The dogs were several hours behind us getting home to the ranch, but they were none the worse for wear.

Horses were judged by how tough they were. Looks helped, but stamina was important, and also the ride. A smooth-riding, fast-walking horse was appreciated. Nobody worried if the horse crow-hopped a bit in the morning. That was accepted. If you could reach Anahim Lake in eight or nine hours without flogging your horse, you were riding a good one. Moffit Harris told me that he made Anahim Lake from Nazko in two days—a distance of about 135 miles. "Good hoss, good hoss," he said.

CHAPTER 10

Trails

The Lunaas pack trail went from Anahim Lake into Precipice Valley, then climbed up and back down into the Bella Coola valley. The last part of this trail was extremely steep. I was told that most of it was dug with pick and shovel by people living in the Bella Coola valley during the Hungry Thirties to pay their land taxes. The last section of the trail into the Bella Coola valley is called the Sugar Camp Trail. I've heard two stories explaining how it came to be called Sugar Camp, but there are probably more. One story is that Capoose, who was an old Indian packer in the area, had two hundred-pound bags of sugar, one on each side of a pack horse. While going up the mountain the pack horse struck a tree, tearing a small hole in one of the bags. By the time Capoose reached the summit of the mountain, the bag was empty and the pack horse was leaning to one side—thus, it was named the Sugar Trail. The other story recounts that the pack train had to cross a fair-sized creek at the foot of the mountain. The bags of sugar got completely soaked during the crossing and then turned into bags of rock-hard sugar, so the camp by the creek was called Sugar Camp. Then the trail became known as the Sugar Camp Trail.

The Grease Trail is now called the Alexander Mackenzie Grease Trail after the explorer who used this route to the sea in 1793. It leaves the Fraser River, following the Blackwater River and its string of lakes all the way to Eliguk Lake, and from there over to the Dean River, on to

Tanya Lake and across the Rainbow Mountains. Then it follows a very steep descent into the Bella Coola valley at what is now known as Burnt Bridge.

Bella Coola is a small village that was settled by the Norwegians in the late 1800s. It had two fish canneries by the early 1900s, and the Union Steamships came to Bella Coola weekly. The Hudson's Bay Company built a post in Bella Coola in 1867. It operated until 1882, when it was purchased by John Clayton.

From Anahim Lake you could travel east to Tatla Lake and Alexis Creek country on a trail that later became Highway 20. The road was greatly improved in the 1940s by Stan Dowling, who was Anahim Lake's first postmaster, freighter and store operator.

Another trail went north to Ootsa Lake and Fort St. James. Mostly, the Indian people used this trail. Travel north became more difficult when the Kenney Dam was built in 1952, and the floodwaters spread and covered the trail and many homesteads.

The trail from the Home Ranch over the Ilgachuz Mountains was cut in 1941, opening a direct route to Anahim Lake that could be used with a team and wagon. Up until then, the only route passable with a wagon was the long trail via the Ulkatcho Reserve. The story goes that Dad told the Indians that he had cut a trail all the way to Anahim Lake, and that there was a stampede going to be held there. In truth, he had cut only the first five or six miles. When the teams and wagons headed out to Anahim Lake, Dad joined them. Everything went well till the trail ended abruptly and the job of cutting the next forty miles began. All the work was done with an axe. Where they could, they followed grassy draws. Some of the trail was high and dry, but some was muskeg. After crossing Pan Creek just above the falls, they faced some steep hills. The only blessing was that it was sandy soil most of the way. At the summit, the trail hit a draw that ran south to the Corkscrew basin. Even in the open country it was solid ground and sandy soil.

A corral was built at the head of this draw for our cattle when we drove them to Anahim Lake to be shipped to Williams Lake. Another corral was built at the lower end of the Corkscrew basin. Later a cabin was built at the foot of the main hills by Pan Creek. A shortcut saddle-horse trail was developed up the creek from the cabin, which avoided the steep hills. It followed the creek up a narrow canyon, quite marshy with steep sides, and at the end of a short climb, to the rim and just a short distance from the corral. Taking this trail with saddle horse would shorten your travel time by a good hour.

It was probably in the mid-fifties that another trail was cut over the pass between the Itcha and Ilgachuz Mountains. This new trail was more gradual and didn't climb nearly as high. It followed a rocky muskeg draw, and it crossed the creek thirteen times to avoid cutting any timber. Over the years a few trees were cut and the number of crossings was shortened, but it was still a godawful piece of trail with mud, rocks and roots. The summit of the trail was Table Mountain, and from there you had a good view of the country before descending to the Corkscrew basin and the Bryant ranch.

These trails were passable only from May through November. In the winter, an alternate trail had to be found. After the snow came we had to go to the Blackwater, follow Ulgako Creek to Eliguk Lake on the Ulkatcho Reserve, west to the Dean River, then south to Anahim Lake. This route was much longer: it took a good four or five days. Later, a trail was cut south from Eliguk Lake to Irene Lake, passing Rainbow Lake to Eldash, the abandoned Holte ranch, and then on to Muskeg Meadow, Lessard Lake and Anahim Lake. This shortened the trip by two days, but the trail was passable only in the winter.

In the spring of 1961, Dad decided a road should be cut from Rainbow Lake to Tanswanket Creek, then westward till it hit the Dean River road. This road would be a year-round trail shorter than the route through the Ulkatcho Reserve. The Indians seemed to like trail cutting and the camping and hunting that went with it. So Dad had no trouble rounding up enough men in May to start the job. The trail they planned to cut was very steep. There were huge boulders and heavy timber to deal with.

They travelled to Rainbow Lake and set up camp while they cut trail. On the fourth day as they neared the bottom of the hill, the men felt they had only one more day of cutting left before they would reach Tanswanket Creek, where there was good horse feed. They told the women to break camp and move down the hill, which they did. The men went on ahead, blazing the trail. They felled trees and cut them into short lengths, then left them for the women to cart off. The women followed with the wagons. About halfway down that section of the trail the men began to tire, so from there to the bottom they only blazed the trail. When the women reached the uncut trail, they had no choice but to start cutting down trees themselves and clearing the right-of-way. Dad found this very amusing, and to this day that trail is called Woman Hill.

Dad and some of the Indians decided to build a new wagon trail over the mountain on the southeastern side of the Ilgachuzes and Pan Canyon. The plan was to have the trail come out at Clesspocket Ranch rather than at the Bryant ranch. It was started off the old trail just before the Pan Creek crossing, about one mile south of the ranch. The first two and a half miles were good—cut wide and following a sand ridge above Pan Creek—but as the trail turned away from Pan Creek, the land became hilly and less cutting was done, leaving a narrower trail. A bridge had to be built over a fast-moving creek with high banks that ran down into Pan Creek.

While this was going on, Dad returned to the ranch for tobacco and a few supplies. After spending the night at the ranch he returned to trail cutting. They had hit swampy country so had to do some scouting ahead. Finding a decent route was getting harder. They were entering a heavy spruce forest, indicating wetter ground. Dad rode home for tobacco again. Finally they reached solid ground and the going was easier. The mile and a half through the spruce was narrow and winding and rough, with a lot of moss, rock and hummocks, but then, for some distance, it was better.

As they approached Pan Canyon, or Moose Heaven, as some people called it, the trail got a lot steeper. The mosquitoes were bad, and there was a shortage of horse feed at this elevation since it was still early summer. Dad returned to the Home Ranch for a couple of days and brought back more tobacco. It was at that point that Mom started calling the project Tobacco Road.

He returned to the trail for a couple more days until they reached the timberline and more open country. The wagons could travel around the scrub pine and boulders, working their way across Pan Creek and other small streams. No cutting was required here and no marks were made. Dad eventually decided to abandon the trail. The Indians continued on to Clesspocket. In the end, this trail was seldom used, mainly because it seemed to disappear seven or eight miles from the ranch, as it was so poorly marked and the terrain was worse than the old trail. To this day, this trail is still called Tobacco Road.

As the years pass and the old trails become overgrown, the original blazes can still be found on the trees if you look closely. Blazed trees are common as they mark where traps were set or mark turnoffs for shortcuts. Some blazing may go through the bush to mark where a moose was killed. Some blazes have no explanation that anyone can remember, but are there because at one time they served a purpose.

Travelling these trails was hard on the horses, and not all of them were well looked after. If mud holes weren't corduroyed, the horses would flounder around, searching for good footing. Sweat would drip from the horses' bodies while mosquitoes, horseflies and blackflies fed on their blood. Many horses had sore shoulders from ill-fitting collars and sore feet from poor trail conditions. Some of the horses were underfed and treated cruelly. Some were beaten when they were exhausted, unable to drag the loads farther. In the winter it was no better: there wasn't mud, but deep snow often crusted on the trails and there was little or no feed. Fortunately we were able to look after our teams decently, but still it was a hard life for them.

CHAPTER 11

Kids' Games and Pets

During the winter months after our schoolwork was done, I would play with the colts that we had weaned. I would halter-break them and gentle them down. We had a pony saddle and a small pony collar that I could use on them. Once they were used to the saddle, I would pack the colts and lead them about. When I was sure the colts were gentle I put the collar on them and then a harness that I had made out of bits and pieces of leather and rope. Ken wasn't into horses, but he used the swede saw and cut trees and windfalls. Then I would skid the cut wood into the woodshed with the colts. Thus we amused ourselves in useful ways— training colts and getting wood.

In the summer, the milk-cow calves were at my mercy. Ken and I built a stone boat, or as some might call it, a drag. Then I broke the calves when they were big enough. I used basically the same homemade harness I'd used on the colts, except that I turned the collar upside-down for the calves. They could pull a lot more than the colts but they were slower. Ken also built me a cart, which was easier for the calves to pull. I'd still start them off on the drag, and then get them to the cart.

One day Dad brought a cow and her calf in off the range. He put the calf in with the milk-cow calves. The cow was put in the pasture to be let in twice a day at milking time so she could feed her calf. This calf was four or five months old and not used to human contact. It took quite a while to gentle him down enough to harness him and hook him up to the drag. I moved him quickly to the cart, and things were going great. But then I opened the gate, and boy, was that a mistake! Once he was out the gate, he took off at a dead run, the cart whipping along behind, and I was bounced out of it. The calf was bawling and running, and the cart hit the ground about every fifty feet or so, only to fly up into the air again. As the runaway calf passed the ranch house, the cart started to break up and pieces of wood were flying up in the air. The calf finally hit the pasture fence, about an eighth of a mile past the ranch house. When I got there, the calf was lying in a willow brush in a tangle of rope and harness, his eyes rolled up in his head and his tongue hanging out. I was told to leave him alone after that, and it was just as well—he was hell on the equipment!

When the mares were in the field on the mowing machine, I had the chance to play with the colts left in the corral. One summer there was a bald-faced bay filly I called Flicka that was especially gentle. She soon followed me everywhere, including right into the house. I would run in one door, then run through the house and out the other door. The colt would follow and we'd race around outside the house and re-peat the performance. Sometimes she would stop in the doorway and whinny for her mother, but then she'd race after me again. On one especially fast trip through the house, she slipped on the floor and slid into the washing machine. Mom issued new rules: "No more tearing through the house!"

When Ken and I were first learning to ride, we had an old bay geld-ing called Alex, which my dad had bought years before in Chezacut. I was told that when we were tiny my parents would put a pack box on each side of Alex, pop a kid in each box, and we would ride along, peer-ing out of the boxes or napping, while they built fence or checked the cows. Alex was a faithful horse and generally well behaved, except when he was at a certain place in the large horse pasture—right on the trail— and this was his bucking spot! If an adult was riding him there, he would really pitch in and carry on. With us kids, he'd make a few crow-hops, but one day he did succeed in bucking us off. I howled the loudest. It was a sad day for us kids when he had to be put down.

After Alex died, we each had a reliable old horse; mine was a bay mare called Hammerhead and Ken's was a gelding called Brewster. We rode bareback until we were probably ten years old. Our dad wouldn't let us have a saddle before then. I think Dad was afraid we would get hung up in the stirrups and be dragged to death, which was what had happened to a friend of his in Wyoming. We kids always had to find a log or a stump to get up on these horses, as they were not ponies. At the end of a ride before we turned them loose, we'd sometimes give them a bath in the creek. But when they were turned loose, they would always roll in the dirt till they were good and dirty again.

We had the usual pets: cats, dogs and lambs. We had a black female cat named Blackie who lived to be eighteen or nineteen years old. Then she just disappeared one day. Blackie was not much of a pet as she got older, because she preferred to live under the kitchen stove, which was about six inches off the floor, where it was warm and she had no fear of being stepped upon. She was a good hunter, which was a plus, but when she wasn't hunting she just lay under the stove, watching the comings and goings. She'd hiss at you if you disturbed her. One day Mom and I were pretending to wrestle. Blackie came out from under the stove and bit me on the ankle and then went flouncing back under the stove. After that I would check the whereabouts of the cat before I started any roughhousing.

We had raised a couple of pigs for pork and had butchered only one. The other pig ran free around the ranch, and she became quite a pet. She enjoyed the arrival of airplanes as much as we did. When a plane landed, she'd head to the strip at a fast trot, complete with grunts and squeals. She would nose through everything that was unloaded and would help herself to anything that appealed to her, so she had to be watched constantly, but she was good entertainment. One day, some visitors left their new chaps by the front gate when they arrived. The pig chewed on them till she was discovered. She got a kick in the rear. She would also visit the henhouse regularly, checking out the bottom nests for eggs. We had to build a new door that allowed the hens free range but kept the pig out of the coop. We became so attached to that pig that she was around for several years. However, one time while I was away she got butchered. I never asked the reason, and I certainly didn't enjoy the bacon.

The next batch of pigs was kept at the barn and not allowed to become pets. One day when there wasn't much work to do, it was decided that Ed Adams and I were going to butcher a pig. (At that time Ed was living on the ranch as a hired hand.) I took the .22 rifle to the barn where the pigpen was. The one pig left in the pen had gotten very large. Ed came along with a sledgehammer and said it would be better if he just knocked the pig out and then cut its throat. I had never seen this done and figured he knew more about these things than I did. Well, he swung the hammer and hit the pig with a good solid-sounding "thud." There was a godawful screech from the pig, which hit the side of the pen so hard that the two-inch planks splintered and broke! The pig went through the opening in the pen and tore out the barn door, squealing loud enough to split our eardrums, and disappeared into the bushes down towards the creek, while Ed and I just looked at each other. It was several days before the pig returned to his pen (which Ed had repaired in the meantime). He seemed happy to be back. The next time butchering came up, Ed used the rifle!

We raised a lamb on a bottle up by the house rather than leaving it in the sheep pen. It slept in the doghouse with the dogs. When the dogs took off barking, the lamb raced along right behind them, bleating loudly. She would even swim the creek when the dogs crossed it, just to be with them. We tried keeping her with the sheep, but she thought she was a dog. When she was weaned off the bottle and had to rely on grass, she seemed to lose interest in the dogs, but she never did mix with the sheep. Ed liked to chew plug tobacco when he took a break from work. Whenever he pulled the plug from his shirt pocket, the lamb would appear for a chew. She seemed to enjoy the chew, but she became such a nuisance in other ways that we had to get rid of her.

I developed a love of cats and had two—a yellow and white striped tom that Dad turned into an "it," and a grey and white striped female. I called them Jimmy and Jackie, and they were well house-trained. They had "their" chair that they slept in, and it was the only chair that they got up on. If someone sat in their chair, the cats would sit beside the chair and stare at the person, meowing loudly until they got it back.

CHAPTER 12

Baby Brother

In March of 1956 Mom left for Quesnel to await the birth of my brother. At the ranch we settled into a different lifestyle without her. There was no home-schooling, we could walk through the house with boots on, and if our hands weren't clean we could still eat! We shared the cooking of breakfast—anyone can make a pancake. It seemed that my dad's favourite food was cabbage soup. He must have brought in a fifty-pound sack of cabbage and a lot of salt pork in preparation for the bachelor months! We ate cabbage soup for lunch and cabbage soup for dinner. I'm sure we ate it steady for a good ten weeks. The thought of it, even today, does not sit well. Dishes were washed at least once a day. Dad was very fussy about soap on the dishes so he supervised, although he never got his hands wet. We swept the floors now and then. The housework suffered, but we still took our baths and we were old enough to wash clothes. Luckily we never got our arms caught in the wringer.

We listened to the messages broadcast twice daily on the local radio station, CKCQ in Quesnel. It was a great way to receive a brief message, and it was entertainment twice a day, something to look forward to. Dad had always listened to the broadcast and demanded absolute silence while it was on, but now we were old enough to enjoy it too. Even if the messages weren't for us, it was a way to find out what was going on with the neighbours. I still remember two messages from back then: "Please

Pan, Robert, Ken, Betty and Diana on the way to the Anahim Lake Rodeo,
1956. PHOTO: RICHARD HARRINGTON

return my blankets. You can have my husband, but I need my blankets,"
and "Can't make it home till next week. Please feed my rooster."

It was during one of these message broadcasts that we learned that
Robert Eugene Phillips had arrived on April 11. Dad grumbled because
he didn't like the name Eugene. I was only eleven, so it was hard for
me to imagine a baby. It certainly didn't make much of an impact on
my daily routine. Mom took the baby and went to Anahim Lake to wait
with Mickey and Lester Dorsey at Three Circle Ranch until the trails

were passable. The trail from the Home Ranch over the mountains to Anahim Lake wouldn't open up until well into May when the snow melted. The trail around the mountains was impossible as well, because the ice on the Blackwater River would be dangerous with the spring thaw.

When the snow melted in the meadows and on the range, Dad started burning them off, and he took me along. Ken didn't much like riding, so he stayed home. Dad said that if you burned before the poplar

Ken, Betty, Pan, Robert and Diana, Home Ranch. PHOTO: RICHARD HARRINGTON

leaves came out, the danger of forest fires was very small, and it was true. Very seldom did the grass fires get into the timber. The occasional tree went up in a burst of flames and the black smoke would billow up towards the sky, but it was rare that we had to fight fire. The ground was soaked from the heavy snows. Burning the old grass made good range: it kept down the brush and rose bushes, and got rid of the bed of "old bottom" underneath, where all the parasites breed. If the layer of dead grass got too thick, it smothered the growth of new, sweet grass, and then the cattle wouldn't graze in those areas at all. Our cattle travelled and fed only where the land had been burned off.

In the mornings, we awoke to the honking of geese passing overhead on their way north, and to the cries of the sandhill cranes as they circled the wild meadows, looking for good nesting grounds. Meanwhile the ducks quacked away happily on the ponds that were formed by the melting snow. The red-winged blackbirds set up their racket from the pine trees and the crows competed with them. The rooster crowed from the henhouse. Everything was happy that spring was coming and the long winter of being cooped up in semi-darkness was over.

In the mornings, we'd check the cows and do the feeding. Dad would start his pot of cabbage soup or add to the one already simmering on the back of the stove. About 2 p.m. Dad and I would saddle up and ride range for the remainder of the day, leaving a trail of smoke behind us. We were up on First Creek, a small creek southeast of the ranch, with smoke climbing high in the blue sky, when we heard a fire patrol plane coming in low over the smoke. Dad headed for the thick timber and I followed, and we held our horses there while the aircraft circled around, then flew off towards the east. Later in the summer, when Dad went to the forestry office in Quesnel, he was told, "The next time you set the whole damn country on fire, don't ride a white horse!" Apparently we were spotted in the timber!

Near the end of May, Dad decided that we could make it through the pass between the Itcha and Ilgachuz Mountains to pick up Mom and our new baby brother. The creeks had been dropping and most of the cows were out on the spring range. The days were sunny and there were few bugs out yet, so it seemed an ideal time to go.

Ken and I would be riding saddle horses, and Prince, my dad's black horse, would be tied to the back of the wagon for Mom to ride home. Queen, the mare I was riding, was young and had been an orphan, so she'd been fed milk from a pail after her mom had died. The morning we were leaving, Dad milked the milk cows dry so that the calves would be hungry and would keep the cows sucked out for a few days. This would be better for the cows, as no milking would be done while we were gone. Two pails of warm milk were given to Queen, and then we were on our way.

Ken, Rob and Diana in front of the bunkhouse, 1960. PHOTO: RICHARD HARRINGTON

A couple of miles out on the trail, Queen got colic. Dad said the colic was probably brought on by the large amount of milk she had consumed. We removed the saddle and she thrashed around, kicking at her belly and rolling around in the pine needles and moss under the trees. Her body was covered with sweat and dirt. After about an hour and a half, she seemed to have settled down a bit so we decided to move on. We left Queen to follow along, and Dad let me ride Prince. I was on cloud nine: to be able to ride a horse that was labelled "not a horse for children" was super! I managed the horse just fine, and that was the beginning of "what Dad rode I rode." Queen followed behind for the rest of the trip with no apparent problems from the colic.

When we arrived at Three Circle Ranch, I was happy to see my mom and baby brother, who would have been about six weeks old by this time. I held him while he studied me with the disinterested stare of babies that age, but soon I was playing with the older boys, Ken and Frank. We then left for the Home Ranch, with Dad driving the team, Rob riding in the wagon in an Indian willow basket, and Mom, Ken and me riding the saddle horses.

Our life changed some with a new baby in the house. There was a lot more laundry after Rob arrived, and a lot more water packing, since the cotton diapers had to be washed in different water than the other clothes. It was a good thing that Mom had that gas washing machine. And once the baby smiles and giggling began, Rob was much more fun to play with.

CHAPTER 13

Indian Stories

For years the Indians had travelled through the Rainbow Mountains to Bella Coola and Kimsquit, where they could trade furs for eulachon grease and salmon. The trail they took was then known as the Grease Trail, running west from the Fraser River. Now known as the Macken-zie-Grease Trail, it passed by the Home Ranch just a few miles to the north.

Anahim Lake was named after Chief Anaham, who was a Carrier Indian from the area. In 1862 the smallpox epidemic nearly wiped out all of Chief Anaham's people. After the Chilcotin war, Anaham's people were moved east near Alexis Creek onto the Anaham Reserve. Stan Dowling, who was one of the first postmasters at Anahim Lake, changed the spelling of Anaham to Anahim to avoid any confusion between the two places.

When Indian families came to work for Dad, they would pitch their tents down by the creek and turn their horses into the pasture (usually keeping one horse tied in camp for the kids to ride). Dogs were tied to trees or to the wagons. To keep a dog from running, they would some-times tie the dog's front leg to its neck.

While the men cut rails, or did whatever work they had been hired to do, the women would set up a smooth log on an angle, hang a moose hide on the log and scrape the hide for buckskin. Or they might have a hide laced on a stretching rack, and they'd work it with a stick to soften

Mary Cassam tanning a moose hide. PHILLIPS FAMILY PHOTO

it for tanning. A few of the women used small sewing machines with a crank handle to sew buckskin articles. Most sewed by hand, sitting cross-legged just inside the tent flaps with a blackened pot of tea beside them. They had a tin cup to dip into the pot. The tea was sweetened till it tasted almost like syrup.

Many of the Indian women used sinew for sewing. The large tendon from the back of the moose was saved when it was butchered. When the tendon was dried and cured, it could then be separated into threads for sewing. A lot of the fancy work on buckskin gloves and moccasins was done with embroidery thread or beads—sometimes both.

Sometimes the women would butcher a moose that the men had hauled home. They would cut the meat into long strips and throw it over a high rack near the fire. It would dry in the wind, sun and campfire smoke. The dried meat was something like hardtack to chew on—unsalted and tasteless. Later, when salt was easier to come by, the strips of moose meat were salted, which made it a lot more satisfying to gnaw on.

Dad sometimes got a cow in a trade, which the Indians would bring him within a day or two. They would arrive with the cow, often driven up with several others that they'd then turn loose to wander home. The cow that Dad had traded for would be branded and left under good fence until she had been fed for a winter and calved out. By then she was accustomed to her new home and usually did not leave to wander back to her old home.

As a child I had always heard the expression "moccasin telegraph," but it was something I never paid much attention to. What it really was, I'm not sure, maybe just people passing on news and information. Somebody who was miles away would somehow know what happened in another part of the country. When they were asked how they knew, there was no explanation, just a shrug.

Helen Squinas told me that she and Andrew were visiting one day over at Tom and Cecilia Baptiste's place on the west end of Tsacha Lake. The Baptiste house was on a poplar knoll overlooking the lake, where the Blackwater River fills the first lake of many on its eastward route to the Fraser. Cecilia grew vegetables near the lake. When she found snakes in her garden, she asked Andrew to shoot them. Helen said that Cecilia stayed outside the garden fence while Andrew went into the enclosure to search for the snakes. He saw one and he shot it. The bullet went straight through the snake's head, hit a rock, ricocheted and hit Cecilia in the stomach! (She was a fairly large lady.) She started screaming, holding her stomach and running in circles. Andrew dropped the rifle and ran after her. The bullet had bruised her quite badly, but it didn't penetrate the skin. Still, it gave her quite a scare.

Something similar occurred to a local Indian lady who had been out hunting squirrels and had gotten quite wet. When she returned home she removed her jeans and threw them over the warming oven of the wood cookstove. She had some shells from her gun in one of the pockets of her jeans. One fell out onto the top of the stove where, after a while, it exploded from the heat! The shell casing struck the lady in the stomach and she, like Cecilia, thought that she had been shot. After a lot of hollering and investigating, she was relieved to find it was only a bruise.

At the end of January, Ella Jimmie went missing at Nazko. She and her husband Freddie quite often worked for us at haying time, and we were concerned. A week later, her badly beaten body was found in the snow. A funeral was to be held at Anahim Lake, as Ella belonged to the Ulkatcho Band, and she was being taken home for burial.

On the day of the funeral, I rode to the Alexis place, where a large group was gathering to travel to Anahim Lake. In those days, the whole Indian community went to funerals. They put out lots of hay for the cattle before leaving, then sleighs were loaded, and amidst the yapping and fighting of the dogs, the children's laughter and the women calling back and forth, one sleigh after another pulled out and went trotting down the trail. There were nine sleighs that left Alexis's place that day, and more would join the group before they reached Anahim Lake. I felt left out as I stood with my horse and watched the last of the sleighs disappear down the trail. The jingling of the horses' trace chains faded away and silence fell. I mounted my horse and turned it towards home.

The Indian people believed it was bad luck if the blood of a wolf touched you. Antoine Baptiste's daughter, Julie, got polio when she was a young girl and was left with a limp. The Indians were convinced that it was because Antoine had shot a wolf and Julie had gotten some of its blood on her hands. When haying was done, the Indians always left a stook of hay in each of their meadows. That way, if any of their ancestors passed by, they could stop and feed their horses. They did not believe in shooting grizzly bears and would never hunt one. Some of them would kill black bears though, and the Kluskus people even ate the black bear meat.

One winter day John Jimmie arrived with a team and sleigh, along with his youngest son, Robbie, who was about four or five. We kids had tricycles and Robbie, having never seen one before, was fascinated. He rode round and round the living room for hours. He was finally pulled from the tricycle and put to bed, but later during the night when everyone else was retiring, Robbie awoke sobbing that his legs hurt. No amount of consoling could stop the crying. John was very embarrassed that his son had kept the household from a good night's sleep. My parents waved it off as part of child rearing.

John Jimmie had five sons: Joseph, Alfred, William, Freddie and Robbie. There were also two daughters: Agnes, who married Edward

Chantyman, and another daughter whose name I can't recall. Joseph lived at Tatelkuz Lake with his wife, Josie. They ran a trapline and raised some good horses. William and his wife, Elsie, lived there too. The rest of the family lived at New Kluskus (about seven miles east of Old Kluskus).

The Francis Cassam family was probably our closest neighbour, if you got right down and measured the distance. They lived north of us about seven miles on the Blackwater River, where Tsetzi Creek runs into the river. Their place was called Blue Lake, being just below Blue Lake, and was set in a depression surrounded by hills covered with thick second-growth pine. The skeletons of older burned trees dotted the hillsides, and there would be the occasional patch of standing old-growth timber that had escaped the fires. When I was young, the Cassams lived in a tiny cabin with their three children, Lisa, William and Wilfred, who were all older than I was.

Francis was a pyromaniac; he started fires wherever he went. He was also a medicine man. He would doctor the sick amongst his people and he made predictions about the future. One time there was a child

Francis Cassam, the medicine man, and Ed Adams, who lived at the Home Ranch. PHOTO: RICHARD HARRINGTON

lost in a fierce snowstorm and Francis told the searchers where the child was, but no one believed him. Eventually they found the child right where he had told them to look, but unfortunately they arrived too late to save the child.

Francis had lost an eye in some sort of accident—probably he ran a stick into his eye while chasing horses. He was fitted with a glass eye, which he always wore. It looked fairly natural. One fall, when he was in Williams Lake, he caught a ride to Anahim Lake with a freight truck. It came over the news on the radio the next day that there had been an accident on Highway 20 near Chilanko Forks, and a freight truck had overturned: "Ross Wilson, the driver, escaped uninjured but passenger Francis Cassam suffered the loss of an eye." We were feeling very sorry for Francis because now he would be totally blind, but we found out later that he had only lost his glass eye! I don't think he ever did replace his glass eye after that.

Francis didn't know exactly how old he was. He had no birth certificate, only baptism papers, and then he wasn't sure how old he was when he was baptized. He thought he must have been about twelve years of age at the time. It was said that he came from Ootsa Lake country. His wife was Mary Baptiste, and she was the daughter of Baptiste Long John.

Francis's fee for doctoring the sick was usually one horse. He would take a cow but preferred horses. He was very hard on his horses and many died of starvation, overwork and beatings in his yard and on the trail. The saddle horses' backs were raw, as were the team's shoulders— probably caused by ill-fitting saddles and collars. This was one of the reasons that he wanted horses, so that he could keep travelling about the country. One time at Anahim Lake he left his team tied to a tree in the hot sun for three or four days. A young lad was told by his father to water the team and he did so, but after filling up on water, one of the horses died! Francis wanted the horse replaced. The young lad was so afraid Francis would take his horse that he hid it till Francis left town. Mary would come and spend a few days at a time with us. She never wanted to unsaddle her horse because its back would be such a mess of open sores. Mom would scold her about it, but it would go in one ear and out the other.

Francis Cassam with his granddaughter, Tillie. PHOTO: VANCE HANNA

Francis was afraid of flying. In later years, the Department of Indian Affairs was flying Indians out of the area for medical treatment. Before boarding a plane, Francis would stand in front of the aircraft and bless it.

Lisa married Harry Squinas and moved to Anahim Lake. William married Rose Paul from Baezaeko, and they built a two-storey house beside the old cabin at Blue Lake. Francis and Mary built a larger cabin on the bench overlooking the old site. Wilfred built a much larger one beside them and moved in Rosalee Alexis. They had two daughters, Tillie and Roseanne. Wilfred was an awfully mean man. He beat the animals and he killed his wife when their daughter Roseanne was just a baby. William and Rose took the girls and raised them along with their daughter, Veronica, and Joseph Jimmie's son, David.

Rose was the best thing that ever happened to the animals at Blue Lake. When she moved there they were well fed and the small herd of cows was looked after. They were all much better off after she came; no more skinny animals with sores all over, or hungry dogs.

Back in the 1940s a family lived on the Blackwater River right next to Jack Thompson's Sleepy Hollow. It was a beautiful spot on the north side of the river, surrounded by poplar sidehills, with a small lake out front. The hay land was on the south side of the river. I can remember only an old fellow by the name of Kluskus Tommy and his granddaughter, Helena Jack. They lived there off and on. While the grass burning was going on one spring when they were not at home, their cabin was burned down. It was never rebuilt and they never returned. I do know that Helena Jack lived after that at Nazko.

The Alexis family lived on the Blackwater River about seven miles northwest of the ranch; Peter and Minnie had a large family. They lived on the north side where the river opens up to form a miniature lake. The neat cabin was built on a knoll surrounded by poplars, willow and the odd jackpine. From the front door you could view the river and the Ilgachuz Mountains. Andrew and Helen Squinas lived just up the trail in a tiny cabin on the river, and this was where the corrals and barn were that were shared by both families.

Tom Baptiste lived on the west end of Tsacha Lake in a very fertile valley that grew red top grasses, bunchgrass on the higher ground and slough grass in the wet spots. Big willows, alders and smaller bushes covered the riverbanks. The north hillsides were mostly poplar, probably due to the yearly spring burning in that area. The Blackwater River twists and turns through the valley; it barely seems to move over the sandy river bottom. The river runs into Tsacha Lake just out from Tom's cabin. When Tom was young, he joined the army and served in the Second World War. At one time he had a wife, Sedul, who died from an unknown illness about 1939 or 1940. Later he took up with Cecilia Peter. Her sister, Christine, and Christine's son, Frank, lived with them for several years as well. After Frank disappeared, Christine moved down with Peter Morris at New Kluskus.

Frank was probably in his teens when he and his mother came to the Blackwater country. He was a tall, very good-looking young man but unfortunately he was deaf and may have been a bit simple. He disappeared in July, just before haying season. People came from all over to search for him on saddle horses. They concentrated their search north to northwest of Tsacha Lake in what is now known as Matthew Creek (or Rozak Creek) and the Laidman Lake area. They found a footprint on a sandbar at Matthew Creek, which could only have been Frank's because at that time there was no one else living in that area. After a couple of weeks, the searchers began to return home as they had haying to do. To this day, even with the logging and mining in that area, no remains have ever been found.

Francis Cassam, with his psychic powers, claimed that he saw Frank catching a grouse with his bare hands and eating the raw flesh. Frank had no matches with him to start a fire; if he had, he might have been found. Being deaf he would have not have heard anyone calling him. Some people believed that he did not want to be found. He had spent his life in the bush so it seemed odd that he got lost. With his disabilities, maybe he became confused and hid from the searchers.

Francis's final theory was that a grizzly bear had attacked, killed and eaten Frank. This was possible as the area was infested with grizzlies. In the kitchen at the ranch, Francis gave us a demonstration of how he thought it might have happened. Francis was the bear and Frank was a kitchen chair. Francis crept quietly up to the chair and then pounced on it while making roaring and growling sounds, viciously shaking the chair till I thought he'd break the legs off it! I tell you, Chief Dan George had nothing on Francis!

Martha Paul lived with Tom and Cecilia for a number of years. Martha was born blind, and she was one of those unfortunate people that nobody wanted unless she served a purpose. She was much more popular when she began receiving a welfare cheque, although she wasn't any better treated. She packed water, sawed wood with a crosscut saw, chopped wood and split kindling. She spent hours on the scrub board, scrubbing and rinsing clothes. Knitting was one of her pastimes. She knit very colourful blankets and tube stockings. Martha Paul gave birth to two children, Marvin and Sally, and her life may have been easier after she had children, as they became her eyes.

Sometimes Tom and Cecilia hayed for us, but not often. Tom did not like to work for a white man, although he did make a good friend and neighbour. While they were working in the fields, Martha and the children would be left in camp. Mom would send us to the camp with bowls of food as she felt Martha and the children where underfed. Marvin would bring the bowls back to the ranch and they were always very clean.

Tom bought a Snow Cruiser snow machine, and he'd take Martha for rides out on Tsacha Lake or over to the Cassams' place. Martha packed a stick and when she felt Tom was driving too fast, she'd hit him on the head.

Years later, after a particularly wild drinking party, Martha wandered off to avoid the fighting and she became lost. When the party moved on, no one seemed to realize she wasn't around. I found her quite by accident three days later, sitting under a tree. I was appalled that she had been there for so long in only a skirt, a cardigan sweater and moccasins, and it was October! She told me in her very broken English that she had left and then been unable to find her way back. I slowly walked her back to the cabin and prepared tea and food for her. She wouldn't eat until she had washed thoroughly; then she ate and fell asleep. While she was sleeping, I went to find someone to take care of her.

One February Antoine Baptiste came to the Home Ranch, as he wanted to buy a cow. He was having a big party at his place, and he wanted a change from the usual moose or fish. Ed, who lived at the Home Ranch then, finally agreed to sell him a yearling steer. A price was agreed on and the steer was butchered and thrown into the sleigh. As Antoine was leaving he asked me if I wanted to come to his party. The beef he would be serving in place of moose appealed to me, as we never ate beef, but I also knew their parties got out of hand, so I had to decline.

One time during the winter Doggan Leon, who lived at Irene Lake, came to the ranch to tell my mom that one of his young sons was really sick and could hardly breathe. They figured it was pneumonia. All Mom could tell him to do was to apply mustard plasters to the child's chest, and this would knock the pneumonia from his lungs. She prepared some plasters for him out of dried mustard, flour and water. She explained how the plasters had to be heated quite hot, laid on the chest and then covered with something warm to hold in the heat. Doggan took this information and the plasters and headed home. Dad stopped in at their place later that afternoon on his way back from Anahim and said the baby wouldn't make it through the night. Luckily he did survive, although he was months in recovering. No doubt the mustard plasters saved the baby's life.

Another one of the Leon children got some kind of infection and was in the hospital for a long time; he was away for so long that when he did get home, he had forgotten his language. He had been watching Westerns on television and he wanted Rob, my brother, to play cowboys and Indians with him. He was to be the cowboy, not an Indian, which gave our parents something to laugh about.

March fourth was George Leon's birthday; he was probably about five years old. His parents, Doggan and Liza, brought him to our place for a bit of a birthday party. My mom had baked a birthday cake and made homemade ice cream; everything was dished up and passed around. George tried the ice cream and whispered something to his mom who burst out laughing! My mom asked what he had wanted, and Liza said that he wanted the ice cream put on the stove and warmed up!

For years the Indians used to make homebrew from dried fruit, yeast and sugar. It was pretty gross stuff, but they would get a real buzz from it. Doggan and Liza Leon came visiting one time, along with Liza's mom, Mrs. Alexis. Well, Doggan had a pretty good buzz on from his jug of homebrew, and it soon became clear that Doggan did not hold much love for his mother-in-law. Mrs. Alexis was sitting on the edge of the wood box. After some time Doggan began to cuss at her and then proceeded to shove her down into the wood box, which was empty. I think at that point my mom intervened. Everyone had a great deal of respect for "Mrs. Pan," so he backed off. But the funny part was when Mom and Liza tried to pull Mrs. Alexis out of the wood box. Her feet were clad in buckskin moccasins and moccasin rubbers, and her long cotton stockings and skirts were under her somewhere! There was a lot of grunting and then finally giggling on Mom and Liza's part before the old woman was pulled from the wood box.

The Leons quite often stayed in the little cabin out back during the winter. In the summer they would have camped outside. My mom had covered the walls of the cabin with brown paper that was almost like brown wrapping paper, and Doggan used to draw pictures on those walls. He made beautiful drawings of moose, bear and deer. He had such a great talent that was never used except for drawing on bunkhouse walls.

One time I went to visit them in the cabin after dark and there was a "bitch lamp" burning (a rag stuck into a can of moose tallow). This provided a small amount of light but it stank because of the cloth and the burning moose tallow. It also smoked a great deal. Later a kerosene lantern with fuel was always left in the cabin for their use.

One May, while the men were off trapping somewhere, Mrs. Alexis, a very elderly lady at that time, passed away in the family cabin. She must have died quickly because back then, when someone was expected to die, they were moved outside. We were in bed that late evening and the dog began to bark, so we got up to find our yard full of horses and riders. Some horses had three children on them. The women and kids had come to our house because they believed it was bad luck to stay in the house after Mrs. Alexis died in it. The horses weren't a problem to contend with as we let them go into the pasture, but bedding down all those people was another thing. Mom somehow managed to make enough beds (some minus mattresses) and then rounded up enough blankets to get them through the night. The next morning Helen Squinas went out to find the men, and the rest of the women and children returned home for the burial.

When the days began to warm in the spring, the sap started to run in the pine trees. It was a common practice for the Indian people to cut large slashes in the bark of the pine, which was at that time easily pulled free from the tree in large pieces. Between the bark and the wood was a thin, whitish skin, which they ate as a spring tonic. (The young girls told me it also was good for ending unwanted pregnancies.) I have also been told that when the sap runs, the inner bark is full of a sweet substance, which is eaten for the sweetness.

When the sap oozed out from these large barkless areas, it hardened and turned yellow with age, and was very good fire starter. You could cut large slabs of pitchy wood with an axe and place them on top of a few boughs with dried pine needles to make a quick, hot fire. The Indian people also chewed the pitch until it was soft and pliable and then used it as a poultice on infected wounds. Often they just chewed it as chewing gum, but I found it a bit bitter! The pitch was gathered and melted in a tin can over the fire, becoming a hot liquid that hardened as it cooled, and was then used to mend the cracks in wooden boats and seal against leakage. Exposure to the sun too long caused it to crack and fall out, so it was only a temporary fix.

In the spring, the Indians would catch muskrats, then skin and boil them in a huge blackened pot on the fire. As the water boiled, the little bodies would roll over, the heads would surface, and those black, beady eyes would be staring up at you. The long hairless tails were often left on as well.

The Indians would ride about in the wintertime wearing just a denim jacket for a coat, and buckskin gloves and gumboots. They'd come in from the cold without removing the jacket, drink tea for several hours, then mount their saddle horse and head off for a two- or three-hour ride home as the sun would be sliding down over the Ilgachuz Mountains and the cold was beginning to get a good bite to it. The Indians seemed to have much better blood circulation than any of us whites!

I believe that welfare was the downfall of the Indian people in Blackwater country. After the government cheques started to arrive, traplines were abandoned and the small herds of cattle were sold. The people congregated on the small reserves with nothing to do but attend church. They returned less and less to their isolated homes. One close neighbour told us that two government men had argued about whether he needed welfare. One said he did not, and the other said he did. Pretty soon, he told us he received a welfare cheque, even though with his few cows and trapline he had been supporting his wife and daughter. But soon that family, too, moved to the reserve at Anahim Lake.

CHAPTER 14

Blackwater People and Other Stories

It was September of 1960 when Ed Adams first came to the ranch. One day we saw a float plane circling the buildings and then it went off towards Stuyvesant Lake. We went to the dock at the lake, but there was no one there. Thinking that the plane hadn't landed, we returned to the ranch.

About 10 a.m. the next day there was a knock on the front door and, upon opening it, there stood a tall, thin gentleman with very sharp features, wearing a business suit complete with white shirt and tie. He introduced himself as Ed Adams. He had flown in the day before with a pilot who landed him on the wrong side of the lake. Ed had been so sick from the plane ride that he just built a fire and spent the night out there.

Ed was born and raised in New York State on a dairy farm that his parents owned for many years, and he'd carried on the tradition. After his parents died, he sold the family farm. His only other sibling was a sister who was a career lady and had no interest in farming. Ed went to Wyoming for a number of years, to the same area that my dad had been in. He heard stories of how Dad had gone to BC to start a cattle ranch so he decided to come to BC as well and ended up in Quesnel, where nearly everyone knew my parents. He then hired a plane and flew to the Home Ranch. He became a true friend to both of my parents, all the kids and especially me.

When he came to live with us he was nearly fifty years old. He had never married and said that he had never had time. In thirty years he'd missed milking on the family dairy farm only once—because he had gone to Saratoga for the horse races and had gotten drunk.

Ed settled into the bunkhouse, took his meals in the ranch house and went to work. He refused wages; he was only looking for a home. Over time he ended up with a small herd of cattle, a team of horses and a saddle horse. He had absolutely no desire to go to town and went only when it was absolutely necessary. One time he stayed on the ranch for five years without ever leaving. He had a dry sense of humour and a soft voice that he rarely raised, and I can't remember him ever losing his temper. He was always very respectful, especially of the ladies. He was kind and generous. His motto was, "If you can't say something nice about someone, don't say anything." He would also say, "If you didn't learn one new thing in a day—it didn't matter how small—it was a wasted day."

After he arrived at the ranch he seldom ever drank, but the odd time he would join other people to have a sociable drink. One day a German visitor asked him if he ever drank, and Ed replied, "Two dairy farms and a sawmill have gone down my throat." With that said, he walked away. He told another visitor that he could back a pickup truck up to his barn in New York any day of the week and load it up with empty whisky bottles.

Shortly after Ed arrived, he asked Rob (who was four years old at the time) if there were any fish in the creek. Rob said he'd seen a big one out eating grass a few days before. Ed just chuckled!

With Ed living on the Home Ranch with us, life was much easier for Mom. Being an ex–dairy farmer, Ed rose early, started the fire in the ranch house and put the kettle on. Prior to his arrival, it was always left to Mom to start the cookstove and open the damper and add wood to the heater. The house might have been cold and drafty, but now it was at least warm when she got up.

Ed packed the water and also cut the wood. Plus, he took over the milking and the feeding of the chickens and tended to the sheep. He also helped feed the cows, cut rails and he worked at the sawmill, so he was a great deal of help to Dad as well.

Our short-horned milk cow calved and got milk fever. She was stretched out in the grass, gazing at the great divide when Ed came along. This was nothing new to him. He stared at the cow for a while and then he went to the shop and returned shortly with a tire pump and some string. With some help he got some air pumped into each teat and then tied them with the string. After about an hour the cow got up and started bawling for her calf.

Dad would fall a lot trees and then go off on a freighting trip to Anahim Lake. Ed was an old teamster, so he'd skid the logs into the mill site, where lumber was cut (after we had hauled hay and fed the cattle). The team literally would run down the skid trails, with Ed leaping from one side of the log to the other, hollering "Whoa!" He finally got tired of the team not listening to his commands, so he tied the lines together and then when he saw a stump coming up by the side of the skid trail, he would yell "Whoa" and drop the lines over the stump! This would cause the team to sit down on their hind ends with a good jerk, and after doing that a few times, he said that now all he had to do to get the team to obey was to whisper "Whoa" and they would stop!

Another time he was using a different team that wouldn't listen; he harnessed and hooked them together and then blindfolded them. He drove them around the corral until they started to move freely, then he drove them up to the side of the barn and called "Whoa" just before they hit the barn! This team also learned the meaning of "Whoa."

He was an expert teamster, loved driving a team and would never even consider getting on the tractor. He thought that any motorized vehicle was a curse on mankind! (In later years he did buy and learn to operate a chainsaw. He could fuel it up, but anything beyond that he needed help with.) Ed would ride saddle horse but preferred to use the team, or to run. He used to run wherever he went—perhaps this was the reason he was so skinny. He always missed the three back loops in his Wranglers with his belt, said it made them last longer. He wore long johns twelve months of the year and never exposed any skin to the sun other than his hands and face. He seldom wore a cap, preferring a felt or straw hat, depending on the season. When the weather got cold, he wore a winter hat with big earflaps that he rarely tied under his chin, so when he was running he looked a bit like Goofy!

He had some neat sayings. If someone was good with his fists, Ed would describe him by saying, "He could whip a buzz saw." He never swore, and would say things like "Lightning to grind," when he became a little impatient, or he would turn his palms out and say, "Well, looky here." When he began to get hard of hearing, he asked me one day, "Why is it that when I was young everyone shouted, and now that I'm old everyone whispers?"

One morning Ed didn't get up early and we feared that he'd died in his sleep. No one wanted to go to the bunkhouse to check. Fortunately he was okay. He said that he just felt like staying in bed.

Alex Fraser was a good friend of my parents', especially my dad. Alex was the mayor of Quesnel for twenty years, and he was the International tractor dealer there. In 1969 he was elected MLA for the Cariboo–Chilcotin district and remained an MLA until his death in 1989. He was the Minister of Highways from 1975 to 1987. He made a great many improvements to the roads in the Cariboo, probably more than any other minister. He was especially helpful to the ranchers and farmers. Alex and his wife, Gertrude, came to a lot of the Anahim Lake stampedes.

After he was elected MLA, Alex had to spend a lot of his time in Victoria, although he and Gertrude kept their home in Quesnel and returned as often as they could. One of the last times that I remember seeing Alex was in 1970 after we had sold the ranch and moved to Tsetzi Lake. We hadn't yet built an airstrip there. Alex and Alec Holley and another fellow had flown to the Home Ranch and then borrowed horses to ride out to Tsetzi Lake and visit with Dad. I met them about halfway up the trail. The horse that Alex was riding was dancing all over the place, and it looked as though he didn't have a great deal of control over it. Alex was a politician, not a horseman. I told him he looked good in the saddle even though his trousers had ridden up nearly to his knees and he was wearing his polished oxfords with pine needles clinging to his stockings. He told me, "I'm scared shitless, and I need another drink!"

Alfred Bryant was the only person I knew who drove a steel-wheeled wagon after the rubber-tired ones became common. I've seen steel-wheeled wagons sitting in people's yards or abandoned behind barns, but he actually used his. He'd take his to the hunting camp in the mountains. The narrow, heavy wheels must have cut through the muskeg something fierce, which would have been hard pulling for the horses.

There was an Indian trader by the name of Capoose who packed out of Bella Coola in the early days. (I mentioned him earlier when I was explaining the origin of the Sugar Camp Trail.) He traded supplies for furs; very little else is known of him. In the 1920s he traded in the Anahim area, west Chilcotin and as far north as Fort St. James. He had a small independent trading post at Abuntlet Lake, north-northwest of Anahim Lake.

Paul Krestenuk, my godfather, was born in November of 1887 in Russia, escaped from a penal colony there and made his way to Canada in 1922. After working and saving his money, he started a freight line in Quesnel with teams hauling trading supplies to Nazko, Kluskus and Ulkatcho. Paul started the trading posts at Nazko and Ulkatcho, but there was already some sort of trading post at Kluskus even before Paul arrived. He travelled through the country, cutting most of the first roads. He corduroyed a lot of muskegs to allow teams to cross. He also built a bridge on the Blackwater River upstream from where Tsetzi Creek drains into the Blackwater. This was probably the first bridge on the river.

Paul had a partner in the trading post at Kluskus by the name of Alex Paley. Alex lived at the trading post a great deal of the time. Paul would travel as far west as Anahim Lake and northwest to Burns Lake and Tetachuck, trading supplies for fur. On his return trips his wagon would be loaded with fur and, depending on the size of his load, he might need four horses to manage the hills, which were very steep. He used a technique for going down some of those steep hills that involved a section of a log that was hollowed out to accommodate the tire of the wagon. Using pry poles and blocks of wood, the rear axle of the wagon was pried up and this hewed-out log put under the tire. The log acted as a brake on the steep hills, helping the horses to hold the loads back. At the bottom of the hill, the wagon had to again be pried up to remove the log. On the next trip out, the log, poles and blocks of wood were hauled to the top of the hill to be used on the return.

In the spring at the Kluskus trading post there would be a gathering of people from far and wide, with hundreds of Indians arriving by horseback. People and horses and dogs were scattered about the village and sidehills. Paul acquired the nickname of "One Percent Paul" at one of these gatherings. When accused of overcharging for his merchandise, Paul said that he bought for one dollar and sold for two. That was one per cent. Paul Krestenuk passed away on May 7, 1969 from tuberculosis.

Andy Holte, one of the original pioneers, with a team of horses. PHILLIPS FAMILY PHOTO

In the spring of 1948, Tommy and Marion Walker, who had a lodge at Stuie at the headwaters of the Bella Coola valley, moved north to Spatsizi. They travelled hundreds of miles with pack and saddle horses to the North Country. They came through the Home Ranch and camped for a number of days, resting their horses and buying more horses from my dad, who always kept sixty or seventy head. Dad was constantly selling, buying and trading horses. The Walkers were accompanied by Albert Casimir and Patrick Jack from Anahim Lake, who looked after the horses and did the packing.

The Walkers either bought or took over the Spatsizi area from the Hyland brothers, who had guided and trapped that area prior to 1948. The name Spatsizi means red goat. Apparently the red dirt near Cold Fish Lake is where the goats roll and bathe themselves—no doubt in the rutting season—thus giving them a reddish hue. The Spatsizi has an abundance of game, which explains why it's known as "the Serengeti of the North." Through the persistent lobbying efforts of the Walkers, in 1975 the area became the Spatsizi Plateau Wilderness Provincial Park.

One sunny winter afternoon, Andy Holte arrived with a team and a sleigh. We were young but I remember the sleigh box was empty but for his bedroll, a set of skis, and a case of dried prunes. Andy had travelled for probably four days, relying on nothing but his friends amongst the Indians and his love of the country—but that was Andy. He was one of those men who rose in the morning and accepted the upcoming day with a lot of enthusiasm.

I was told that Andy, his wife, Hattie, and two sons and two daughters had arrived in Anahim Lake in 1921 from the state of Washington. He had already established Eldash, his ranch north of Anahim Lake, when my dad came to the country. Rich Hobson said Andy reminded him of Will Rogers. Andy loved to travel the country by horseback and sometimes with a team. Time meant very little to him. One story goes that Andy had bought a kitchen stove for the ranch house but when he got it home he discovered that he didn't have the wrench he needed to assemble it. So he saddled up and rode twenty miles south to the nearest neighbour's to borrow a wrench. While drinking coffee with the neighbour, the conversation turned to horses and they agreed that this was a good time to go after the wild horses on Sugarloaf Mountain.

Soon Andy was headed in that direction without a thought to Hattie, the kitchen stove and the ranch. Three weeks later he returned to his ranch, having forgotten all about the wrench!

So it wasn't surprising when Andy showed up on our doorstep one day, four days from home with only a pair of skis and a box of prunes — and he hadn't even brought the mail. I guess he had harnessed his team with no real destination or plan in mind. The skis he gave to us kids, which we loved. The prunes he probably gave to Mom. He spent a few days visiting with us in his quiet, polite manner, telling Mom and Dad the latest news, what the rustling for horses was like and how much hay people had left, how many coyotes he had run down and the price of fur. Then one day he just harnessed up his team and with a wave of his hand he drove out of the yard and headed for home — that is, unless he got sidetracked along the way!

The last time I saw Andy Holte must have been shortly before his passing, in the late 1950s. I was checking cows three or four miles out of the ranch by the old pack trail. As I sat on my horse on a fairly large grassy meadow, a horse and rider came loping out to meet me. It was Andy — he'd ridden along the old pack trail from Anahim with the Home Ranch in mind. We rode on down to the ranch and he spent the night, saddled up in the morning and rode back up the trail.

CHAPTER 15

Cattle Drives

For years, our cattle were driven from the Home Ranch to Anahim Lake. Starting in 1952, we took them to the fall sales in Quesnel. While the Frontier Cattle Company was up and running, the cattle were driven to Vanderhoof, where there were stockyards, and from there they were put on railcars and taken to the BC Livestock Exchange yards in Vancouver. (The BC Livestock Co-op had purchased these yards in 1943.)

Our first drive to Quesnel was in October of 1952; Dad estimated it would take sixteen days to get there. Dave Dorsey and John Bragg came from Anahim Lake with the Dorseys' and the Bryants' cattle and perhaps some others as well. Because of the distance we'd cover, no calves were taken on this drive—only yearlings, cull cows and old bulls. Jack Thompson arrived with his cattle several days before the departure date. He'd agreed to help on the first few days to get the cattle started.

The cattle were moved out at daylight while frost glittered on the grass and the air was crisp. Breath from horses, riders and cattle rose in the air. The cowbell sounds mixed and rang out—each bell having its own tone. The weather was beautiful and everyone was in high spirits.

The wagon left hours later after all the chores were done. We were to be gone for a good month so there was much to do. The cow was milked for the last time and then turned into the field with her calf. No meat could be left in the meat house, as it would attract the bears. Any

Moving cattle at Hobson's Rimrock Ranch. PHOTO: RICHARD HARRINGTON

Ken and Diana riding bareback and Betty in the chuck wagon on a cattle drive, 1953. PHILLIPS FAMILY PHOTO

perishable food had to be taken with us. Lots of feed was put out for the chickens, but still they would have to fend for themselves before our return. The cats were put outside too.

By late morning we were on our way. Mom drove the team and wagon loaded with camp supplies, and food and clothing to last us for more than two weeks. She had baked many loaves of bread, gathered vegetables from the garden and packed sugar, jam, peanut butter, canned milk, coffee, tea, cheese, salt, macaroni, rice, lard and margarine along with some fresh meat. Additional meat would be hunted along the way. We kids were too young to chase cattle so we rode bareback on our horses, Hammerhead and Brewster, following the wagon. We helped Mom set up camp in the evenings and dismantle it in the mornings.

The first night we camped at Paul Meadow, a brush flat on the plateau above Tsacha Lake, sixteen miles east of the Home Ranch. There was a good amount of feed there and a creek, which acted as a natural barrier. The cattle were driven across the creek and camp was set up near the crossing. Listening to the bells at night, we could tell if the cattle were moving, feeding or lying down. This would have been the hardest camp to hold the cattle in, as it was the first night and they were close to home and homesick. If we were going to have any trouble, it would be here. On some drives a cow or two would manage to slip away in the night. Most times they were caught. A horse was kept close to camp for this purpose. I think my dad lay awake till daylight, listening to hear cattle moving, a splash in the creek or a branch snapping as a cow circled the camp. That first night proved uneventful and dawn came to the world once again—crisp and cool—the skies showing the promise of a second beautiful day.

In the morning the cattle were at the creek crossing, bells ringing in the stillness, an occasional cough or low mooing. After coffee and a hasty breakfast, the four men (Dad, Dave Dorsey, Jack Thompson and John Bragg) swung into their saddles. They turned the herd east and began the climb for several miles to a higher timbered ridge and then a gentle, very rocky descent into the next valley where Antoine Baptiste lived with his mother, Mrs. Long John. In the valley, Kushya Creek wound through swamps, hay meadows and bush flats without so much as a ripple before it started its rather steep descent to the Blackwater River. When we reached the Baptiste place, the cattle were put in the hay meadow under fence. Mom, Ken and I set up camp on a rise above the house while the men cared for the horses, and then we went to the house to drink tea and visit. Jack Thompson had left us about noon to head back home. The drive that day had been about ten miles.

The third dawn once again promised a gorgeous day. The cattle were ready to travel early. It was eight to ten miles to the old Indian village of Kluskus, which had been abandoned for a number of years. The trail was not nearly as rocky along Squirrel Lake. A couple of miles before the village, we crossed the end of Squirrel Lake and wound through the big spruce. The old trading post appeared just before we crossed back over the creek on our right. Only ten years earlier there had been a lot of activity here, but now it stood deserted, the door hanging on one hinge. Many of the windowpanes were broken, grass and weeds grew up through the cracks in the porch and already small pine and spruce trees had sprung up in the yard.

After crossing the creek we came to a grassy flat that ran to our right, out to Kluskus Lake. Further to the right on a bench of land overlooking the lake was the cemetery, dotted with pine and the odd cluster of willows. Dry grasses waved in the wind. Some graves had a small wooden fence around them with a wooden cross, which would have been painted but now the paint was peeling. Many graves had small houses erected over them, known as spirit houses. There were very few granite headstones. I liked to visit this graveyard every fall when I was growing up. I thought it was a peaceful and beautiful resting spot. My dad thought so as well; years later, he requested his ashes be scattered here.

Across from the graveyard and on higher ground was another grassy bench with a huge bare hillside above it. The church sat here, its steeple rising high above the building. A number of badly deteriorating buildings were scattered around, and some half-finished log buildings. In 1952 the church was in good shape, probably partially due to the fact that it was painted, which helped to preserve the wood. The steps leading to the entrance were wide and solid. At the top of the steps, in the entranceway, you could look way up and see the huge bell hanging inside the steeple. We were told not to ring the bell for fear of spooking the cattle, but that we could ring it in the morning once the cattle had gone down the trail. We couldn't wait! Upon entering the church, we found that it wasn't really that large. It had beautiful stained glass windows, candle holders and many statues of Christ and the Virgin Mary. A small picket fence and a step separated the altar at the back from the rest of the church. We found a trunk containing the priest's robes and many books written in Latin for the mass.

Later we set up camp by the creek while the cattle grazed out on the flats with their bells ringing. Horses were hobbled here and there, with one horse staked out by camp for an emergency. Campfire smoke rose in the air as everyone wandered about, gathering wood and hauling water.

The fourth morning was another beautiful day. It was only about five miles to Chantyman's Crossing, which was the home of Lashaway and Jessie, and their son, Edward, his wife, Agnes, and their children. Before we left the village, we stopped at the church and pulled the long hemp rope that hung from the steeple. The sound of that beautiful bell reverberated out over the valley and the water.

The trail ran along Kluskus Lake. This was mostly poplar country with some pockets of spruce. There were massive sidehills and grass grew everywhere. When the swamp meadows were wet, the Indians hayed these areas where it was not too steep. Along the lake the trails were sandy and we found that the team could trot right along, the trace chains jingling.

Before we reached the Chantymans' place, we went through a gate, crossed the foul-smelling water at the end of the lake and then climbed a bit to where the sidehills again rose up. We set up camp near the house. Once again there would be visiting back and forth. Lashaway was a tall, confident, good-looking man and he was a very hard worker. He raised horses and good Hereford cattle. Dad bought cattle from him and quite often bull calves for herd sires.

While we enjoyed the warmth of that October day, Mary and Francis Cassam passed by, along with Tom Baptiste with teams and wagons—all headed for home. In Mom's diary she noted that the blackflies were very bad that day so it had to have been quite warm.

The next day was a day of rest for the cattle. Mom would have kept busy in camp making an extra-special dinner and airing out the bedding. John left to go look at Pan Meadow, which was six or seven miles to the northeast, as he was thinking of buying land. Dave and Dad may have shod some horses or gone hunting. We kids would have climbed some of the hills and then proceeded to roll rocks down the sides.

The seventh day brought clouds and cooler temperatures. Lashaway had gathered his big yearling steers to be driven on to Quesnel with ours. About three miles past the Chantymans' place we came to some corrals and a barn, and a cluster of old log cabins, where several families lived. The John Jimmies had moved there from Tatelkuz Lake; Chief Morris and his family and Thomas Chantyman's family lived there also. This little settlement had a number of names, such as Clay Clee, Stink Water or New Kluskus, depending upon whom you asked.

The next stop was Round Lake, which was Lashaway Chantyman's other home—about ten or twelve miles away. Here the cattle were hard to hold: the water was bad, and although there was no shortage of feed, they didn't like it. The cattle grazed till dark, watched by Dave and Dad, and then they were corralled for the night. Surrounded by spruce and swamps, it was not the nicest place to camp, but the cattle could only travel so far and the days were short.

The following day we faced a rough trail, with a lot of mud, rock and corduroy sections. The cattle were trail-broken by then and at daylight they were ready to travel down that ribbon of trail, which seemed to stretch on and on. We camped that night at Rocky Mountain. This was Bill Orr's hunting area and he was camped farther over with his string of horses and big canvas wall tent. One of the hunters with him was Rex Bartlett from Marysville, Washington, and he came over to visit. This was the beginning of a friendship between Rex and my parents that lasted close to forty-five years.

The next morning the cattle were already on the trail when the men caught up to them. Bill Orr broke camp and travelled with us along the Coglistiko River on a very narrow trail for a number of miles. After we crossed the river two or three miles farther on, we made camp at Bill's base camp. There was a large wild meadow below the cabins and the cattle were content. It was a fun evening spent with Rex and his hunting companions.

The morning brought the shortest day yet: we covered only about three miles. It was hardly worth breaking camp, but we moved cattle and camp to Moffit Harris's place on the Baezaeko River. The feed was better and the cattle were under fence so everyone could rest easier. Rex and his friends stopped for tea on their way out with their moose. Later on, Ronnie Harrington caught up with us; he had been staying at Jack's place, helping him hay. He unsaddled his horse and hobbled it in the field with ours. It was nice to have visitors and hear news of home.

The next afternoon we reached Nazko. Ronnie stayed with us for the rest of the drive to Quesnel, helping Dave and Dad with the cattle. (John had returned to Anahim Lake.) Dad had rented pasture on the Nazko Reserve for the cattle. While we were putting them into the pasture, Bill Leake came by with Stella Robertson. They lived farther down the valley; Stella lived two or three miles below Bill. We spent the night with Buster and Lee Lavoie. Lee and my mom became fast friends and remained so for many years. We also stopped for a visit with Paul Krestenuk, who by this time was no longer freighting in the backcountry. He still traded for fur, but he now raised cattle and operated a store close to the Indian reserve.

Driving the cattle from Nazko over to First Creek was a bit of a challenge; we were now on a road to Quesnel. There was little traffic on the road, but we still met the odd vehicle, which of course the cows had never encountered before. People back then stopped and shut their motors off when meeting cattle. As the cows were pushed past, many of them wanted to smell the vehicle, and they would crowd it. Others would balk at passing or run by as fast as they could.

At Joe Spehar's place we had to cross the Nazko River on a bridge. This was the first bridge that the cattle had encountered and it took some time to get them onto it. Then we faced a very steep climb out of the Nazko valley and up Pennington Mountain, then a short descent into First Creek, where there was a hay meadow. We put the cattle in the meadow and returned to Joe Spehar's to set up camp by the Nazko bridge. Emma, Art Lavington's wife and a friend of my mom's, came on a saddle horse and spent the night with us.

The twelfth day we left early under cloudy skies. We went to a fairly high pass between Nazko and Quesnel, called the Summit. Camped there with their cattle were Major Franklin and Joe Spehar. It rained hard that night. In the morning the cattle were moved out together— they had all mixed together during the night anyway! It meant more riders and easier work. That day we made it to an old homestead that was known as Bouchie's. No one appeared to live there, so we pitched our tent and camped for the night. Art Lavington and Tom Cooper stopped by for a visit.

The next day we made it to Puntchesakut Lake. A family named Quanstrom lived there, and they let us use their extra cabin. The cattle were pastured nearby. The weather had turned warmer. When we met people on the narrow road, everyone would stop to visit. The cattle had gotten used to meeting vehicles by now, so all was well.

The following night we stopped at Corky Evans' place in a beautiful little valley. (It's now known as Bobkat Ranch.) It had a sloping field where the cattle were turned out. We were invited to stay in the large cabin.

We were about nine miles from Quesnel the next night, and were invited to stay with Doris and Jack Campbell. Pasture was rented nearby for the cattle. We were now encountering barbwire fences along the roadway. None of the cattle had ever seen wire before, so when they saw a nice patch of grass they just went to it, crawling through the wire as though it wasn't there. The wire creaked and stretched, staples came loose; sometimes the wire broke when a cow became tangled in it. Once one was through the fence, several others always followed, and then a

Diana and Pan driving cattle. PHILLIPS FAMILY PHOTO

rider had to find a gate to take his horse through to go run the animals back in. It was slow going, and tempers were lost. At this stage, we would have been in the Nine Mile, Meldrum Lake area.

The last day of the drive finally arrived. The cattle passed through West Quesnel and then crossed the wooden Fraser River bridge into the stockyards, which were across the railway tracks beside the Quesnel River. During the sale, the cattle were worked with saddle horses. My dad was one of the riders, as well as Ronnie Harrington, Lashaway Chantyman and sometimes Art Lavington or his brother, Dude.

The team and the kids' horses had been left at the Campbells' place. In Quesnel we stayed at what was called the Log Cabin Auto Court, where Baker Creek runs into the Fraser River. Staying there also were Mickey and Lester Dorsey, Art and Emma Lavington and Alfred and Caroline Bryant, so the party was on! The first cattle drive to Quesnel was completed, and it was a success! We arrived back at the Home Ranch on November 7 after encountering some pretty good weather on the return journey. We had been gone five weeks.

In later years we made changes to where we stopped, depending on where pastures were available. For several years we stopped on the Nazko Reserve because we got pasture from the Chief. Hannah Weber was then teaching on the reserve, so we were able to stay at the school where she had her living quarters. Later we bypassed the reserve and pastured at Joe Spehar's place on the Nazko River by the bridge. This meant the cattle had to walk a couple of miles less on the day we moved to First Creek, as Pennington Mountain was a very steep climb up from the river and, if the day was warm, it was slow going.

We used to stay with the Quanstroms at Punchesakut Lake, then later at Foudy's place, and a few times we stayed with the Knauf family as well. At Nine Mile we'd stay with the Campbells, and later we stayed at the Cotters' place, where Byron Cotter still lives today. From there we'd go to what is now the Quesnel Golf Course. At that time Milt and Penny Thornley had a farm there, and we would turn our cattle out in the field where the golf carts now run about. We drove our cattle to Quesnel till the Nazko road was gravelled. After that we started trucking out of First Creek, as the cattle would become too sore-footed on the gravel road.

In the fall of 1961, when Rob was five, we were in Quesnel for the annual cattle sale and banquet. We were staying at the Log Cabin Auto Court as usual. Len Cave had joined us there after the drive. I was off doing something or other, and Mom was at the laundromat. Len and Dad were supposed to be babysitting Rob. They decided to run some errands in Len's pickup truck and took Rob with them. Well, one of their errands was a stop at the International dealership, which was owned and operated by Dad's good friend, Alex Fraser. They left Rob in the truck because they were only going to be a minute. Rob finally got tired of waiting, so he got out of the truck and crossed a couple of streets, as well as the Fraser River bridge. When Mom got back with the clean laundry, he was playing outside our cabin. Mom asked him where Dad and Len were and he told her they were across town and that he had walked home. Mom was horrified that he had wandered through town on his own!

In the meantime, after several drinks of Crown Royal with Alex at the dealership, Dad and Len had left to find Rob gone from the truck. They panicked and called the RCMP, who in turn put a missing child report on the local radio station, CKCQ. Of course it all turned out okay, but Dad and Len were busy making excuses to Mom. Len usually mumbled a lot and kind of laughed, but not so that day.

In the summer of 1962 we had a bunch of cattle at Sleepy Hollow, so in September Rick Boland and I went down there to bring them home. There was a roan cow there that gave us a hard time, running off in the trees and quitting the bunch. About a mile and a half from the ranch she got on the fight and kept trying to take on our saddle horses. We roped her, tied her to a tree and left her there for the night. When we returned in the morning, she wasn't in a much better mood but we did manage to get her home.

A few weeks later we left on the cattle drive—Dad, Rick and I. Mom and Rob brought the chuck wagon. The cows went okay on the first day, but during the night thirty-one head of cattle got by camp and were on their way back home—the roan cow wasn't one of them. Dad went back after the missing cattle, and Rick and I went on the ten miles to Antoine Baptiste's place with the main bunch. The roan started giving us a hard time again a couple of miles from Antoine's place, but with hard riding and a lot of swearing, we managed to get her through the gate. She then proceeded to run down to Kushya Creek, where it was really muddy, and jumped in with about six or seven yearling steers right behind her. They were all wallowing in the mud, but the steers finally managed to climb up the bank onto the hay meadow. The cow appeared to be bogged in the mud with only her head above water. Rick and I had to go find a crossing that wasn't boggy and round up the steers. Once the steers were back with the herd, we went to see what could be done about the cow in the mud. She had managed to get free, and as we returned to the creek she was running across the hay meadow towards a steep spruce hill that had a rockslide about halfway up.

Whipping our tired horses, we caught up with the damn cow that ran merrily on. The cow then turned and charged our horses. Bellowing, her bell ringing and manure flying—she was having a great time. We ended up just under the rockslide where she made up her mind to stand and fight, and that she did! Rick and I weren't ropers, and the thick and bushy spruce certainly didn't help matters. We approached the cow on foot, as the horses were fairly useless in there amongst the shrubs and huge rocks. Rick finally managed to rope her but then she started chasing him—branches were breaking as he ran behind trees and scrambled over the rocks. Thomas Chantyman showed up at this point. He was riding a small grey mare that didn't have an ounce of fat on her frame, and she looked very tired. He was on an old high-cantled saddle with a bare metal horn. The saddle skirts were curled and the stirrup leathers nearly worn through. The cotton cinch was held together by no more than a half-dozen strings; the broken strings swung back and forth under the mare's gaunt stomach.

Thomas indicated that he would take the rope, which Rick gladly passed to him on his mad dash by. Thomas dallied up to the horn and turned the mare around, about the same time that the cow hit the mare from behind—her head ended up between the mare's hind legs. The cow lifted that skinny mare into the air and down the hill they went! The cow was bellowing in rage, the mare was running as fast as she could on her front legs while the cow ran her like a wheelbarrow. Thomas seemed quite unconcerned about the situation he was in. I thought, "Oh my god, a wreck looking for a place to happen."

Pan with Gyp, the dog, on a cattle drive, 1956. PHOTO: RICHARD HARRINGTON

Rick and I grabbed our horses and caught up to them as Thomas and the cow reached the meadow. The fight seemed to go out of the cow after that and she became quite manageable. We took her to the rest of the herd and she never caused any more trouble for the rest of the drive.

Dad caught up to us at about eleven that night. He and Len Cave had the missing cows. Some of them had made it all the way back to the ranch, so there were some pretty tired cows.

The next morning Len left for the ranch, and the rest of us pushed on to Kluskus with the herd. Kluskus was about eight miles farther on. After fighting with the cows all evening, we repaired an old corral in the dark and corralled them so that we could get some sleep. This was one of our worst drives—the cattle wouldn't settle down and the weather was cold and stormy, with a lot of rain and hail. At night everything would freeze solid while you shivered in your sleeping bag till daylight, then rose and went after the horses. The picket rope would be frozen like a metal pipe, and the horse would be humped up and shivering too. The horses didn't want that frozen saddle blanket thrown across their back or the frozen cinch pulled up against their girth. Everything cracked and popped with the frost. The cattle wouldn't cross the frozen creeks until we rode our horses back and forth a few times, breaking down the ice, and even then, they argued about it!

It wasn't any easier for Mom and Rob; they had to deal with the frozen tent and the horses' frozen harnesses. The ropes that we used to stake our horses were the same ones they had to use to tie down the wagonload. The wind froze Mom's hands as she tried to prepare the meals over the campfire. I know her arthritis was really bothering her by this

Pan, Betty and Diana setting up camp, October 1956. PHOTO: RICHARD HARRINGTON

time. When we finally reached Nazko, there was a message for her that her best friend, Marguerite Gunson, had passed away after a brave fight with cancer. Mom left for Quesnel that night. This left us short-handed, but no one said a word, as we knew the sadness she felt.

After the cattle sale, there was always a banquet and dance in the Billy Barker Hotel put on by the cattlemen. This was the first year that I was allowed to attend. Lloyd Bennett was to be my escort, and he liked to dance as much as I did. The music was great and the liquor flowed. The cowboys fought up and down the stairs and on the dance floor. Women screamed at the blood and tables collapsed and glasses broke. Dr. Bill McIntire was an excellent doctor and a party animal, and he exchanged slug for slug with the feistiest of the cowboys. Me, I had a wonderful time and couldn't wait for the next one!

When it came time to leave town, Mom decided to stay on with the Gunson family for a while to help out after Marguerite's death, so the rest of us went on home. At my urging, Yvonna Robertson came along with us. She was a few years older than I was and had become a good friend. In those days, I was finding ranch life terribly lonely.

On another cattle drive Rick and Dad took the cattle, and I took the team and wagon. Roger Nygaard was along on this drive as he had been around the ranch for several weeks and wanted to go with us. Mom stayed home and Rob was away at school. I hated to leave Mom there, but she was used to being left at the ranch alone, and Ed Adams would be around. Ed helped us get the cows started, and then he was going to go back to the ranch.

On the second day, things started out well. Rick and Dad had left with the cattle and Ed was on his way back. Roger and I broke camp and headed out on the trail. About three and a half miles out, we reached the summit between Paul's Meadow and Antoine's place and started down-hill. It wasn't all that steep, just extremely rocky. Roger was riding saddle horse behind the wagon. The team of mares, Ruby and May, normally worked well together, but May could get antsy and she certainly was that day! She didn't want to hold the load back with the tongue whip-ping back and forth as the wagon eased over the rocks. I put my feet up on the front of the wagon box with a line tight in each hand. I tried to slow them down and make the whole process easier on their necks.

Left to right: Jay Leake, George Chantyman, Pan and a ranch hand on a cattle drive, 1956. PHOTO: RICHARD HARRINGTON

May started swinging her butt back and forth, so I gave her some slack and she kicked over the tongue! "Oh hell, we're in big trouble now," I thought to myself as they took off. The wagon was bouncing so badly I couldn't stay in the seat, and then suddenly the whole outfit flipped upside down!

Roger said that the team didn't drag the wagon far before they tore loose from it and went racing off through the timber, with trees breaking and harnesses ripping as they parted company. I had gotten hit on the head and was lying unconscious on the ground. Roger thought that I was dead. He decided the dead should be covered, so he stopped long enough to grab a sleeping bag from the mess of the overturned wagon, threw it over me and then raced off down the trail to catch up to Rick and Dad. I must have come to, as I remember them returning for me. Antoine brought his wife and daughter in his team and wagon, and I was laid down in the wagon with my head cradled in Josie's lap. Eva was just a baby. She was staring at me with her lower lip sticking out, not knowing whether she should cry or keep quiet. Rick went back to the Home Ranch, changed horses, and then on to Anahim Lake to phone for a plane. (Tsacha Lodge was closed for the season, so no phone there!)

I had a bad cut on my head and a concussion, but I was awake after a few hours. My glasses had disappeared and were never found. Mom took out another team and wagon with Ed, who had gone along to help her, and they went out and picked up the supplies from the wrecked wagon. She arrived at Antoine's later that night. Surprisingly there was very little damage to the wagon or its contents. The camp stuff was in the bottom of the wagon box with the tent and sleeping bags on top, and the whole thing had been tarped and tied.

The next morning Rick arrived with Dan Schuetze in a Beaver aircraft. They landed at the east end of Tsacha Lake. Rick stayed to hunt down the team while Dan flew me out to the Bella Coola Hospital, where I spent three days, and then another week with Ken, who lived in Bella Coola, before I felt like myself. Other than some pain, my time in the hospital was enjoyable. It is the only hospital I have ever been in where people come just to visit with the patients—it doesn't matter whether they know them or not! Each day I looked forward to the afternoon visiting hours, and I met many nice people in those three days and visited with both friends and strangers.

It took Rick several days to locate the runaway team. He found Ruby near Tsacha Lake. She still had her harness on and was headed for home. May was really spooked and much harder to find. She was finally located downriver from Antoine's with only her collar and halter left. Rick returned to the ranch to take Mom's place as she had gone on the drive in place of me.

While he was alone at the ranch, a terrible storm blew in one day so he was indoors reading a wrestling magazine. He didn't notice how bad the storm was until he glanced out the window and saw the cat blow by. Soon after, the shake roof lifted right off the house! The log fence was tossed about like matchsticks and hundreds of trees were blown down.

Once while we were camped at Rocky Mountain during a drive, a helicopter flew in with a reporter from *The Canadian Magazine*. He wanted to interview Dad and take pictures of him and the cattle. Dad loved the limelight! He would have stood on his head if he had been asked to. He told stories and laughed, his face glowing with all the attention. He posed for pictures: on his horse, off his horse, by the fire, making coffee, pretending to shoe a horse or whatever they wanted.

As we neared Nazko there was more traffic, mostly moose hunters. Dad always rode on ahead and stopped the traffic to let the cows go by, while he visited, drank beer and swapped stories. When the hunters moved on, he would catch up at a lope, and then he would ride on ahead to stop the next vehicle. No wonder he called the cattle drive "the annual picnic"!

I've looked into records of the Quesnel cattle sales from the 1940s and '50s to get some sense of what was going on before my time. I couldn't find any record of the first sale, apparently held in 1944. The second sale, in 1945, was a two-day sale and 686 head of cattle were brought in by seventy different owners. Top prices were paid for feeders, and that was $10.75. Cows brought unexpectedly high prices as did the fifty bulls that were offered. Now the cattlemen believed that they could do just as well selling locally as shipping to the coast. Much work was done on the yards—expanding the pens and putting in water. Electric lights were installed so the cattle could be worked at night.

In 1946, the number of stock doubled to 1,363 head. A top price for feeder steers was $11.80. The longest drive was that of Andy Christensen and Alfred Bryant from Anahim Lake, who drove 308 head over the 200 miles of the new Baezaeko Trail, cut early that summer. They had left Anahim Lake on October 2, arriving on the 22nd. The trail conditions had been excellent with plenty of feed and water, and the cattle arrived in top condition. Dad made a drive of about 160 miles with 125 head (as a partner in the Frontier Cattle Company), and the Lavington brothers from upper Nazko came in driving about 100 miles with their stock.

Owing to the Canada-wide strike in the meat-packing plants in the fall of 1947, only 547 head of cattle came to the sale that year. Matt Hassen from Armstrong was the auctioneer. The highest price paid was $14.80 for Dad's yearling steers. Bulls were selling for $6.85 and cows for $7.10. The largest contributors were Pan Phillips and Herald Dwinell, who drove in 230 head of prize fat stock. They had left Batnuni on

October 6 and arrived in Quesnel on the 23rd with the cattle in top condition. It was reported that "Mrs. Phillips and two small children accompanied the drive, travelling in a chuck wagon."

Quesnel Cattlemen's Association's fifth annual cattle sale in 1948, held at the improved PGE stockyards, had 1,112 head being sold. The average price per head was $127.00. Bill Lehman from Anahim Lake had the longest drive, bringing twenty-five head of cattle. They had been on the trail twenty-three days, fording rivers and crossing mountain ridges. The drovers and cattle were caught in an extreme blizzard on a high plateau and had been lost for some time, but otherwise the trip was a pleasant one. Mrs. Gerty Dolvin's drive had come in from Nazko.

Not much was written about the 1949 sale, except that the Anahim Lake cattle drive was the longest in British Columbia and the cattle were expected to be on the trail for a month. Top price was $26.60 for seven prime steers. Top price for heifers was $19.00. Bulls were selling for between $14.00 and $15.35.

Anahim Lake ranchers started on their drive in late September 1950 with 275 head, expecting to arrive in Quesnel on October 19 for the eighth annual sale. An equal number of cattle was expected from Blackwater and Nazko. There were a little over a thousand head of cattle and prices were better. Joe Spehar from Nazko bought nine heifers belonging to Art Lavington for $31.00, the top price paid at the entire sale. Feeder steer were as high as $28.00, and top-grade Hereford cows brought $20.00. Five registered Hereford bulls were sold for prices from $500.00 to $775.00.

The 1951 prices were slightly better, with yearling heifers bringing as much as $36.00 and prime steers reaching $32.80. Cows ranged from $17.80 to $25.50. A few calves were offered but no price was mentioned. The heaviest bull ever weighed in, at 1,900 pounds, was one of Bert Smith's of Batnuni. Joe Spehar bought the most expensive registered Hereford bull, offered by Len Wood of Armstrong, for a top price of $1,400.00.

The 1952 sale prices were down from the year before. Steers were selling at $25.60 and heifers at $22.25. Cows brought $14.00 and the calves that were offered brought $27.00. The highest-selling bull brought $1,050. There was only half the number of cattle driven from Anahim Lake as in previous years. The prices in 1953 were even lower. The top price paid for steers was $17.80. Heifers topped at $15.75. Cows ranged between $5.60 and $9.10. The drive from Anahim Lake was boasted as being the longest in British Columbia, but a gentleman by the name of Mr. Allan pointed out that the cattle drive bound for the Grand Trunk construction camps back in 1912 was no doubt longer than the drives to Quesnel from Anahim Lake.

The sale in 1954 saw prices only a cent or two above the year before. Calves were in sharp demand but the top price offered was only $16.00. For the first time cattle were purchased for shipment to Edmonton. Four

Pan at the Quesnel stockyard, 1956. PHOTO: RICHARD HARRINGTON

carloads left the yards for the packing houses in Alberta. In 1955 sales manager Abe Wells visited the cattlemen of the Vanderhoof area. As a result, thirty-five head of cattle from that area were offered at the sale. While this was not a significant number, Mr. Wells felt that the next year would bring more. With the improvements on the Nazko road, Helmuth Penner commenced hauling stock in from the Nazko area for the sale. It's recorded that Pan Phillips from the Blackwater and Bert Smith of Batnuni combined their drives and were expected to arrive the day before the sale with 250 head. The average price for steers was $14.95, while the average in 1954 was $14.24 and in 1953, $14.15. Prices for calves were strong with the average at $15.10. Yearling heifers averaged $12.08, while cows averaged $8.10.

The last year the Phillips family drove cattle all the way to Quesnel was 1956. That was the year that Richard Harrington joined us to photograph the drive. Rob was six months old, and Mom brought him along. She bought a kerosene heater for the tent so that it was cozy and warm for baths, changing and playtime, before he had to be bundled up for the outside weather conditions. Harrington sold his photos of the drive to magazines across Canada, and some of the pictures appeared in his books. This brought a lot of fan mail to the Home Ranch.

CHAPTER 16

Haying

Haying season started around the end of July. First, the horses had to be found, rounded up and brought in from the range; this might take four or five days as there were no fences, just open country. If it was hot and the flies were bad, the horses would stay in the thick timber during the day. If you were lucky, you might hear their bells ringing and you could find them that way. If you put a bell on your saddle horse, the range horses would come to you—hearing the bell, the horses thought it was more horses. The younger horses are much more social than the older ones, who would rather stay in the shade.

The teams were kept in a large pasture. Many of these horses were mares with spring colts on them, and they were used only for haying. The first few days of haying, the colts would be afraid to nurse under the traces, and they'd be constantly getting caught in the harnesses. They'd get spooked whenever you got near them. By the end of summer they were pets and you had to push them out of the way.

The teams used on the mower were most often geldings. If a mare was used, its colt had to be locked up in the corral. The older mares left their colts more willingly, but the younger ones were sometimes a bit of a problem. With their baby squealing and running about the corral, trying to jump the fence, they were reluctant to leave. After a while they would become used to the routine, but the nursing was still a problem as colts nurse often. I've seen mares come in at lunchtime or in the afternoon when the teams were changed, with milk squirting from their bags and soaking their hind legs.

The mowers used for haying were heavy and hard to pull. A team certainly earned its keep pulling them, while the sweat rolled off their backs and the flies swarmed. Often pieces of burlap sacking were cut in strips and tied to the nosebands of the halters. The strips hung down over their noses, and when the horses tossed their heads they kept the flies off their faces. If the flies were really bad, the teams would always be trying to rub against one another, or on the neck yoke or the tongue

Diana on a sloop of hay. PHILLIPS FAMILY PHOTO

of the mower, often causing the bridles or lines to tangle together. Quite often we brushed used oil over their face, nose, ear and neck areas to keep the flies off. This helped, but sweat soon washed the oil off.

After the hay was mowed, it was left to dry for a day or two, depending on the weather. Wild hay dries much faster than cultivated hay, and it doesn't have to be as dry when stacked loose. Next it was raked with a team pulling a hay rake. The colts were allowed to follow the mares on the rake, and they would trot alongside until they got tired, then drop behind, heads down, plodding along. Eventually they would

Pan raking hay. A horse team certainly earned its keep during haying season.
PHOTO: VANCE HANNA

stop when they realized that their mothers weren't leaving the area, and they'd sleep in the sun. When they wanted to nurse, they would come to the mare. The team would be stopped so that the colts could drink, as that was easier than having the colt run back and forth in front of the mare, stopping the team anyway.

With the horse rake you went around the mowed field, dumping the hay each time the teeth of the dump rake became full. Each round after that you dumped in the same place, thus forming the windrows. As the area of unraked hay became smaller, you used fewer of the wind-rows. When a row was no longer used, you straddled the row, dumping

Derrick poles and haystack, Home Ranch. PHILLIPS FAMILY PHOTO

the hay into piles called stooks. It was from these stooks that the hay was hauled to the stack. After the stooks were left for a couple of days, they settled into a smaller pile and this was much easier to fork onto the loads of hay. The stooks also shed some of the water if it happened to rain.

The third step was to haul the hay, but first the derrick poles had to be put up. These poles were probably sixty feet long. They had to be straight, solid wood, peeled and then left to dry. Several hundred feet of cable was used to pull these poles upright and keep them standing. The first cable was half-hitched on the top of the poles in the middle where the ends of the poles were crossed. The second cable was a bit shorter, and it was tied to one of the poles at the top. Once this was attached, two pulleys with hooks were added. Then the cable ran through a pulley tied to the other pole, ran down to the ground and then through a second pulley anchored to the bottom off one of the poles. The excess cable was left on the ground; this was where the team was hooked up to draw the load of hay up. There was enough slack in the cable so that the two pulleys with hooks hung close to the ground. The first cable was tied to stakes, driven in where the top of the poles lay on the ground. The bottoms of the poles were spread about thirty feet apart, and a stake was driven in to keep them from sliding when the poles were raised. Next, a team was hooked to the other end of this cable and this pulled the poles into an upright position.

When raising the derrick poles you had to put up "squaw" poles, which were about fifteen feet long and were tied at the top and anchored to the ground. The cable used to raise the derricks was then put on the top of these. The squaw poles were raised first and anchored in an upright position. This would get the cable in the air when the derricks were being raised; otherwise, the derricks would skid along the ground.

The cable tied to the stakes had to be just the right length to allow the poles to come up and lean forward a bit. If the cable wasn't long enough, the team had to hold it until the slack was let out a bit. If the cable was too long, it risked the bottom of the poles kicking out if it leaned too far. The odd time the cable was not tied to the stakes, because it had been forgotten. When we pulled the poles up, down they went in the opposite direction, hitting the ground with a terrible bang, which scared the team and caused great confusion. If all went well, the team was unhooked and that cable was anchored to a second set of stakes with slack, so that when the pulleys with the hooks were hooked into the slings with the load of hay and the team hooked to the cable at the base of the pole, the team pulled on the cable and tightened it, the poles swung forward while the load of hay was raised, and then it swung back so that the load could be dumped by a trip under the slings.

The slings were made of cable with poles as crosspieces to keep them spread and free of tangles. They consisted of two pieces, joined in the middle by the trip. The two ends had rings and were tied up on the top of the hay rack where, after the rack was loaded with hay, they could be reached. The pulleys with the hooks were hooked into each ring. It sounds complicated but it's really not.

We used what we called slips, or sloops, to haul the hay. These were built with two log runners and a hayrack on top. The slings were spread out on the rack floor, the trip set and the trip rope carefully coiled under the trip. If the trip rope wasn't carefully coiled and it fell between the cracks, the trip would be set off. Then when you hooked up to unload, all you got were two slings. All the hay that fell back into the rack had to be forked off and the slings set properly before the hay could be forked onto them again.

The stack man was the person on the stack when the load came up. The load swung back and forth with the trip rope hanging underneath, thus enabling the stack man to dump the load to the front or the back of the stack. When he pulled the trip rope, he had to duck to avoid the slings. Being stack man was the most dangerous job in the field; men had been killed doing this. When the stack was still low, the stack man could jump down to the ground and jump onto the stack from a load of hay. As the stack got higher, he was pulled up to the top with the pulleys while hanging onto them. Most often he'd slide down a derrick pole to get off.

The sloops had a piece of cable from one runner to the other with a loop at the centre. The doubletrees on the team had a hook on them, which was hooked into the loop. It was easy to unhook the team, and then hook them to the loop of the derrick pole with the cable; switching the team from the sloop to the derrick was fast.

One summer we had a Scotsman working for us by the name of

Diana loading hay on sloop, 1965. PHILLIPS FAMILY PHOTO

Alex Logan. For some reason, I found every chance to quarrel with him. He was rather hotheaded and waved his arms when he was angry. We were finishing up a stack of hay in the fall—just the two of us—using the team of mares, Nora and Juliet. We'd ride the mares to and from the field with their harnesses on. Juliet took little steps and was choppy to ride, but she was very gentle. Nora would walk right out and was better to ride, but goofy! If she saw any movement above the blinders, she would buck. I always rode Nora.

On a day when Alex had really gotten on my nerves, I told him he could ride home on Nora. I jumped on Juliet. As soon as we were mounted and headed home, I continued on with whatever the issue was. Alex immediately started waving his arms, and when Nora saw this, she lit into bucking, big time! The hames on the harness were straight metal, no brass balls on these. Alex flew up into the air, and when he came down his belt caught on the hames. At one point his feet were straight up in the air and his head was down by the mare's shoulder! After several pitches he broke loose and hit the ground. I laughed all the way home—after we traded horses. Alex jogged along behind on Juliet and licked his wounds.

Sill Meadow, our hay meadow, was about three miles northeast of the main ranch. We would hay there every year. It was natural wild meadow with a beautiful view of the Ilgachuz Mountains to the south. To the north you could see the Naglico Hills with Mount Tsacha and Mount Davidson behind them. Tsetzi Creek ran slowly through the east side of the field. Sometimes we would ride back and forth from home every day to do the haying. When we did that, we hobbled the teams

Diana stacking up stooks. PHOTO: VANCE HANNA

at night and left them on the meadow until morning. Other times we camped right there till the haying was finished.

When we camped, one of us would knock off work early to go fishing in Tsetzi Creek. The creek had a lot of brook trout, which made a quick supper easily cooked over a campfire. We would camp near what remained of an old cabin, barn and corral. The Sills had once lived there, before Dad arrived in the Blackwater country. We rebuilt the corral to accommodate a milk cow since we often brought one with us. We'd put her calf in the corral and leave the cow to graze free, letting her in twice a day to milk. The cow hated it, but she wouldn't leave her calf. She got even with us by grazing close to camp and leaving behind those large, oozing cow-pies that you're apt to accidentally step in at night while on a trip to the bushes in the dark!

One summer Ivan Demeniko stayed with us to help with the haying. He had escaped from Russia during the war after being wounded a number of times and suffering horrendous ordeals. He had managed to find his way to Canada and British Columbia. He spent some time with us and then he homesteaded at Cottonwood Creek, which was about eighteen miles to the west.

One afternoon Ivan, Dad and I were building a new sloop for haying, just over the hill from camp. Whoever was in camp was shooting camp robbers (Canada jays). One of the bullets ricocheted, and with a "zzzing" it hit the ground between Dad and Ivan. Dad leapt up and started swearing and jumping about, but Ivan never stopped working. He told Dad, "Don't worry, it missed you. Worry when it hits you!"

I always got the teams with a green horse. An unbroken horse would be paired with a gentle hook horse, with the green one tied to the gentle horse by the halter. This usually worked because the gentle one would stop on "Whoa," but not always. Sometimes there would be a runaway, with the team running all over the cut hay and often ending up in the uncut hay. Dad would stand up on the tractor yelling at me because the team and sloop were mashing down the uncut hay. I generally gave him the finger as I ran by, telling him what a lovely team he had. As soon as he knew I was on the fight, he'd smirk and go back to mowing the hay. The team never ran too far before they became winded, as the sloops are hard to pull. With sweat dripping, nostrils flaring and sides heaving, they could be coaxed back to where they had started. Their shoulders would be quivering from overwork, so all they could do was stand for a while.

One time we nearly wiped out the derrick poles when the horses ran under the cable. Rick was on the stack yelling, "Holy jumpin'!" The stack was too high for him to jump off, and if the derricks fell on the stack, he had nowhere to go!

CHAPTER 17

Change Coming

In the late fifties, change started coming to the Home Ranch. In the past, Dad had relied on ranching—buying and selling cattle and horses—supplemented by work as a guide to big-game hunters. With the purchase of a portable sawmill in 1959, he began to sell lumber. He'd deliver the lumber where it was needed and also freight in other goods to the lodge that was being built at Tsacha Lake.

Before Dad bought the portable sawmill in 1959, any lumber we needed had to be cut with a whipsaw, which is very labour consuming. Having lumber to build was a real treat. After the cows were fed, and if the weather was decent, the men would cut, fall and skid logs to the mill site. Dad did the falling with the David Bradley chainsaw he had purchased a year or two before—it was one of the best purchases he ever made. Ed would skid the logs to the mill site with a team of horses. Ken would limb the trees and he'd help to cut the lumber.

The Department of Indian Affairs bought a lot of lumber from Dad for the Indian people to improve their homes. Dad would deliver it personally with team and sleigh to whoever was allotted the lumber, then bill the department for the lumber and delivery charges.

Around 1958 some folks by the name of McLean took the first steps towards establishing a fly-in fishing camp on the south side of Tsacha Lake where the Twin Lakes Creek spills into Tsacha Lake. I visited the camp a couple of times and once overnighted there. The land was most-

Pan and Betty, Home Ranch, 1960s. PHILLIPS FAMILY PHOTO

ly covered by thick spruce and underbrush—a great place for swarms of hungry mosquitoes. The McLean family built a couple of small, sod-roofed log cabins during the two summers they spent there before selling the place to Harold and Eva Lionberger from Portland, Oregon.

When the Lionbergers took over Tsacha Lake Lodge (now Mackenzie Trail Lodge) from the McLeans, Dad sold them the lumber they needed to build the lodge and cabins. Dad and Jimmy Holte had also gotten a contract to haul all the supplies needed at the site, which included fuel, roofing, furniture, boats and motors, stoves and windows. Everything needed for the building of Tsacha Lake Lodge was hauled from Anahim Lake during the winter. Both Dad and Jimmy put half-tracks on their tractors. With sleighs behind them, freighting long hours, they moved much more than would have been possible with teams. Jimmy was a guy who liked to waste the day and work all night, so they were often on the trail at night. I'm not sure my dad fully enjoyed these working hours. We never knew when they might show up; sometimes

Jimmy Holte standing beside the tractor with half-tracks, Home Ranch, early 1960s. PHILLIPS FAMILY PHOTO

they'd arrive home in the middle of the night. I always enjoyed it when Jimmy was around. Sooner or later he'd pick up the old guitar and sing a few songs for us. Jimmy was blonde, blue-eyed and round-faced, and he loved to laugh.

Harold and Eva Lionberger drove in from Anahim Lake with their power wagon—the first vehicle in Blackwater country. They drove it around the mountains to the Home Ranch in March of 1960, following the well-packed snow trails made by the tractors. This was the first time that we learned the actual mileage: from the ranch to Anahim Lake on that trail was seventy-seven miles.

Antoine Baptiste and his son Isaac began building the log lodge in 1961. Jed Campbell from Quesnel brought his Cat bulldozer all the way from Nazko the same year to build the airstrip for the lodge. It was the first Cat and the first airstrip in Blackwater country.

During the winter, we built an icehouse where the old storehouse had once stood. We cut blocks of ice from Pan Creek and buried them in sawdust from the sawmill. Now we could have ice in the summer. The icehouse was built with a seven-foot ceiling and a very steep pitched roof, so there was a large loft up above. I cut out a moon-shaped window in the front of the loft and put a door on the backside, with a ladder for access. That was my summer sleeping quarters for a number of years.

Somehow Mom obtained an old-fashioned icebox. It was solid wood and quite an attractive-looking thing. It was about three feet high, and two and a half feet deep. The top had two lids that opened up. There was a wooden rack for food and underneath was an area for storing a block of ice. As the ice slowly melted, the water dripped from a drain under the icebox.

In March 1960, Dad turned fifty. Mom, Rob and I accompanied Dad to Anahim Lake for his birthday. (Ed and Ken stayed home to feed the cattle.) The trail was still hard, so we took the tractor with the half-tracks and made it to Jimmy Holte's place on Lessard Lake in one day. It would have been two long days with team and sleigh. The weather was beautiful, clear and warm with gentle south winds. Mom, Rob and I sat up front on the sleigh seat and watched the countryside pass by. We spent the night with Jimmy and Theresa, then went on to Anahim the following day to visit around town and do some shopping. Somehow it was decided that there would be a party at Lessard Lake for Dad's birthday. I can't recall just how many vehicles left Anahim Lake for Jimmy's place, but there were several with a lot of people crammed in. The road hadn't been ploughed, just packed down hard by the tractors. D'Arcy and Judy Christensen came along with baby Cary, who was five months old at the time. D'Arcy was driving an old blue panel truck, and they'd packed in several more people. Thelma and Earl McInroy brought their musical instruments. Dave and Jean Dorsey, Tom Mathews, Frank Dorsey and Ted Williams were all there. Someone had come into town that day with a team and sleigh and a preemie calf, which they felt needed constant care, so they brought it along with them to the party. The calf was in the back of D'Arcy's panel truck, competing for space and losing badly as it got pushed one way and then another.

Jimmy had built a new log house beside the old one. It was pretty well finished, but they hadn't moved in yet. They did have a wood heater in the new house, so that's where the party was held. Jimmy, Thelma and Earl played the music and sang while people danced, sang, visited and fought. A couple of the local Indian ladies were doing a lot of jumping up and down on the cellar door, which was located on the floor. Both of them ended up in the cellar when the hinges on the door gave way. Jimmy laughed and slapped his leg. Then he sang a song for the occasion, making up the words as he went along. The preemie calf had been brought in and laid by the heater, but after several hours the poor little thing was panting and making gurgling sounds. Whoever owned it had forgotten to take care of it. Finally it was taken outside and knocked on the head. When daylight arrived, a tired-looking bunch of people got back into their vehicles to start the eighteen miles or so back to Anahim Lake and feed their livestock. There were a few black eyes and some hangovers, but everyone agreed that it had been a fine party!

We had to leave for home right away as well since the weather had stayed warm with no frost and we knew that the trail would soften up. Ken turned sixteen a week after Dad's birthday. He was not happy living on the ranch. His heart was in machinery and trucks, not cattle and horses. So a few days after Ken's birthday Dad took him to Anahim Lake, where he caught a ride to Bella Coola with Hodson Freight Lines to look for a job. The last thing he said as he was leaving the ranch was,

"I hope I never see the ass-end of a cow again!" Ken managed to get a job right away working for Northcott Logging, where he worked for two years at the mill, then went into the bush for a year. After that he signed on with the Department of Highways, where he worked for five years. News from Ken was rare as he was not a letter writer. Over the next few years we'd ask anyone who was from Bella Coola or had been down there for news of Ken.

Spring finally arrived and the calving started, so this helped take my mind off Ken being gone. I spent more time with Rob and spring work kept me busy. The lambs came, along with the calves. We had a small flock of sheep, and the ewes had to be sheared. The horses' feet needed to be trimmed. Horsehair was worth a lot of money back then. Mane hair was worth about a third the price of tail hair, so we'd pull tail hair, the longer the better. I'd pull the tails carefully so they looked good and the horses would have something left to fight flies with. Dad would grab his jackknife and when he got done, the horses would have very little left, just a hair-covered bone going thump, thump, thump against the rump.

I can't remember a spring that we didn't have colts. In fact, I can't remember a time when we didn't have a stud, sometimes two—Dad loved horses. Each year, we used to break a few horses to ride. Usually Rick Boland did a lot of the first riding. Dad would go out with them on a gentle horse. He usually snubbed Rick's green horse. He'd take the lead rope from the green horse and wrap it around his saddle horn for the first few miles before he'd turn them loose. After a hard day of riding they'd come home tired. When the green horse began to slow down, Dad would put branches under its tail or throw his hat under it, anything that might make it buck. While Rick would be crashing around through the trees, fighting with a horse that was green broken, Dad would be laughing his head off. The horses would usually be ridden every day for a few weeks and were then considered broken. Some were sold and others we kept.

Rob suffered bad burns to his back when he was out doing spring burning close to the house. Apparently he lit a patch of grass on fire, turned his back and squatted down to light another, and the tail of his flannel shirt caught fire. Mom heard his screams and ran outside to see what was happening. She saw Wilfred Cassam, who was visiting, rolling Rob around on the ground. Mom didn't know what was going on till Wilfred explained what had just happened, and then she was very grateful to him for what he had done. He no doubt saved Rob from much more serious burns.

Richard Harrington and his wife, Lynn, returned again in 1960 for more photos, which brought another landslide of mail and new friends and pen pals. A lot of people wanted to visit us after reading Richard's articles and seeing his photos. Some were young guys looking for a chance at a "Grass Beyond the Mountains" of their own. Dad would pore over the maps with them for hours, talking about the country and which areas were promising and which were hopeless. People would write letters with hopes of a response from this family that led an unusual life in the remote Blackwater country. Others would want to send their kids to live with us. We received about every type of letter you can imagine. I answered a lot of letters and Mom did too.

CHAPTER 18

Schooling

In the fall of 1960 I decided that I wanted to go to school rather than continue with correspondence courses at home. I was already a year or two behind. Arrangements were made for me to go to the school in Nazko and board with Clarence and Elsie Leake at Rainbow Lake. There were about ten kids living with them, including their youngest son, Larry. The teacher lived in a trailer on the same property. In the mornings she would give the girls a ride to the schoolhouse in her car, but the boys had to walk the three miles. If the weather was nice we sometimes walked home with the boys.

I started school in late October, so I'd missed more than a month already, but it was a good experience for me. The grades went from one to eight. There were only three of us in grade eight: Peter Gillis, Charlie Johannsen and me. There were more kids boarding at Bill and Frances Leake's place down the road, and that pretty well made up the entire school population. There was also a school on the reserve for the Indian children.

One of the girls at the Leakes' house, Linda, used to have epileptic seizures, and one time she had a seizure on the way home from school. Thank heaven it was warm weather so we could lay her on the ground at the side of the road. When she came around we helped her get home, although she was quite groggy. Another time, she had a seizure in the cellar where Elsie had sent her to get potatoes for supper. Larry and I were sent down to get her, as Elsie wouldn't go down those rickety stairs for anything! We tried picking Linda up but then we'd get a fit of giggling and drop her. After a while Elsie (who was standing at the top of the stairs) lost her temper, but we knew we were safe, as she wouldn't come down those stairs. We made her promise that she wouldn't punish us when we came up, and we finally succeeded in carrying Linda up the stairs and laid her on her bed.

One day we were just finishing breakfast when we heard Clarence above the kitchen ceiling in the attic. The ceiling consisted of plywood nailed onto two-by-six boards. The attic had no floor—you had to step from board to board. Between the two-by-sixes Clarence had put in sawdust for insulation. That morning, Clarence missed his step while he was over the kitchen area. He was a big man and when he stepped into the sawdust, the plywood ceiling gave way with a loud crash, the plywood landed on the kitchen stove, and an avalanche of sawdust fell into the kitchen. When the air cleared, we looked up and there was Clarence, straddling a two-by-six with a leg on each side—moaning and swearing! Elsie put her hand over her mouth to keep from laughing because he looked so funny and then she herded us kids outside, suggesting that we leave for school early. We were enjoying the show and had to miss the end, but when we returned from school the ceiling was back up, there was no evidence of sawdust and the incident was never mentioned again.

One of our favourite pastimes was to give the teacher a bad time. She had a small car, and one night we blocked it up about an inch off the ground. The next morning when we got ready to go to school, she started the car, put it in gear and nothing happened—just grinding gears and screaming tires. If it had fallen off the blocks she would have run right through the house, as she was pointed that way. We girls were killing ourselves laughing, but by now the teacher was crying. A fellow came over and told her he thought she had better take the car off the blocks before she blew the motor.

Another time we pushed the car down the hill and out onto the frozen lake, after dark of course. I think she needed help to get it back up on the road that time. One Halloween night at the party at the school, we pushed the car out in the pasture and she couldn't find it in the dark.

One weekend, the teacher was going to Quesnel to get the brakes fixed on the car and I went along with her, as Ken was working in Quesnel and boarding at the Schofields' and I could stay there. Near Udy Creek there was a steep hill with a sharp turn at the bottom to get onto the bridge. Well, she was driving too fast and we were flying down the hill when she let go of the steering wheel, covered her eyes and cried, "I have no brakes!" What a ride! We shot down the hill, going like mad, hit a pile of brush and logs and suddenly, we were airborne. We landed out in the jackpine and luckily we weren't hurt. She was bawling, "Oh God, oh God!" but it was obvious He had done all He could. I went back up to the road, as I knew Bill Leake was behind us. When he came along, I flagged him down and he was able to tow the car back to the road. I can't remember just how much damage there was to the car, but we were able to drive on to town.

While staying at the Leakes' house and going to school, I often went into town with Clarence and Elsie for the day. One day we were returning to Nazko on the narrow, snow-covered road, in the dark. We'd been following a car for some time, unable to pass, when the car came to a stop in the middle of the road. The back door of the car opened and a man stepped out onto the road, dropped his britches, squatted down and in the headlights of our vehicle he went about his business! Elsie was extremely embarrassed, her face going bright red. I studied my hands and looked out the side window, anything rather than look ahead. Clarence just laughed. Finally the man stood up and Elsie said, "Oh, thank God!" But it turned out he'd just gone to retrieve a roll of toilet paper from the back seat and there he was, squatting down again. Elsie shrieked and covered her face. Finally the man stood up, pulled up his pants and stumbled into the car, slammed the door and the vehicle drove off. The things you see on a country road!

The barn at the Leakes' was built into the side of a hill, with the front door at ground level. The back door, however, had about an eight-foot drop to the ground, which was handy for cleaning the barn, and also for us kids to tease a ram that they kept. When the ram was mad enough, he would chase you. You then ran for the back door and swung out onto a ledge on the side. The poor ram would leap out into space and land in the manure pile. He would pick himself up, give a vigorous shake and trot back up the hill so the performance could be repeated. Maybe he liked it? We did, but after five or six leaps he would lose interest, and we would have to wait for another day.

The Robertsons lived farther down the valley, about seven and a half miles or so. I had become friends with their daughter, Yvonna, and I would visit there as often as I could. She also had a younger brother, Rod, plus an older brother and sisters as well, but they had already left home. They lived very simply in a bare log cabin, but things like that don't matter if you feel welcome.

One time their long-haired cat was sleeping in an open china cupboard and had its tail hanging over the edge. Rod took the coal-oil light and brought it up under the cat's tail so that the tail was down in the glass globe, close to the flame. You could immediately smell hair burning! It took a couple of seconds for the sleeping cat to notice, but when it did, the cat let out a screech and swept the cupboard bare as it was leaving. There was china raining down and breaking on the floor, and Rod was bent over with laughter.

I went home for Christmas and spring break. At Christmastime everything was covered with snow, there were Christmas carols on the radio and Mom was always busy in the kitchen baking all sorts of goodies. Rob still believed in Santa Claus, so he was excited waiting for the big day. I had to see all my animals, plus spend some time hunting squirrels.

After Christmas I went back to school and stuck it out till June, when Mom, Dad and Rob came to get me. They drove the team and wagon from the ranch to Nazko. When I saw Rob I was so happy, I cried. I had missed him so much and it was so good to be going home. I tried to get back into correspondence courses, but found that there was too much work to be done on the ranch and too many distractions. So one day I just gathered up the books, notebooks and paperwork and dumped it all into the wood heater—thus ended my school days!

CHAPTER 19

1961–1962–1963

The sixties brought big changes to life on the Home Ranch. The building of an airstrip practically on our doorstep at the Home Ranch had the biggest impact on our daily lives. Before Dad put in the airstrip, we had only limited contact with the outside world. There were no telephones or TV, just letters going back and forth in the mail. Going to the stampede at Anahim Lake and our fall cattle drive to Quesnel were the two times a year that we left the ranch. We had company now and then: local people would visit on saddle horse, and a few visitors came by float plane, but nothing compared to the volume that started arriving once the airstrip was built.

I met my half-brother Homer for the first time when he made his first visit to the Home Ranch with his friend Clyde Stagner in June 1961. They spent about a week at the ranch before we left for Anahim Lake and the annual stampede. I was sixteen by this time, so I was allowed a lot more freedom. I partied and danced all through the stampede with my fun-loving older brother and his buddy. Homer was told to watch out for his kid sister, but I'm not sure he ever thought about watching out for me. I was one of his party buddies.

The concession stand at the stampede was built on a rise above the arena, allowing a good view of the rodeo. Dad and D'Arcy Christensen ran the stand for many years. Both Dad and D'Arcy were frugal so they got along just fine. The coffee was served in Styrofoam cups, which they

Betty with orphaned lamb, 1960s. PHILLIPS FAMILY PHOTO

filled right to the brim, as coffee was cheaper than milk. They would put only one hole in the can of milk so that it had to be shaken to get the milk out. They sold coffee, soft drinks, hot dogs, hamburgers, chocolate bars, chips, chewing gum and cigarettes. They also had a breakfast menu of ham, eggs and toast, but if the run of customers was heavy, the chances were good that you got a couple of slices of untoasted bread.

Dad sometimes judged a few of the events, and this got him out of the concession. D'Arcy found excuses to get away as well. They opened for the breakfast trade and stayed open till the rodeo was over in mid-afternoon. Then the stand was shut down till they opened up again for the dance hall trade in the evenings. They would sometimes hire help but not very often—they would have had to pay wages after all, and that would have cut into their profits.

The summer of 1961 was hot and very dry. There were wildfires around the whole countryside. In mid-August a fire started in the area of Irene Lake, which was thirty or so miles to the west of the Home Ranch. It swept up the side of the Ilgachuzes, and then worked its way along the mountains to the southeast. By mid-afternoon huge columns of smoke rose skyward under a hot sun. The fire continued to burn over a number of days, getting closer and closer to the ranch. We were in the Quesnel Forest District, and their crews had too many fires to deal with already. A crew from Southbank District finally arrived and began cutting fireguards between the fire and the Home Ranch to keep the fire along the base of the mountains. It was now within three miles of the ranch. Ashes rained down on the buildings. The smoke was thick and made for sore lungs. My mother cried a lot and prayed a lot, and feared our home would be burned.

Ken flew home from Bella Coola to give us a hand with whatever had to be done. We decided to move the cattle to Sleepy Hollow. When I thought about it afterwards, I don't know why we wasted our time—the cattle would have just kept moving ahead of the fire anyway. Ken and I were to move the cows that grazed in that area. The smoke and roaring flames didn't seem to bother them at all; we found them grazing close to burning trees. Of course it was very hot. The cows travelled okay for a while with Ken and me pushing them as much as possible, but they came to a standstill about two and a half miles out from the ranch in a ravine going down into Airplane Lake (also known as Cluchuta Lake). We hollered, yelled and beat on them, but they wanted to rest. Even the dog couldn't seem to get them going. Ken lost his patience in a thicket. He was kicking his horse and beating the cows with a stick when he stirred up a hornet's nest! Well, horse and rider broke out of the trees on a dead run, but not before Ken was stung a number of times about the face and especially the mouth. This did get the cattle moving and Ken was much quieter for the rest of the trip because he had great difficulty talking, and I think it hurt to yell. His face soon became badly swollen, especially his lips. He looked as though he could have eaten corn through a picket fence.

The fire burned for weeks, all along the mountain, but we were out of danger when it passed on towards the south. The fire crews manned the fire lines till the rains came and the fire burned itself out. Life slowly returned to normal, the fire crew left and Ken returned to Bella Coola.

In late summer Len Cave came through with several pack horses on

Betty and Pan, 1960s. PHILLIPS FAMILY PHOTO

his way down the Alexander Mackenzie Trail to Bella Coola. He wanted to start a business leading trail rides in the area. He was hoping this trail would be one he could do in the future with paying guests. At the time, I was breaking a good-looking chestnut gelding, a three-year-old that Len talked me into letting him take on the trail. He had five three-year-olds and an older gelding with him. He assured me the trip would do the colt good and that he'd be broken when he got back. Weeks later he returned. The colts were definitely broken, in spirit as well. It had been a hard trip on the young horses. The days had been long. In the high country the feed had been frozen down, as by then it was September. Going down the steep descent into Bella Coola had taken a number of days, and with no feed. Len was the first person I knew who did the trail from the Blackwater to Bella Coola with horses.

After we got the sawmill, and with Ed there to help, Dad decided that they were going to build a frame house. The foundation had been laid earlier in the spring and the lumber had been cut the winter before. Mom was excited about the prospect of a better house, one built to plan, without the constant avalanches of dirt falling from the ceiling. The hay that had originally been laid on the punching to keep the dirt in place had pretty well disintegrated over the years and it didn't serve its purpose any longer. We'd put a ceiling in the kitchen so the cooking and eating area could be kept clean, but other parts of the house were prone to these sudden avalanches of dirt. The old house was warm (since the plywood floor had been put down), but nothing was level and nothing was square. Of course the old house didn't have a foundation—one corner had been put on a hummock and the other on a horse bun! Over the years the bottom logs rotted and the building settled. The windows got lower and lower, and every so often the doors had to be removed and the bottoms trimmed so that they would open smoothly. The floor sloped to the north, so when you washed it, it was best to be on the south side if you wanted to keep your feet dry. It seemed that most of the other ranch houses had similar problems; it was a way of life. The women dreamed of a modern home like their city friends had, but they never expected to get one!

First off, Mom and Dad couldn't agree as to where the house was to be built, so they bickered over that. Who won that round I'm not sure, but more than likely it was Dad. If Mom quit bickering, she lost ground awfully fast, and so on and on they went. The lumber had been cut and stacked, and in June when Homer and Clyde had been there they had put the walls up. Then it sat for a good year because the floor plan could not be agreed on! At some point, Dad decided a frame house was too expensive and a log house would be cheaper to build. So the frame walls came down. Ed pulled the nails and stacked the two-by-fours in his spare time. Len was supposed to help him, but Len preferred to use his charm and not his muscles, which worked for him most of the time — with the women, that is.

For the next few years, logs were cut, peeled and stacked to dry and then construction would begin again. Roger Nygaard from Bella Coola began the log work. Mom had a floor plan but it was totally ignored. Windows were cut out wherever Dad took the notion, and that applied as well to the two doors. A log wall was constructed inside, about one third the way down the length of the building and that pretty well wrecked Mom's floor plan, so she lost interest. Then Dad would say, "Jesus Christ, I build her a house but she is never happy!"

The house was never finished inside, although the roof did get put on and windows installed. It was used for storage and the overflow of visitors in the summertime.

Before freeze-up in the fall of 1961, Dad ploughed what would be our future airstrip on a ridge of high ground that ran east and west, in the fields east of the buildings. It was probably seventy-five feet wide and about 3,500 feet long. Turning the heavy sod was a slow process, but the fall was mild so the job did get done, and it was left to set over the winter.

Andrew and Helen Squinas would often visit during the winter with their daughter Judy, who was Rob's age. They would arrive with their team and sleigh, their blankets and dogs and whatever buckskin and beadwork Helen was working on at the time. Helen was a big-boned woman with very ruddy, red cheeks. Unlike most of the Indian ladies, she was very forward. Dad would tease her a great deal, and she generally had a quick comeback for him. She wasn't shy, whichever way the conversation might lead.

They would spend several days, Helen in the house with Mom,

drinking tea and smoking cigarettes when they weren't doing housework or cooking. Judy and Rob would play in and out of the house. Andrew would help out around the ranch or go hunting.

One day Rob and Judy were playing in the woodshed with a couple of hatchets. Mom asked Helen to check on them, and Helen felt they were fine. Shortly afterwards Rob came to the house crying and Judy followed behind, her face covered in blood. They had both been chopping in the same hole with the hatchets and Rob had struck Judy on the head, cutting an artery. The blood flowed freely. With every pump of her heart, the blood gushed. Towels were used to soak it up. As the towels became soaked, they were thrown into a tub of water. We tried everything to stop the bleeding. Judy was slowly becoming pale and cried against her mother, more from fright than pain. Finally someone came up with the idea of sprinkling flour onto the cut. More flour was applied as the blood surfaced, till at last the blood coagulated and stopped flowing, much to everyone's relief. The next day it was a huge chore to get the dried blood and flour out of her long, thick hair without disturbing the scab on the wound.

In spring it was always a treat to hear the birds sing. I loved to hear the kingfisher down by the creek and the call of the sandhill crane. One knew then spring had truly come. The cranes would fly in big circles, hundreds of them on their flight to their summer nesting grounds. Sandhill cranes return to the same area year after year. They are very territorial and will not share the nesting grounds with other cranes; there is only one pair of sandhill cranes per wild meadow. They hatch one or two babies, about the size of a gosling with yellow downy fuzz. The babies grow very quickly. I found one that was hidden in the grass, about two weeks old, and it immediately took off running, stumbling through the grass and weeds. I chased it, and finally was able to grab it with both hands—this was a mistake, as it bit me on the finger, nearly breaking it! I quickly put it down, and it disappeared into the grass. Its parents ran back and forth near me on their very long legs, flapping their wings and making croaking sounds while trying to lead me away from their young. I was glad to leave them alone after that bite!

Once, after the stampede, we passed through Alfred Bryant's place and stopped for coffee. He had a black and tan bitch hound, about eight months old. He talked Dad into taking her home with us. I'm not sure why Dad agreed, as we certainly didn't have any use for her, but home she came. I suppose it gave Rob another dog, and he did enjoy the dogs.

Len Cave arrived at the Home Ranch with his dog. He had pretty well moved from his place at Tatelkuz Lake, as he had sold it to Barry Wilwand, an ex-RCMP officer. So Len had his stuff at our place and his horses at Sleepy Hollow. Rob spent a lot of time playing with the dogs, tying them all together with the bitch in the middle. He had them down by the creek when a fight started between the males, and they all—including Rob—fell in the creek. Rob was screaming, the male dogs were fighting and the bitch, as well as Rob, was trying to get away. I cut them loose and consoled Rob, suggesting perhaps he shouldn't play on the creek bank. A couple of months later, the bitch produced eleven puppies! It took her all day to get the deed done in the hay manger of the barn. Dad spent all day drowning puppies and swearing. He shot the bitch soon afterwards. I don't think drowning puppies was something he wanted to do again, and he knew that would happen if we kept her around.

While checking horses one spring we found one of our work mares had run quite a large snag into the fleshy part of her chest, close to her leg. It had started to get infected. We managed to get her home, but had no idea how to get the broken-off stick out. As luck would have it, Jimmy Holte arrived the next day with a veterinarian from Washington by the name of Ray Bradbury. Ray was interested in the country, so Jimmy had taken Ray along to sightsee while he hauled a load of freight to Tsacha Lake .After opening the wound and cleaning it out as best he could, Ray removed the shattered remains of the snag. The mare recovered, thanks to Ray. It seemed Ray had arrived at just the right time.

A similar thing occurred one summer while Dad was haying. For some reason the tractor caught fire in the electrical system. He was able to put the fire out but had no idea how to go about replacing all the burned wires to get the tractor running again. Haying had just started, and the weather promised to be good. That same afternoon a couple of fellows from Alberta rode in and stopped at the Home Ranch for a visit. One was a mechanic and understood wiring well, said there was no problem and had the tractor running in no time. Dad couldn't thank the guy enough for his help.

It must have been in late March when Dad fell ill. He stayed in bed for a good week with no improvement. The RCMP Beaver ski plane was flying in the area and stopped by. They had room in the plane and offered to take Dad to the hospital in Prince George, where he spent several weeks.

About a month later Frank Burns from Quesnel flew Dad home in his four-seater aircraft, accompanied by Vic Felton. It was late April and spring was well underway. Frank's plane was on wheels and he landed on the ice on Stuyvesant Lake early in the morning, and they all walked home to the ranch. We had breakfast, and then Mom decided that she was going fly out with Frank to go to town for a while for some female company. Dad took the tractor and sleigh to haul everyone back to the lake. He skirted the field looking for snow for the sleigh. It was better in the timber, where there was more snow left. When they reached the lake Dad drove the tractor out onto the ice, which had melted away from the shore a little. The day was already hot. The plane was parked about fifty yards from shore. When Dad was halfway to the plane, the ice began to roll ahead of the tractor! Instead of heading for shore, he panicked and stopped. As soon as Dad stopped, the tractor started to sink. Someone quickly unhitched the sleigh and pushed it away. One tire went through the ice completely, and then the tractor kind of turned on its side and quietly slipped under the ice! Dad was absolutely grey. It was our only tractor, and I knew he couldn't afford another one.

Frank was panicking as well, since his plane was sitting just a few yards away. He, Vic and Mom got in. He fired it up and rolled away, gathering speed. The plane soon lifted off the ice and climbed skyward. Rob, Dad and I began our walk home without speaking. The birds were singing and the ducks were quacking noisily on the fields where the large pools of water gathered, and the cattle were contentedly grazing. The snipes cried loudly as they ran along the edge of the water, and a kingfisher called out. It was a beautiful day—that was about all that could be said about it at that point.

The airstrip that Dad had ploughed the fall before was ready to be worked up and seeded, but now with the tractor gone, it would have to be done with teams.

About two weeks after the tractor sank, the winds broke up the ice on the lake, and within a day it was gone. Frank Burns put his plane on floats and flew Warren Kerr and Willie Martin out to the ranch. Willie was a diesel mechanic who worked for Alex Fraser at his dealership in Quesnel. They brought out cable and blocks to use along with what we had. With a rowboat and a large hook, they hooked onto the back end of the tractor, which fortunately was resting on its wheels and was in only about eight feet of water. The worst part was that the bottom of the lake was muddy. When they had everything ready, Dad hooked the team onto the cable and blocks that they had rigged between the trees. The team slowly moved forward and with the doubling of blocks they were able to draw the tractor out onto the shore. Once it was on dry land, Willie gave the fellows directions and they took the tractor completely apart, cleaned everything thoroughly and then put it back together and drove it home that night! I thought the grin on Dad's face would split it, he was so happy. I think that they may even have celebrated a little that evening. Now with the tractor back running, it was easier to get the runway packed down; it had already been disked and levelled.

Frank flew Mom home when he came for Warren and Willie. Rex Bartlett also came back with Mom for a visit. Len Cave returned about the same time, to stay for the summer. Calves had to be branded and turned onto the range, horses sorted and feet trimmed. We had to decide which animals would be kept in and which ones would be turned out on the range till haying time. Rick would be back soon, so we could break some more horses.

With the airstrip up and running, there were usually two or three planes a week that stopped by, mostly just for a coffee and a visit. A lot of the time someone would be bringing us something we needed. Most visitors from town brought treats we were not accustomed to— fresh fruit, town ice cream, vegetables we couldn't grow in our garden, and beer—this beer thing was unheard of, as no one ever packed beer on a saddle horse.

Life for Mom was made easier with the planes. She was able to get out more than twice a year to visit her many friends. Riding saddle horse had become hard for her, and the wagon was no joy, so she left the ranch only a couple times a year before the airstrip was built. Now she was able to fly to Quesnel and spend time with friends and enjoy the luxuries that town had to offer. I think her health had begun to fail after so many years of hard work. She seemed to have lost her happy-go-lucky ways. Mom suffered from arthritis and was in a lot of pain—more pain than any of us were aware of.

We flew out quite a lot. Rates were fairly reasonable, and a lot of people had private planes and would fly for the price of gas. The Home Ranch was very isolated, and this opened up a whole new lifestyle. A hard eight- to ten-hour saddle horse ride to Anahim Lake was now a twenty- to twenty-five-minute flight.

With the airstrip so close to the house, we saw the planes landing and had enough time (at least for me) to change jeans, comb hair and be prepared for whoever our company was. The Quesnel Flying Club had a plane, and a lot of the young pilots flew out to the ranch just to get hours logged on the plane. This was fine for me. I enjoyed the company of the young men. If they had an afternoon to kill, we would go riding. Not everyone enjoyed riding, but they rode because there wasn't a great deal else to do. Sometimes they would take me flying, but I never was a happy flyer. Then again, it was something to do. If they rode with me, I would go flying with them.

This was all well and good if there wasn't much happening in the work department. If it was haying time, Dad hated to see the young fellows arriving because I would usually leave the field and then the hay crew would be short, and he would be angry.

Bud and Mary Wellmon had come up from the States the summer of 1963 on their honeymoon and in search of land. After meeting my parents at the stampede, they decided to come back with us to the Blackwater. There were no spare horses and the wagon was heavily loaded, so the two walked behind the wagon all the way to the ranch amidst the swarms of mosquitoes. What a honeymoon! Mary was eighteen and Bud not much older. They lived with us for a number of weeks while Bud rode about the countryside looking at various wild meadows. Mary lived in fear that one day he wouldn't come back from the wild bush. My mom would console her. When they left we did give them a ride back on saddle horses to their truck, which was parked in Anahim.

In late August two families from Washougal, Washington, arrived by float plane: Ray and Mary Jean Malfait and their daughter, Laurene, and another couple of friends of theirs, Joe and Dolly. Ray was looking to buy a cattle operation in BC and had heard somewhere that our place might be for sale. At that time Dad was not interested in selling. They stayed for a week and it was a fun time, especially since they were ranchers and horse people like us.

Dolly was a hairdresser, so every day a couple of us would get our hair shampooed and curled—this was a real treat for Mom and me. We seldom ever got our hair done. Usually Mom and I would cut each other's hair and give each other home perms, but that was about the extent of any hair care other than shampooing.

We needed meat, so I took Ray and Joe hunting. We ended up in a swamp that had been burned many years before. There was the odd tree standing, but most of the big spruce was on the ground rotting, and the new growth of spruce had a pretty good start. There were a lot of moose signs in this area, but no moose to be seen. Suddenly, Joe said that he saw one. I couldn't see it, but I volunteered to hold the horses while they went after the moose. They took off, slopping through the wet spots in their riding boots, and they returned about thirty minutes later, wet to the waist. There were no moose to be had that day.

The first guiding of American hunters out of the Home Ranch took place in the fall of 1963. This was something that Dad and Len had hoped to develop into a business. Dad had applied for a hunting area, and Len was licensed to guide under Dad. There was only one party of hunters that fall, the Cranes, from Portland, Oregon: Horace, Jean, and their daughter, Kay, who was also a hairdresser. Kay was just a year older than I was, so she was someone with whom I could have girl talks. We were haying, so I was busy during the day, but in the evenings we spent as much time as we could together. Len took Horace and Jean hunting and they both got a moose. It was one of the best summers that I had ever had; I hated to see it end.

CHAPTER 20

Big Kids at Play

In the fall of 1963, Mom and Dad headed off to Illinois to visit Dad's family, and Rob was put in a dorm in Anahim Lake so he could attend public school. I think Mom just couldn't cope with home-schooling any longer, and she wanted so badly for us to have our education. Mom had never graduated and neither had Ken or I. Rob was her last hope that one of her children would graduate from school.

Yvonna Robertson rode up from Nazko that fall to stay with us. She was riding a roly-poly, red and white paint mare. My saddle mare had never seen a paint horse before and was scared of it. The paint galloped after her, and my mare jumped the fence and headed for the high country. I didn't get her home till the November roundup when we brought the horses home to winter range. I've heard animals are colour-blind but this seemed to prove otherwise.

Rick and Ed, Yvonna and I were left on the ranch. It was a good thing that Ed was there to pick up the slack when Rick, Yvonna and I took off. We spent a lot of our time riding colts. We girls did get meals on, and the dishes were done. The house was kept in reasonable order, and we did the laundry. Rick was interested in boxing and wrestling, and the evenings when he wasn't playing cards, he was busy reading his wrestling magazines. Rick always seemed to have Yvonna in some kind of wrestling hold, while she yelled bloody murder, threatening to kill him—but of course she never did.

There was to be a dance in Anahim Lake in November and of course we couldn't miss it, so the three of us left early in the morning. November days are short on daylight, and with the snow, the trails can be hard to find in the dark.

Our pack horse for the trip was a big half-Clydesdale mare of mine that Rick had ridden a few times. He knew that she could be a bit cranky. Rick had a good grip on the halter while Yvonna and I packed. We were just throwing the diamond hitch when the mare grabbed Rick on the top of the shoulder with her teeth! She lifted him into the air and gave him a vicious shaking. A horse bite is one of the most painful things, and Rick had gotten a good one! But daylight was burning — no time to lick one's wounds: we had about thirty-five miles to cover in the snow to the Lehman ranch and a mountain to cross — there was a dance to attend!

By pushing our horses hard, we made good time. There was about a foot of snow on the top of the mountain and the weather was fairly mild. We arrived at the Lehmans' about dark. We were always welcome there and knew that there would be feed for the horses.

Mike Lehman took us into Anahim Lake the next day, and I spent time there with Rob. Ev and Bill Lampert were running the dorm and acting as dorm parents. We rented a cabin from the MacInroys, as we needed a place to crash before and after the dance.

It may have been at this dance that two of the local Indian ladies got into a fight. They were wearing the traditional, long homemade skirts in vivid colours, moccasin rubbers and cardigan sweaters. Neither lady would have won a beauty contest. They probably were friends till they got drinking, but now it was fight. The crowd gathered around them, and no one behind could see what was happening. One pulled a knife and stabbed the other in the abdomen. Blood spilled onto the floor and the fight was suddenly over. The piano player, Anita, who was on stage, had a good view of the fight and someone on the floor asked her who had won. She replied, "Oh, the pretty one!"

Several days later, with the forecast saying that a storm was coming in, we decided we had better head for home before the snow got too deep to cross the mountains. We left the Lehmans' early in the morning, along with Vic Hulley, who worked for the Department of Indian Affairs and had some business to attend to in the Blackwater area. The Lehmans stuffed several large gunnysacks with hay and gave us oats for the horses. We put all of this on the pack horse—who wouldn't argue with Jane Lehman—and then we headed out in the heavy falling snow.

There was a lot more snow the higher we got and it was slow going. The lead horse had to break trail and the horses behind used the same foot holes. Every mile or so the horse in the lead would go to the end, while another horse took the front and broke trail. Darkness was close and we hadn't reached the top yet, so we went into Alfred's hunting cabin at Chateau Camp, about a mile off the main trail. We tied our horses up, fed them half the oats and divided the hay amongst the five of them.

We started the heater in the cabin and soon it was toasty warm. There was wood stacked against the cabin wall and we melted snow for drinking, and then proceeded to devour the huge lunch that Jane had packed for us. The snow continued to come down in large, dry flakes, and the world was silent and still.

Crawling into our sleeping bags early, we lay on the foam-covered bunks. The fire crackled and occasionally a block of wood fell inside the heater. The horses were moving about under the trees and their hoofs made a crunching sound in the snow. Finally I fell asleep, but I awoke later to the pitch-black and the breathing of my cabin companions. It sounded as though they weren't sleeping either, but no one spoke. Even the horses were silent. There wasn't even the sound of wind, so I knew it was still snowing.

Finally daylight started to filter through the windows and we got out of our sleeping bags and stared outside. It had snowed a good six inches more during the night!

We rolled up our sleeping bags and ate the last of our sandwiches. Vic decided that he would return to Anahim Lake, as there would probably be too much snow for him to get back when he finished his business in the Blackwater. We all saddled up, fed the last of the oats to the horses, packed the pack horse and rode out to the main trail.

Vic rode off in a southerly direction. His horse was hesitant to leave ours, but it was also anxious to get home to feed. The horses were all hungry and we had about seven or eight miles to reach the summit, then going downhill would be easier. We would lose elevation fast and the chances were that there would be less snow.

The snow was soon up to the horses' bellies. We switched lead horses often, and pushed steadily on. It was slow going. There seemed to be a whisper of wind. Hopefully, it would soon stop snowing! It wasn't always easy to know where the trail was; there was a lot of open country that was sparsely dotted with scrub pine trees. Sometimes only the tops of the trees showed through the snow, others looked like deformed snowmen. The trees of any height were weighed down with snow.

When we were pretty sure that we were halfway to the summit, we stopped the horses where there was some dry windfall. The horses needed a rest. Digging under the snow and trees we found some pitchy wood pieces and started a small fire. We weren't very cold, as we had warmed up clearing the snow, but it was something to do. The horses were covered with sweat and frost. Trickles of steam escaped from under the saddle pads as their bodies cooled.

We waited an hour and then moved on. Once we passed the corral, I knew it was going to be hard to find where the trail left the draw and went into the heavy timber. The branches of the trees were so bent down with snow that we couldn't see the blazes. Thank heaven the horses knew where to turn! Soon we were in the timber.

We'd climb up one hill, only to drop down and then climb another, each hill higher than the one before. As we neared the summit it wasn't as hilly, only a steady climb. Our saddles were filled with the snow that fell from the heavily covered branches overhead. Our chaps saved our legs, but not the seat of the saddle or our pants.

Finally, with happy grins, we crested the last hill. We had intended to rest the horses there, but they kept right on going without being pushed. They too knew that the worst was over and home wasn't far away.

By the time we reached Pan Creek, the snow had let up to just a very fine fluff coming down. We broke through the ice as we crossed the creek. Darkness was less than an hour away, and we still had twelve miles to go, but there was less snow the farther we travelled. The tired horses seemed to get a burst of energy. The pack horse even wanted to get ahead and break trail instead of dragging along behind! Our stomachs told us that we'd missed lunch and that suppertime was fast approaching.

Hours later, under a clear sky with twinkling stars, we rode into the corrals and pulled the saddles from the horses. While Yvonna and I took care of the tack, Rick forked a huge pile of hay from the barn loft and spread it around for the horses. It was minus twenty-one degrees when we arrived home. The place looked mighty good in the glow of the gas lantern as we stomped into the kitchen. The teakettle was singing on the back of the kitchen range. Ed had been reading by the kitchen table. He lowered his book and peered over his reading glasses at us. "Mercy!" was all he said, but he was grinning!

Well, the brats had made it home. Was it worth it? Of course it was! We had made it to the dance, and Yvonna and I had learned a new dance called "the Twist," plus the fellow who taught us the Twist was a good-looking young man who had just moved into the country.

The news on the radio at noon on November 22, 1963, was shocking. President John Kennedy had been shot that morning in Dallas, and he was dead! John Connally, the Governor of Texas, who had been in the car when the president was shot, had been wounded. Lyndon Johnson was sworn in as the United States' thirty-sixth president. There was also a message from Mom that day. She said that they had arrived in Pittsfield, Illinois, five days before and were having a good time.

At the Home Ranch, the horses had to be brought in from the winter ranges, and the cattle had to be checked. It took a few days to find the horses. They would start home once the snow started to get deep, but the creeks were freezing, and horses are scared of ice. Usually, some of the older horses would break the ice and then most of the others would follow them across, but often a younger horse would not cross and would be left behind. When we did the roundup sometimes we would be able to find the strays, but not always. If a stray horse kept travelling, we could cut across their tracks while we hunted for them, but if they holed up in some thick spruce swamp, they were rarely found. There were miles and miles of country for them to hide in. The snow got three to four feet deep and the temperature dropped to minus thirty or colder, and daylight lasted only seven hours, max. It was then clearly time to give up the hunt and let nature take its course. If it wasn't too hard a winter, a few might make it through the cold, dark months. Sometimes we would find their bleached, scattered bones in the spring, and other strays we would never see another trace of!

Once while burning range in May I found a young Clydesdale two-year-old who had spent six months alone in the high country and had survived. He was thrilled to see another horse but afraid as well. He would come running up fairly close, then race off and disappear, only to return again. This went on for half an hour or so before he just settled down to follow a short distance behind my saddle horse all the way back to the ranch.

One day we hooked up some Clydesdale colts—any horse that wasn't broken, Dad called a colt, even if it was seven years old. At first we just drove around the ranch, but the colts were going so well that Yvonna and I decided to go to Anahim Lake again, around the mountain with the team and sleigh. We would have a well-broken team after a week on the trail. We loaded the sleigh with hay, sleeping bags and some food and headed out.

The first part of the drive to Peter Alexis's place—about seven miles—was pretty poor, but most of it was downhill, and we didn't have much weight anyway. After we dropped down off the plateau that the Home Ranch was on, we skirted the edge of Tsilbekuz Lake for half a mile or so. This lake was the most westerly of a string of five lakes. A few miles farther on we crossed Shag Thompson's old place. This property had been sold to Bill Lampert, who lived in Anahim Lake. Next we crossed the Blackwater River, which was frozen solid and packed with tracks from Peter's cattle, as he watered them there and fed them from a large stack of loose hay on the north side. From here on, the trail was well used, not only by the cattle going back and forth, but also by sleigh traffic from the east that travelled on this route once the mountains became snowed in.

Having been alerted by the yapping dogs, Peter came out to greet us and invited us in for tea. We tied our team to the hitching rack and then we edged our way, very carefully, around the dogs. His dogs were lean, large and not very friendly looking.

In the warm one-room cabin, Minnie, Peter's wife, greeted us from the stove where she was preparing the tea. She was a very clean housekeeper. The bedding was on the floor, as there were no beds, but it was neatly rolled back against the walls. The floor was swept and nearly bleached white from many scrubbings. The log walls were unadorned with the exception of a calendar and a picture of Christ, with prayer beads hanging from the corner of the frame. Their younger children giggled in the corner and were told to hush. Their older son, Roy, and several girls in their teens remained quiet.

Minnie brought us each a mug of strong, hot tea that was sweetened with a large quantity of sugar. We sipped the tea and visited with Peter, discussing the weather, trapping, the price of furs and local news, which wasn't much. Peter often visited with Ivan Demeniko, who was about six or seven miles farther up the trail at Cottonwood Creek, so we learned news of Ivan's activities.

We left Peter and Minnie's, going only a short distance to another smaller log cabin, barn and corral and more yapping dogs. This was where Helen and Andrew Squinas lived. Helen came outside and yelled over to us, asking if we wanted tea, and if we'd stopped at Peter's. We told her that we had just had tea and would stop for a visit on our way back. Helen said that Andrew was out with the dogs, chasing after a lynx. I eyed all the mongrels by the cabin and wondered, just how many dogs did they have anyway?

It was better trail now, so we trotted right along, the sleigh runners sliding easily on the wet snow. We came to Cottonwood Creek, which was partially open, but it's so shallow that there was no problem getting across. A bit farther on we crossed Ivan's sleigh tracks. He was hauling hay from his hay meadow below Geese Lake on Ulgako Creek and over to his main place on Cottonwood.

The next few miles were timber, and then we crossed some brush flats close to Geese Lake. Farther on we came out on an opening, which was dotted with poplar trees and sloped towards Eliguk Lake. The creek coming out of Eliguk Lake ran eastward and was the last of the water heading for the Fraser River. From here on, all water ran west to the Dean River.

Less than an hour later we arrived at Doggan and Liza Leon's cabin on Tilgatgo Lake. We called it Irene Lake, but because of the pronunciation, the Indians called it Island Lake. Their cabin was small, about thirty by thirty feet, and there were very few windows so it had a dark interior. It did have a covered porch, from where you had a beautiful view of the Ilgachuz Mountains—they seemed almost close enough to touch. They had a couple of corrals but no barn. We put our team and sleigh in one of the corrals for the night, as I knew that there were loose horses around that would eat our hay if they could get to it.

The cabin was full of people. Mac Cahoose and Timothy Sill were there with their families, plus a number of other people. There were twenty-three people happily gathered about sitting on bedrolls and blocks of wood. In the centre of the cabin, a wood heater and a kitchen stove were back to back, sharing the same stovepipe. When wood was added to either stove, we could see a shower of sparks going up the pipe.

A cribbage game was in progress on a tiny table by one of the two windows. The cards they used were old and worn. Cribbage was a favourite amongst the Indians; they were excellent crib players. It was in similar surroundings that I had learned to play cribbage, and I had played many a game while sipping hot, sweet tea and chewing on moose jerky.

We ate a supper of boiled moose meat and rice. Because we were company, and probably because we were white, Yvonna and I were served first. The men were served next and then the women and children last. Later, when the people started shaking out their bedding, I told them that we would sleep in our sleigh. We buried our sleeping bags in the hay.

We slept poorly, as the team ate on and off all night, sometimes close to our heads. The grinding of the horses' teeth as they chewed was annoying, and their hoofs crunched on the snow. Luckily, the dogs had pretty well all been tied up to keep them from killing each other. With every family having a half-dozen dogs at least, there would have been a lot of fighting otherwise. The hoot of the owl was a comforting sound.

The cabin door must have banged every fifteen minutes all night with the comings and goings of that many people. It was only during the last couple of hours before daylight that things seemed to finally quiet down. The horses rested, and the cabin door banged less often as dawn began to break through the trees on the hills to the east.

After a breakfast of coffee and pancakes we harnessed up the team and headed out. There was considerably less snow around the Leons' place than around the Home Ranch, and Eldash, the Holtes' place, was not known for having a lot of snow. I decided that we had better go home, because if we continued on we would be running the sleigh on next to nothing.

The horses travelled fast heading for home. Helen had tea on so we stopped for an hour there, and this allowed the team to cool down and rest a bit. We then went on and arrived home in the dark. The weather was mild and it was nice riding through the snow in the dark, listening to the sounds of the sleigh and team.

On another nice day, Yvonna and I decided that we'd drive down to the Alexis place, using another colt that we'd harnessed up with a gentle hook horse. I thought it would be a good trip with the sleigh, as it was easy pulling and it would be only fourteen miles round trip. We'd take a break and have tea at the Alexises'. For some reason the tailgate on the front of the sleigh box had been removed, but I decided we didn't need it anyway.

About three miles along the trail there is a fairly steep hill; it has some dips but drops down all the way for a couple of miles. Once the team started trotting, they'd trot right down to the lake unless you held the sleigh back. We were travelling right along—the hook horse didn't want to hold back, and the colt wanted to run. I had my hands full keeping them just under a lope. Lumps of snow flew up in our faces as we sped along. Rounding a corner, one of the runners struck a rock that was under the snow, and this caused the sleigh to bounce sideways, knocking Yvonna out of the sleigh! She landed on the doubletree, grabbed the sleigh tongue and began hollering bloody murder. I had my hands full and, although she wasn't in the safest place if one of the horses kicked, she could ride the hill out if she held on, and she was definitely doing that! The snow and ice particles flew into her face, smothering her yells. When the ground levelled off near the lake and the team slowed down, I reached down and hauled her back into the sleigh. The profanity rained down on my delicate ears. Her face was red and dripping wet and so was her hair, and somewhere she'd lost her toque. I thought the whole thing was funny and told her she was lucky she hadn't got pooped on! I couldn't wait to relate the story to Rick and Ed when we got back.

CHAPTER 21

1963–1964

When Mom and Dad returned from Illinois in mid-December, things got back to normal. Yvonna had to return to Quesnel before Christmas so she left with Dad, who was going to Anahim Lake. From there, she would catch a ride to Williams Lake and take the bus to Quesnel.

Alfred Jimmie came up from Kluskus and traded for the half-Clydesdale mare that we had packed to Anahim Lake in November. He said that he would bring me a heifer calf when he weaned his calves in the new year. I'd been building a herd since I was ten and had my own brand.

While checking on horses east of the ranch I found a mare of Len's that he had lost when he was hunting earlier in the fall. The mare was skin and bones and seriously sick, and she had a half-starved colt at her side. I did manage to get them home, but we knew that the mare wasn't going to get better. Since we had just had a milk cow freshen, we decided that we would do away with the mare and raise the colt on a bucket.

I had a lot of fun raising that colt. When I hunted squirrels or checked traps, the colt always followed me. He stayed at the corral when I wasn't doing something with him, so he knew he was a horse. But I was his mama. When he got older I had to stop taking him out with me, as he had the habit of running up behind me, knocking me down, and then running right over me, leaving me in a heap on the ground.

Rob was home for the holidays. Mom decided to put him back on home-schooling, and it was good to have him with the family again. Rick had decided to stay at the ranch for the winter and not return to logging.

On Christmas day the Quesnel radio station, CKCQ, would broadcast special messages at noon. We would sit around the table listening, sometimes for an hour, and we always received our fair share of messages.

Sometime in February Mom fell on the ice and broke her ankle. She had to wait until the next morning to be taken to Anahim Lake, which was three days away by team and sleigh. From there she would have to travel ninety miles by truck to Bella Coola, to the hospital. This definitely would not be pleasant for Mom: she would have to get in and out of the high sleigh box and deal with outdoor bathroom facilities along the way. Dad took her as far as Anahim Lake and got her a ride to Bella Coola. He then loaded up with freight and came home to await word from Mom that she was back in Anahim Lake and ready to come home.

It was nearly a month before Mom came home. She had a cast on her leg and ankle. Shortly after she returned, she became seriously annoyed at the awkwardness of the cast. She promptly sat down and, using a bread knife, cut the cast off! She limped for a while but eventually she recovered completely.

One beautiful spring day, I put on my new cowboy hat. We had been skidding logs at the mill and had stopped for lunch. After eating I took the team to water, as it was warm. I had a big dumb horse named George, and he was sharp-shod. It was a tad windy, and my hat blew off. It landed under George's feet and he stepped on it, right into the oozing dung! I kicked him in the chest, and he did a couple of steps backwards, not lifting his feet much—just enough to roll the hat along so that he could step on it again. By the time I recovered my hat, it had eight holes in it and was soiled beyond cleaning! That was the last cowboy hat I ever bought.

It was an early spring. We had lots of sunshine, lots of wind and very little rain. The airstrip was dry and ready for aircraft traffic by mid-April when Len Cave arrived with his own plane—a yellow Piper PA-12. Len had taken flying lessons at the coast that winter and had gotten his pilot's licence. He felt that in order to develop the business of hunting for big game, you needed a plane.

Len and Ed immediately started bringing in logs to build a hangar for the plane. The hangar was to be about halfway down the runway on the south side. They worked hard on it for ten days and then Len decided he had to go to town. He left on May 6. He returned two days later on a clear but very windy day. Rick and I had taken some mares and colts to the bull pasture to put with a stud that Dad didn't want on the range. Ed and Dad were out near the airstrip. Mom and Rob were at the house doing lessons.

I'm not sure to this day just what really happened, but because of the wind, and probably lack of experience on Len's part, on the approach to the airstrip the plane dived into the ground, killing Len instantly!

Dad and Ed were on the scene within minutes, but there wasn't anything that they could do. Len was gone. Gone was a friend who had filled our lives with laughter. He could never be serious for very long, he was constantly teasing and always up to something. He'd pick up a broom and pretend it was a guitar, and he would start singing an Elvis song. He couldn't carry a tune in a bucket but he would still make everyone laugh.

This was my first close-hand experience with death, and I probably grew up a lot that day. I certainly saw the world from a different point of view after that. It was a very trying time for us all.

Since we had no way to contact the authorities, Rick left at 4:30 a.m. the next day to ride to Anahim Lake and the nearest phone. Dad went with him as far as the Alexis place to make sure he crossed the river safely. Rick and Dad each led a spare saddle horse and once they crossed the river, Rick took off with both of them, leaving with reasonably fresh horses for the ride to Anahim Lake—seventy-seven miles—a long trip even under good conditions.

As it was springtime, a lot of the trail was mud and in the shaded areas there was still snow with ice underneath. With the frost coming out of the ground as well, the horses could easily break through and stumble. Rick switched saddle horses every hour and a half as he crossed creeks, skirted bogs, climbed ridges and dropped off hills to rocky valleys. The wagon trail he was on wound its way west and then eventually turned south along the Ilgachuz Mountains, with the Dean River on his right. At Lessard Lake the horses were exhausted, so Jimmy Holte loaned Rick a saddle horse to continue on to Clesspocket Ranch and the nearest phone, which was still another eighteen miles or so farther on. He arrived there at dark and nearly fainted as he dismounted. He had completed the fifteen-hour ride without stopping to eat. He stayed at Clesspocket overnight and then returned the next day, on a much slower trip.

Two days after the crash, Len's brother, Toby, arrived along with Warren Kerr. Later the police flew in, and the following day the Department of Transport arrived in a Beaver airplane. They damaged a wheel on landing so we were blessed with their company until the RCAF aircraft took two of the men out. One of the DOT fellows stayed on for several days before he was picked up. They left their damaged plane at the Home Ranch until parts could be found in Timbuktu or someplace.

While the crash investigation was going on, we had mares foaling and calves still coming every day. It sure helped to keep busy.

Towards the end of May, I took three horses and rode to Nazko to pick up Yvonna. I then spent a week in Quesnel before returning to Nazko to find that two of the horses had taken off and headed for home. I still had one horse, so we borrowed another one from the Leakes and rode home in two days—about ninety-five miles.

When we arrived home we discovered that Rick had run a big splinter into his hand. Requiring medical aid, he once again did a one-day ride to Anahim Lake. This time he went over the Ilgachuz Mountains and he said it was a pretty rough trip, as he had to hold his hand in the air to ease the terrible throbbing.

I had to return the horse I had borrowed from the Leakes and pick up the pack outfit that I had left behind when my horses had gotten away in June. So Yvonna and I shod up some fresh horses to prepare for another trip to Nazko.

We reached Nazko on the third day, pastured our horses and found out what excitement Nazko had to offer, which wasn't much. We decided that on the return trip we would go through the Titetown, Dry Lakes, Poplar Mountain area, travelling the north side of the Blackwater. I had been this way only twice—once back in 1949 when we'd gone to Batnuni and once when we'd driven cattle this way in the fall in the early fifties, meeting up with the Smiths at Titetown. Yvonna and I were lucky: someone offered to haul our horses to the Piltzes' place on the Blackwater (where the Nazko River met the Blackwater River). This was to be our starting point. Having the horses hauled this far saved us a day's ride down a dirt road. It was the first time my horses had ever been hauled, however, and I'm not sure they were impressed.

The second day we made Poplar Mountain and camped. We staked our horses nearby. When we awoke in the morning it was pouring rain and everything was soaked. I, at least, had gumboots so my feet were dry while packing up. Yvonne's riding boots were soon soaking wet and made squishing sounds with every step that she took! We got into a quarrel, and she suddenly declared that she was going back to Nazko. I told her it would be a damn long walk with her saddle on her back, because she was riding my horse! That ended the discussion, and we finished packing and took off in silence, which lasted most of the day.

It would have been a pretty ride once we hit China Lake, as it is beautiful poplar country following the Blackwater River all the way to Euchiniko Lake, where Bunch Trudeau lived at that time. But we didn't see much of it as it poured rain all day, clearing shortly before we reached Bunch's place. She made us coffee and served it with delicious cinnamon buns, dripping with sugary syrup. This put us both in a good frame of mind.

After a good night's sleep we continued on up the river, passing by Jerry Boyd's place, now long deserted. Dead Man Crossing was just west of there. Where the name came from I'm not sure, but I remember a story that years ago a man tried to swim his horse there and because the big coat he wore was loaded with gold coins, he drowned when his horse was taken downstream in the undertow. I'm not sure how much truth is in that story. Chantyman Crossing was the next one on the river, but it appeared to be very deep, dark and very wide. We continued on to Church Crossing, where it was gravel bottom and quite shallow. There we crossed and followed the trail up through the thick spruce and poplar for not much more than a mile, coming out on the wagon trail about two miles from the Old Kluskus village. We made camp farther on at Squirrel Lake, and then made it to the Home Ranch the next day.

While Yvonna and I were at the stampede that July, we met Charles and John Smithgall from Atlanta, Georgia, who were friends of Bud Wellmon's, the young honeymooner who'd stayed with us. After talking to Bud about his trip the year before, Charles and John wanted to do it. They had come up several weeks before and bought horses from Lester Dorsey, paying seventy-five dollars apiece, with the promise that Lester would buy them back in the fall. Lester had already taken them on a trip into the Rainbow Mountains. We girls reluctantly agreed to take them with us to the Blackwater. We felt they'd slow us down too much. We liked to travel fast. Their horses were loaded heavy. We had a pack horse, but it was loaded light. When we reached the summit of the mountain, we told the bewildered young men they'd have no trouble from there and loped off, leaving them behind. (I had forgotten we had done this till my memory was refreshed by Charles and Bud on reaching the same spot during a pack trip with them in 2006, forty-two years later.)

By the time the guys reached the Home Ranch hours later, Yvonna and I were in bed, but my parents had more manners and waited up for the weary travellers to give them supper and bed them down. Charles told me later that Dad fed him large quantities of fresh cow's milk, which kept him up most of the night, much to Dad's delight!

We always got a moose for the haying season so that there was plenty of meat. Dad usually did this, but for some reason Yvonna and I were sent out hunting one evening up by Shag Creek. I wasn't a hunter and hated to kill things, but we needed meat. While walking along the rim, I spied a cow moose. She was alone so I assumed she was dry. Dropping down off the rim and wading through the creek, I worked my way up close enough for a good shot. I fired and knew I had hit my mark. I followed her for the finishing shot. When Yvonna and I began to dress her out, we discovered her udder was full of milk! Yvonna told me of the time her sister Doris had shot a cow with a calf, and the calf kept charging Doris, who finally had to climb a tree. In the end she had to shoot the calf as well, for her own safety.

We had not seen a calf, but we were in a lot of willow and alder bushes, making for poor visibility. All we needed was a moose snorting down our necks—even a small one was dangerous. We finished dressing out the moose and laid the quarters out on a bed of moss to cool and stiffen so they would be easier to pack out the next day. There was no sign of the calf and none the next morning when we returned with the pack horses. Something must have taken the calf earlier, before I shot the cow.

CHAPTER 22

Bear Stories

In the spring of 1949 or 1950, Dad had taken a ride to the bull pasture, which was situated about four miles southeast of the ranch on a plateau above. This was a wild meadow that had been fenced to hold the bulls in the spring before we turned them onto the range with the cows. The trail to the pasture crosses the creek several times, then follows a rim-rock above Shag Creek for a mile or so before swinging away from the creek.

On the way back, while Dad was riding along on his horse Silver, a big white gelding, he glanced down to the creek and noticed a couple of grizzlies fishing below a high clay bank. Not being able to resist the chance for some fun, he dismounted, tied up his horse and walked to the edge of the bank. As the grizzlies splashed in the water chasing the spawning trout, Dad threw a rock and struck one of the bears, which in turn slapped the other bear. After a snarl or two they went back to fishing. Dad proceeded to strike one of them again with a rock, causing it to raise its hackles and stand up on its hind legs! Fishing was serious business and these grizzlies didn't need this interruption. I'm not sure how long he teased them, but long enough for them to begin boxing with each other and roaring loudly.

Dad's dog Gin, who had been chasing rabbits, heard the racket and looked to see what all the fuss was about. When Gin started barking at the two roaring grizzlies, they looked up and, seeing the dog and the man, scrambled up the bank after them, rocks and dust flying! Dad sprinted for his horse, untied him and leapt into the saddle. As Silver raced down the trail, dodging trees and leaping windfalls, the bears followed—one running on the high side and one right behind. On the left side of the trail was a drop-off to the creek and on the right was a steep hill. Gin did his best to distract the bears from Dad by barking and trying to nip at the bears' heels.

Soon they reached the slope where you drop down to the level of the ranch. It's fairly steep, with loose sand and then clay. Normally you walk down this portion of the trail, but not on this day! Silver slid to the bottom on his hindquarters in a cloud of dust while the two enraged grizzlies slid down as well. When they reached the bottom, no one waited for the dust to settle or the rocks to quit rolling. They continued going at breakneck speed through the willows and spruce towards the gravel-bottomed Shag Creek. In three bounds, Silver hit the water twice and was out the other side! Now the running was a bit better as the ground was level and sandy and the trail was wider. In a few hundred yards the horse, rider and dog broke into a twenty-acre field known as the timothy patch. At that point they realized that somewhere after the creek the bears had stopped their pursuit. The horse was thoroughly soaked with sweat and his nostrils still flared as he panted for breath. With only a half-mile to the ranch, he slowed to a lope. Silver had run as fast as he ever had in his lifetime!

The grizzlies could have downed the horse and rider with one powerful swing from a front paw, but that day they'd been lucky—the bears had meant only to teach them a lesson. I'm sure they taught Silver one, but as for my dad, I'm not so sure. My mom said that when Dad came into the house that day, he was very white and couldn't talk for a few minutes. It had been a wild ride and he knew that the bears had only been playing with them. If they'd been serious, he would not have made it home!

A few weeks after this incident, just we were leaving with the team and wagon for our early summer trip to the rodeo in Quesnel, Silver cut himself quite badly. We left him to fend for himself, hoping his wounds would heal without getting infected.

As we neared home on our return several weeks later, Mom sug-

gested that she take the saddle horse and ride ahead to get the stove going and start supper while Dad continued on with the slower wagon and
us kids. She was only three hundred yards from the pasture gate when
the horse snorted and danced sideways. She thought that perhaps he
could smell a bear and that at last she would get to see a grizzly, as she
had yet to see one! She kept watching both sides of the trail. The horse
was getting more and more nervous—snorting and tensing his muscles
indicated he was scared. Suddenly the horse reared, nearly upending
my mom. Four grizzlies filled the trail fifty feet or so in front of her—all
facing Mom and her horse! The smaller bear scrambled for the bushes,
slowly followed by the other three. Mom spurred her horse into a lope
and reached the second pasture gate, but at first she was too scared to get
off her horse and open it.

Finally she dismounted and went through the gate. Glancing back,
she could see one of the grizzlies back on the trail, standing on his hind
legs, watching her. She mounted her horse again and started to lope the
horse for the safety of the ranch house. The horse skidded to a stop, as
there were two more grizzlies on the trail ahead, but they hurried away
without hesitating when they saw Mom. By this time my mom had seen
all the bears she ever wished to see. Ahead was the garden fence and
beyond that the ranch house. As Mom reached the garden, a grizzly
sow with two cubs crossed her path. On reaching the tree line, the cubs
tried to climb a spruce tree but were repeatedly knocked to the ground
by the mother bear. After being knocked about a few times, the cubs
finally realized that they were to keep travelling and the three vanished
into the bushes. Beyond the garden she saw the remains of Silver—just
some bones and white hair.

After tying her saddle horse at the hitching rack, Mom stopped at
the woodshed to gather an armload of kindling and other wood to light
the stove for dinner. On her way into the house, she realized that as we
neared the ranch, we kids would no doubt run ahead of the team and
wagon, excited to be home. She knew we were in danger because Dad
did not know about the grizzlies!

Mom dropped her firewood and went in search of a rifle. She
grabbed a .30-30 and a handful of shells (not even checking to see if they
were the right shells for that gun). She went back outside and untied the

horse, but the horse was not about to leave the yard or let my mom get back in the saddle! After a couple of moments fighting with the horse, she decided it was best to continue on foot. Running down the trail with rifle in hand, she met us at the pasture gate. Dad assured her that he was aware of the bears and that he wouldn't have let us off the wagon. She was the one in danger! She was badly shaken and climbed up into the wagon to ride on back to the house.

About dusk, the sow and cubs returned but were scared off by the dog and activity around the house. When darkness fell, some of the bears returned to Silver's bones, growling and munching not fifty feet from where we sat eating our supper. Gin just barked from the safety of the porch. Dad finally slammed down his knife and fork. He had had enough of the growling outside the window! Taking his shotgun, he opened the window and fired a few rounds. The bears didn't leave, so he fired a few rounds with the .30-30 and struck one of them. At that, they all fled and silence settled around the ranch house.

The following day, Silver's remaining bones were gathered up and hauled away. Mom said that the strong smell of the remains meant that the horse had probably died of infection, and the smell of rotting flesh had attracted the bears. They seemed to be gone for now.

Several nights later, Gin started barking. Mom went out on the walkway, and as her eyes adjusted to the dark, she spotted two grizzlies just outside the yard fence—a really large one and a smaller one. She went inside and told Dad, who took up the .30-30 and hurried outside. With one shot he dropped the smaller one. He hit the larger one five times, but it managed to escape into the night. That seemed to be the end of the bears, at least that summer. We kids were once again allowed to play outside and life went back to normal.

In the fall of 1959 we had problems with bears getting into the meat house. When we first discovered the screen torn and a quarter of meat gone, we made snares and hung them over the window, leaving a quarter of the meat inside.

One evening we were playing Monopoly around the kitchen table and drinking tea. Stan McKee, who worked for us that summer, had gone to the bunkhouse early as usual. (I think the younger people tired him out.) Suddenly the dog tore off the porch barking, and we could hear Stan hollering from the bunkhouse that there was a bear in the snare. All the guys grabbed their rifles and ran towards the meat house. There was a lot of shooting going on—Ken, Rich, Maurice and Dad were all firing away. When the shooting finally stopped, I went down to see what had happened. The air was thick with the smell of gunpowder. The guys were standing around a big black bear, hanging from the snare. The bear had blood oozing from dozens of holes. He would have choked to death from the snares, and there really wasn't any need to nearly destroy the meat house with gunfire, but the men felt that they'd dealt with the problem.

Two days later we had a grizzly problem. One of the guys had nearly run into a grizzly while out in the night for a pit stop. This bear couldn't be lured into a snare, so it was decided we would hang meat from a tree close to the cabin. A rope was tied to the meat, then the rope was run through the window, where a windowpane had been removed, and tied to Stan's sleeping bag.

A few nights later, we heard a muffled shot from a 12-gauge shotgun, and a couple of minutes after, Stan appeared at the house. His hair was sticking out in all directions and he was visibly shaken. He wanted to know how the shotgun worked! Apparently he had awoken to his sleeping bag being tugged. He grabbed the shotgun and stepped to the window. The dog was beside him, as he had taken the dog inside so that it wouldn't bark when the bear appeared. The shotgun was lever-action. He ran the lever ahead and back as quietly as possible, as he could see the outline of the grizzly twenty feet way, pawing at the meat and trying to pull it down. He aimed out the window and pulled the trigger. Nothing happened, so he tried again: and again nothing! Getting a bit excited by now, he threw the lever ahead rather hard the third time (what he needed to do in the first place), pointed the gun at the floor and pulled the trigger. The gun went off, barely missing his foot and the dog, but it blew a fair-sized hole in the new floor of the bunkhouse. The bear disappeared into the darkness. We calmed Stan down and assured him that the lever-action needed rough handling and that it had to be pushed ahead till it clicked. It was several nights before the bear returned, but when it did, Stan hit the grizzly with a full load of shot, and although the bear ran off, it never returned.

Rob was playing near the meat house one afternoon the following year when he ran into the house and reported that a bear had gone into the meat house through the screened window, and come out with a quarter of moose meat. This happened near haying time, so Dad had just killed a fat moose. I arrived home shortly after on a young mare. Hearing the story, I rode down to the meat house, crossed a muddy slough and went up to the five-log-high snake fence for a look for the bear. I had the two dogs, Gyp and Spot, with me. They ran on ahead and dashed under the fence. The bear came roaring out of the brush and went after the dogs, which kept darting back and forth under the fence. There were also two very small cubs nearby that tried to climb up a jackpine tree. The mother bear kept slapping them out of the tree and fending off the dogs. The bear wasn't all that large and she was a very dark colour. I couldn't tell if she was a black bear or a grizzly. I wanted to get out of there, but the mare I was riding seemed almost hypnotized at the scene unfolding in front of her. I finally got her moving by using the halter shank to whip her over and under, and we raced off with the dogs in close pursuit.

A short time later, Tom Baptiste and Peter Morris arrived. They wanted to know if the bear had been a black or a grizzly. I told them I thought it was a black, so they went after her. By this time the bear had moved the meat and her cubs across the creek, and she was on the fight! She charged Tom, so Peter shot her and both her cubs, as they would not have survived without their mother. However, I caught supreme hell from both of them because she was actually a grizzly. Indians wouldn't normally shoot a grizzly because they believe it's bad luck. In this case, they felt they didn't have a choice!

That same fall, Dad and I were up Shag Creek hunting for cattle when, across a mud lake, Dad saw a grizzly digging roots. He started grinning. After tying his horse in the trees, he crawled on his hands and knees to the lakeshore, carrying his .22 rifle. I stayed on my horse in the timber where I could see out. Dad shot and hit the bear, which then slapped itself, stood up and looked around. The wind was in our favour so the bear could not smell us. Dad was snickering and having a great time. He shot the bear two more times, and it repeated the performance of slapping itself and standing up and looking all around. Eventually the bear must have decided that the "stings" from the .22 were too much, and it took off with his rolling lope and disappeared into the spruce timber.

In the spring of 1964, shortly after the cattle went to range, a bunch of them returned, tearing down fences to reach the safety of the ranch. They had really been spooked! After taking a close look at them, we discovered that a big steer calf had puncture wounds on his rib cage. A bloody froth was bubbling out of the wounds with every breath! There was only one animal capable of hitting a calf hard enough to break ribs and puncture lungs—it had to be a bear, and most likely a grizzly, as blacks were uncommon where these cattle grazed. The calf was destroyed and the cattle, reluctant, were driven back to the range.

I rode to Tsacha Lake Lodge, as there was a radio telephone there. The lodge was now open for the season. I phoned what would now be called Predator Control and explained that we had a bear problem. Over the next two days we lost another calf and a cow, and the cattle came home again, breaking through the pasture fences and drift fences. Unfortunately, we had to push them back to the range because our pastures were limited. The fields near the house were needed to grow hay for winter feed.

The guys spent nights with the cattle, building fires to keep the bears away. With fires and someone there with them, the cattle would stay. This was the fist time that my parents missed the Anahim Lake Rodeo. They had a serious bear problem to deal with. Even Rick stayed home to help.

Yvonna and I took saddle horses to the Lehmans' and then caught a ride to Anahim Lake. We made it to the rodeo, hit all four dances, missed a lot of sleep and rode home on the Monday after partying and dancing all Sunday night and into the early hours of Monday. We were home, but totally drained, so we slept for two days. The bear problem had been dealt with by Milt Warren from Prince George, who had come out with poison and hounds. For now, everything seemed peaceful.

I had to take a horse to Nazko. Yvonna and I decided to take it back before the haying started. The day before we left, the bears killed another cow. The guys were back on lookout, watching for a predator that slipped silently through the forest and range, on a quest for meat.

Bears' favourite time to kill is just after dark or just before dawn. They carry their kill to a place near water and with higher ground close by, so that after they have fed they can climb up and guard their kill from above. They then bed down to sleep away the heat of the day, keeping a watchful eye below.

Milt came to the Home Ranch again and got another grizzly. This one was smaller than the first one. We hoped this would be the end of the problem as we now had haying to do. We were also planning to hay at Sleepy Hollow, as Ed had bought the place from Jack Thompson. After we finished haying at the Home Ranch, the guys all went down to Sleepy Hollow, including Charles and John Smithgall. Yvonna and I stayed at the ranch and watched the cattle.

We had just got into haying when the cattle returned home for the third time! They were scattered so badly it was hard to know which ones were missing! Calves were too scared to return to where they had last nursed to try and find their mothers, and the cows were reluctant to go searching for their calves. Some of the pairs were separated for days and others never did find each other. I rode to Tsacha Lake to phone Milt once again.

This time when Milt arrived, I went with him to find what we could, as the guys were busy haying. He had two hounds with him, and the first day we left them chained at the ranch. We followed the cow tracks back to where they'd been when they were attacked. It wasn't hard to find the kill or the remains. The ravens and crows that gathered around the remains scattered as we approached, circling and squawking. Bald eagles sat atop trees and watched the goings-on.

Fortunately, the carcass we found still had enough meat for the bear to return for another feeding. Milt loaded it up with 1080 poison and we walked up onto the rise just east of the dead cow. It was a knoll covered with second-growth jackpine about waist-high and a lot of bleached windfall from an old fire. Sure enough, there was a bed dug into the soil and gravel where the bear had rested. It had no doubt just vacated the bed when we were making our way up there. Milt said that this is when most bear attacks occur! I wondered just what we were doing out there, armed only with a couple of .30-30s. But he had been at this for a long time, so I trusted him. We returned to our horses and rode home.

The next day we returned to the poisoned carcass to find very little left! Milt had brought his favourite dog, King, along on a leash. We left our horses tied and Milt circled the area with King until he picked up the scent, and then we were away. The bear travelled one way and then another. It was sick by now: it was vomiting and had a bad case of diarrhea. It dug holes, pulled up trees and scattered windfall as it travelled. It covered many miles in his pain, but it died only about a mile from where it had taken the poisoned bait. It was a fairly large bear we found, and Milt started to skin it while I returned for the horses.

Somewhere along the way, King had eaten some of the bear's vomit, even though Milt had been watching him carefully. The dog had already had his first convulsion by the time I got back with the horses. The 1080 poison works on the nervous system, and the vomit from a poisoned animal is as deadly as the original bait. I know it broke Milt's heart to have to shoot his own dog, but he knew that would be an easier death than to die by the poison. Milt delayed his trip back to Prince George so that he could return the following day to the site where he had shot his dog. He brought the body home in a burlap sack and buried him just north of the ranch house, beside Dad's beloved dog, Gin.

The following spring, coming back from Anahim Lake, we were near Irene Lake; I was riding a saddle horse ahead of the wagons. Rick and Dad each had a team and wagon. At the turnoff to the Leons' place, I could hear a cow bawling in fright, so I decided to investigate. It didn't take me long to locate the cow making the noise. It was a young heifer lying in a hollow in amongst the scattered jackpine. Beside the cow was a beautiful silvertip grizzly, about two years old, trying to figure out just how to kill the cow. The heifer was on her knees dragging herself at a snail's pace as she tried to escape the biting and clawing that the grizzly was inflicting upon her. She had been having calving problems and had lain down too long, so that her hindquarters were paralyzed and she couldn't get up. The Leons had gone to town, so there had been no one home to check on the heifer.

The bear had probably already eaten her calf, which no doubt had been born dead, as we couldn't find it. Now that it had a taste of beef, the bear wanted the cow as well! I yelled at the bear. When it saw me, it ran off through the trees. I didn't have a rifle with me, nor did anyone else. However, we decided that rather than leave the cow for the bear to torture, we would cut her throat, which Dad and Rick did. Me, I stayed with the teams and tried to think of more pleasant things. As I sat on the tailgate of one of the wagons, the young grizzly came up the trail to within a couple of hundred yards from where I sat and then headed off through the timber.

The following year, 1965, Rick and I were doing a check on the cattle before leaving for Anahim Lake. We were concerned about the number of bear signs and the uneasiness of the cattle—we didn't know if they were still spooked from all the killings the previous summer or if there were more problems. We were riding through an old burn in a swampy area when one of us spotted movement low down in the grass. It was a cow lying on her back, and she had been there a number of days. The bears had eaten her ears, brisket and udder, and then they punctured her stomach so that she didn't bloat (bloating would have been a blessing, as at least then she would have died!). The gaping wounds were all crawling with maggots. I threw up till I could throw up no more. Rick got the job of shooting the poor cow.

It appeared that we were into our second summer with serious bear problems. The cattle were so spooked that they often didn't come home, but scattered onto parts of the range where they had never gone before—looking for safety or trying to hide. We would find big, fat cows dead after they had had a long battle with a grizzly. From reading the signs, you could see where the bear had pulled the cow down, then she'd escaped and was brought down again and again until the bear finally killed her. It looked as though those bears were doing a lot of playing with their victims. Then when the cow was down, they would rip the stomach open and go for parts like the liver, which must be a favourite of bears.

Once again we were back to trying to keep the cows together. We built fires at night to try and keep the bears away. Early one afternoon Rick went out alone to start the fires. While he was gathering wood he was charged by a very small grizzly with a huge head and large feet with long claws. It was definitely a mature bear, but appeared to be a dwarf. Rick had his .30-30 and had time for only one shot as it came at him. He hit it in the head and luckily it split the skull and dropped the bear nearly at his feet. This seemed to end the bear problem for that summer.

In 1966, which was the third summer of the bears killing cattle, we handled them on our own. We obtained some 1080 poison and poisoned whatever carcasses we found. This helped to control the grizzlies somewhat. Rick was lucky enough to run into two grizzlies that were following the cattle and he shot and killed both of them.

Rick had a big Airedale terrier dog named Mickey that loved to fight. Mickey always leapt on my dog and the fur would fly. While we were watching the cows one day there was a lot of rain and the creek levels had come up. We were crossing a creek on saddle horses and saw there was a logjam below the crossing. With the higher water, the dogs were in danger of being swept into the logjam, so we took them across on the horses, holding them in front of us. When we got to the other side we let the dogs off, but it had got to the point where my dog didn't want to get off the horse because of the fighting. Rick would always jump off his horse and then try to stop them. One time when he picked up both the dogs and threw them into the water, he lost his balance and fell into the water as well. The dogs kept right on fighting over top of him, and I laughed my head off.

One day a horse kicked Mickey and broke his leg. We fed him Aspirins in chunks of meat until he fell asleep. (I half-heartedly hoped that the Aspirins would stop his heart, but they didn't!) We then splinted and taped his leg and when he woke up, he ripped the splint and the tape off. He dragged his leg around for five or six weeks and then started using it again. He seemed to make a full recovery.

Connie King, who had a ranch west of Anahim Lake, was attacked in 1968 by a grizzly and was badly mauled. Connie had been on foot, looking for his cattle in some spruce swamps when the mother bear attacked him. She had a kill nearby and her yearling cubs were feeding on it when he walked in totally unaware of the situation. He suffered the loss of one eye and his face was badly disfigured. He managed to crawl home after the bear left him for dead.

It was about this same time that Maddie West was hunting on foot for her horses near Anahim Lake and she got between a grizzly sow and her cubs. She told me later that her father had always told her not to run, so she stood perfectly still while the bear circled around her. She said the smell of the bear was so bad and she was so scared that she started to run. The bear hit her just once—a swat on her back that laid her wide open and required some 250 stitches to patch up—but luckily she survived too.

Antoine Baptiste was heading out to do some late spring ice fishing one year. He tied his skinny saddle horse to a tree and then went out onto the lake to fish. When he returned to the shore, there was a grizzly waiting for him! It chased Antoine up a tree, where he spent the rest of the afternoon while the bear walked around below. Antoine said that the bear probably never bothered the horse because it was too skinny—Antoine would have made a far better meal, as he was a rather heavy fellow! Luckily the bear didn't attempt to climb the tree or shake him out of it. The bear finally wandered off in the evening. Antoine then climbed down, untied his horse and headed for home.

William Jimmy and another fellow from Kluskus were out trapping beaver in the spring on saddle horses, just after the snow was gone. The ground was still frozen. They were crossing a frozen swamp when a grizzly suddenly appeared and took after them. They were whipping their horses as fast as they would go, with the bear easily gaining, when William's horse broke through the frost and fell, throwing William off. The horse scrambled up and took off while William lay dazed on the frozen ground! That bear stepped right on William's hand as he lay there, but lucky for William it kept right on going—it wanted those horses! William picked himself up and walked home. The other fellow and the horses made it home safely too.

P.L. West was out hunting horses on foot, when he too was chased up a tree by a grizzly. He ended up tying himself into the tree and spending the night there—he was afraid that he would fall asleep and fall out. In the morning the coast was clear so he climbed down and went on home.

There were another two fellows who were out surveying or timber cruising when a bear began to chase one of them. He quickly climbed a tree and the bear kept going. The fellow was so weak with relief, he fell from the tree and broke his leg!

CHAPTER 23

Summer 1964 to 1967

Our house was very busy the summer of 1964. Rick, Yvonna, Charles and John Smithgall, and Rob and I were in and out constantly. Len Cave's brother, Toby, brought his son, Allen, out to spend some time with us, and as he and Rob were about the same age, they spent hours together at the creek fishing. Rob loved to fish and hunt. Then in August, Jack Phillips—no relation to Dad—brought his daughter, Beverley, out for a week. She was about the same age as Rob and Allen, so she tagged along with them.

The three of them were at the creek fishing when Beverley caught a fairly nice rainbow trout. While Beverley was busy with something else, one of the boys (probably Rob, as it is a Phillips trait to tease) pushed a table knife down the throat of her fish. They then told her that she had to clean her own fish. So she opened it up and discovered the table knife! The boys were laughing at her as she came running to the house to tell us that her fish had swallowed a table knife. We tried to tell her that it wasn't possible and that one of the boys must have put it there, but she was near tears, saying, "No, no, the fish swallowed it." I don't know if she was ever convinced that the boys did it or if she left the ranch still believing that she had caught a fish with a knife in it. I do know that the boys had a good laugh.

Summer was ending and Charles and John were returning to Atlanta. Mom took Rob to Anahim Lake and put him in the dorm to attend school. What a long way from home it was for a little boy of eight years old!

The bears finally seemed to be leaving us alone and we had no idea just how many cows and calves we had lost until the roundup was done. It was a big job trying to gather in the badly scattered and still spooked cattle after they were chased all summer by bears.

Toby came back on September 28, and we buried Len's ashes on the northeast side of the hay meadow, on a knoll with a good view of the mountains and the Home Ranch. We also planted a blue spruce, which Toby had brought along, as a monument to Len. It was a sad day, but the healing was in progress and time was helping. Life must go on.

On October 14 we learned that Jimmy Holte and Dick Poet had been killed at Fenton Lake in Tweedsmuir Park. Their Beaver aircraft had crashed while taking off from the lake, due to bad weather conditions. Jimmy had been a special friend to my dad. Together, they had bought the half-tracks for their tractors to freight with. After Jimmy's death, my dad never used the half-tracks again. It seemed his heart was not into doing it without Jimmy.

Rick and Ed were shoeing horses for the cattle drive. One was a young four-year-old mare that we had used some during haying, and I planned on using her on the drive. The guys had her in front of the shop and were having some trouble with her. I rode out with another saddle horse and was gone only about thirty minutes. When I came back the mare was lying on the ground in front of the shop. I sat quietly on my horse and watched her. She didn't seem to be breathing, and no one was around. I jumped off my horse and kicked her, but she still didn't move! Then the guys started laughing their heads off from inside the shop where they had been watching me through a crack in the wall. They said that while I was away she had started fighting and then suddenly fell over dead. We thought it must have been her heart.

Rick, being a wrestling and boxing fan, was in seventh heaven when Cassius Clay beat Sonny Liston in the seventh round in Miami Beach. He thought Cassius was the greatest boxer ever born. Dad would find all kinds of faults with him just to torment Rick, who would defend him. They would argue back and forth for hours.

After the cattle sale in October 1964, when I was nineteen, I decided that I wanted to try something other than returning to the ranch for the fall. There was a cooking job at the Bracewell Ranch in Tatlayoko in the Chilcotin, so I decided that I would give it a try for a couple of months.

At the beginning of November on a dark, grey day, Lloyd Bennett drove me to Tatlayoko. We arrived at the ranch after dark. Alf Bracewell met us at the door. Alf was a fairly tall, lean man with a twinkle in his eye; he was wearing an engineer's cap and had a week's growth of beard. He asked us in and made coffee. In the dim light from the kerosene lantern, two little, fair-haired boys stared at me with big, serious eyes. Kevin, the older one, was in school, so he was probably six or seven, and Alex was about three. The kitchen looked like bachelor quarters, made worse in the dark. There was a counter dividing the kitchen from a big living room, but beyond that it was dark. A staircase led to the upstairs and at the back there were a couple of bedrooms.

Alf's wife, Gerry, ran a guiding outfit so she was away all fall in the hunting camps and came home only when she brought the hunters out at the end of the hunt. Alf did some logging and ran the ranch, but with the children he was tied down, so they needed someone at the house to care for them.

When Lloyd said that he had to be getting back to Quesnel, it took all the strength I could muster not to say, "I'm going with you, don't leave me here in the middle of God knows where, with this bearded man and these two kids who just stare at me!" I watched the tail lights of Lloyd's pickup fade down the driveway and then I went indoors. Alf said that he would show me my room, so I followed him upstairs with my stuff. When daylight broke it wasn't nearly as bad as I had first thought. The place was nestled in the beautiful, narrow Tatlayoko Valley. Giant fir trees were scattered about the yard, their tops permanently bent over by the constant winds. The house was the usual log house, and with some cleaning it was soon comfortable.

I didn't know just exactly what was expected of me when I came down to the kitchen that first morning. The boys were staring at me. Alf showed me where things were as I prepared the breakfast. I asked him how he would like his eggs cooked, and he replied, "Anyway I get them, as long as it doesn't look like someone blew his nose on them!" We made it through breakfast and Kevin left for school. Alf said that maybe I could do something about the laundry in the basement.

I cleaned the kitchen and then checked on Alex, who was still just staring at me. He wouldn't respond to my comments. I went down to the basement for another shock: there was a laundry chute from the main floor, and the laundry was piled to the top of the chute. God, oh God! I couldn't believe my eyes, but I got busy.

By the time Gerry got back from the hunting camp at the end of that first week, the house was in order and the laundry was caught up. The boys had lost their shyness and acted normal—ripping round the house. Alf had shaved, and I discovered that under the beard was a nice-looking face to go along with the twinkling eyes! I felt right at home with Gerry, as she was a very capable horsewoman, packer and hunter. She stayed home only one night and then she was gone again.

By the end of the second week, Alex was calling me Mama without realizing his mistake. He was a lovable little boy who really missed his mother, and I took her place supplying cookies and kisses. Kevin was always a bit more reserved.

Gerry had two older boys about my age, Bari and Marty, whom I met sometime later. They both worked at Lignum Mill, down by the lake, and they lived in a cabin nearby. In the evenings they would pick me up and we would go look for things to do.

I had made good friends there in the valley and I hated to leave, but the hunting was over and the job ended, so I was going home. Dewey Mulvahill picked me up and drove me to Chezacut, where I spent several days at Randolph Mulvahill's ranch. Dewey then drove me to Alexis Creek, dropping me off at the general store to wait for Hodson's freight truck to come by later in the afternoon. I could catch it for a ride on to Anahim Lake.

The weather was turning colder and the east wind blew, the temperature dropping steadily. I waited at the store all afternoon, but no freight truck came. It was obvious by five that it wasn't coming. I was trying to decide what I would do, when a lady came into the store and we got to talking. I explained my situation and she invited me to her place for the night. I ended up staying there for several days as the weather got colder and colder. By the second day it was down to forty-four degrees below.

Finally, Ken came up from Bella Coola to get me, as the freight truck was not running in those temperatures. It reached seventy-two below in Redstone! By the time I eventually reached Anahim Lake I had missed Rob's Christmas concert that I'd promised him I'd be home for.

Mike Holte, Jimmy's oldest son, had come to Anahim Lake with the tractor and half-tracks to pick up two brothers and a sister who were staying at the dorm, so Rob, Ken and I caught a ride to Lessard Lake with them. Theresa and the youngest daughter, Linda, had also come into town. It was so cold going home that we had to huddle under blankets in the sleigh to keep from freezing.

It was very cold and dark when we got to Lessard Lake. The house was freezing cold so Theresa started the fires, and we were soon all standing around the heater. There was a hot water tank behind the kitchen stove. The water jacket was in the firebox of the stove, and this was used to heat the water tank, but the weather had been so cold that it had frozen. When Theresa built the fire in the stove, the pressure built up until the water jacket exploded. Then the side of the cast iron water jacket blew out the side of the stove and went through a two-inch plank counter! Everything on top of the stove flew into the air. The gas lantern that had been hanging from the ceiling on a piece of wire was parallel to the ceiling for a second. The bang made your ears ring! After a stunned moment, as the ashes, soot and dust started to settle, everyone scrambled for the door only to be met there by Theresa, who had been outside and was hurrying in to see what had happened. The soot and ash slowly drifted down, and then out from under the wrecked stove came a cat with a tail the size of the stovepipe! The cat completely circled the room, half-running on the walls, and then shot into the bedroom.

We helped Theresa move into the house next door. After the place was warmed up, we packed the dishes, food and bedding over. The following day, Dad arrived with the team and sleigh in the late afternoon. I couldn't even recognize the horses as they were so white and covered up with frost—they looked like greys. Dad was all bundled up, just his eyes showing, and there were icicles on his nose that he occasionally knocked off with his big mitt. The temperature hadn't warmed above thirty-eight below all day, and although the winter sun shone, there was no warmth in it. By 3:30 the sun had dropped behind the Rainbow Mountains and the cold intensified.

The next morning, we left Lessard Lake at about 10:30 with the thermometer sitting at forty-one below! Rob, Ken and I crawled into the box that Dad had built on the sleigh; the box gave us some shelter from the wind and helped us keep warm. Mom had sent extra blankets, mitts and coats so we bundled up with everything we could get on. Dad sat up on the sleigh seat bundled in his parka with a blanket wrapped tightly around his legs and a kerosene lantern between his feet to give him some warmth. The team didn't offer any argument in the cold. They liked to move to keep warm, and so they did their job and Dad did his—they worked together like a well-greased gear. The team automatically swung wide on the corners and would hold the sleigh back on the hills without tension on the lines; going up the hills they dug in and pulled side by side.

The first night we spent at Irene Lake with Edward Leon; he was the only one home. Dad had left some hay there for the horses, so they were well fed and watered. He didn't baby his horses, but when it was this cold he would cover them with blankets and he left their harnesses on, as this was easier than putting a frozen harness on them in the morning. The next morning dawned clear and cold at thirty-eight below. The horses knew that they would be home that night, so they stepped along faster than they had the day before. It warmed up a little, to twenty-nine below. We stopped at the Alexises' for an hour to rest the horses.

The last eight miles were slower going with the climb up to the plateau where the Home Ranch was. We arrived home after dark. Mom was waiting for us with the smell of freshly baked bread and supper simmering on the stove. Rob hadn't been home since early September, and it had been nearly three months for me—the longest I had ever been away from home. Ken had not been home for over a year.

In January 1965, my mom's brother George passed away from a brain tumour. Mom had now lost all her brothers and two sisters. There was no way that she could get out in time to attend the funeral and be with the family, so she dealt with it as best she could.

Ivan Demeniko, who lived alone at the Cottonwood Creek homestead nearby, had lost a number of cattle through the ice. He was also struggling with illness. This was all more than he could deal with, so he visited us a lot. He would ride the fourteen miles back and forth to feed his cattle every few days. By mid-April he agreed to seek medical help, and he left the Blackwater for the coast. We kept track of his cattle as best we could until they went to summer range and then we hoped for the best.

On a long day-ride, I rode to Lessard Lake on my way to pick up Rob who was back in the dorm going to school but coming home for spring break. The next morning Mike Holte and I went to Anahim with the tractor to pick up the kids from the dorm. It was a warm day, and by afternoon it was downright hot. I can't recall who the old Indian lady was that we gave a ride to, but she climbed into the sleigh box right up at the front end. We hit Lessard Lake, and about halfway over, the ice began a gentle roll ahead of the tractor. Luckily Mike just kept going as fast as it would go. I nearly had a heart attack. The kids and I sat on the tailgate in case we had to jump, and I tried to tell the old woman to get to the back in case the tractor went through the ice. She just stared at me. I don't know if she was deaf or didn't understand English. When we reached the shore, I nearly collapsed with relief. We stayed the night, and then Rob and I rode home together. It was a great trip as the swamps were still frozen but there was no snow, so we were able to take every winter trail available to us. This cut off miles, but it was still a long ride, and we arrived home late in the day with very tired horses.

When it came time to take Rob back to Anahim Lake, the river crossing at the Alexises' was unsafe. The ice was still on the river but it was rotten. We decided to go to the Cassams' place and cross, as the river was swift there and it would be free of ice. This meant an extra sixteen-mile ride, so we put together extra food and blankets and packed them on the saddle horses, as there was no way we could make it to Lessard Lake in one day with the extra distance.

It was raining the morning that we left and most of the snow was gone in the timber, but the frost was coming out of the ground, making it hard going for the horses. We rode the seven miles to the Cassams' to the crossing. William Cassam had a raft that he used to push us across, and one horse was led behind the raft—it would hit the water and start swimming, and then it could touch bottom about halfway across. A second trip had to be made to get the other horse across. We then mounted up and rode nine miles, passing through Sleepy Hollow and on to the Alexis place, where there wasn't anyone home. At the Squinases' the cabin was open, so we stayed there. There was hay for the horses, and we had something to eat and then went to bed early, but neither of us slept much. The geese were calling noisily from the river and the ducks were quacking and splashing about as well.

We got up early, ate some sandwiches, saddled up and started for Lessard Lake. It was a beautiful day, so this made up for the day before when we had gotten soaked in the rain. When we arrived at Lessard Lake, Rick was there. He would return with me to the Blackwater. The next day, Rick and I took Rob and the Holte kids to the dorm. Mike took us down with the tractor. The roads were muddy, so it was a miserable trip to town.

On the return trip, our horses had caught distemper, so they were sick and miserable. We pushed them every step of the way to the Alexises' place. When we arrived there, the river was filled from bank to bank with raging spring runoff—there was no way that we were getting across! We spent the night with Helen and Andrew Squinas and rode to Sleepy Hollow the next day. By this time, I was sick with a bad head cold, and I decided that I'd better go home. Rick rafted me across the river and I started walking for home. Rick remained at Sleepy Hollow with the horses.

It was seven miles to the Home Ranch, and it was a very steep climb out of Sleepy Hollow and then downhill to Tsetzi and Airplane Lakes. I was so tired and feverish that I lay down on some kinnikinnick (a low-lying evergreen) on a south-facing slope by the lake in the warm sun, and I fell asleep. When I awoke after an hour and a half I felt much better and walked up out of the valley onto the plateau above. I was somewhat concerned about a fresh grizzly track that was ahead of me on the trail, but after a couple of miles the tracks turned off, much to my relief. I arrived at the ranch and went to bed, where I slept for twelve hours straight. A few days later, when the water level dropped off in the river, Rick came on home with the horses.

In June, Rick and I camped at Tsetzi Lake and built a log cabin there. Rick had given up on the wild meadow south of Tsacha, but still wanted some place to call his own. He felled and I skidded the logs with a team, then we both peeled them. He also had a boat, so in the evening we'd fish on the lake and escape the mosquitoes by going out on the water. But neither one of us was a fisherman. It was only an hour to the ranch, so we went home often for Mom's cooking. We had a lot of company at the new cabin, as the locals all came to see what was happening and then returned again and again to see the progress we'd made.

Later that summer, Rick and a couple of friends—both named Dave—joined us for our annual trip to the stampede in Anahim Lake. Rick and Dad were driving the teams and wagons, I had my own saddle horse, and Dad outfitted the two Daves with some young horses that had been started, but required firm hands. We left the ranch without mishap, but things didn't last—one horse or the other was putting on a show of bucking or spooking and trying to run into the trees. For the first few miles the guys did well. The mare was the worst: she not only wanted to buck, she was goofy as well—anything would set her off and the further we went, the worse she got. After six or seven miles the gelding settled down. We were going up the draw at the foot of the mountains where the trail crossed and re-crossed the creek. The mare started bucking good and hard. Now, this wasn't any sandy rodeo arena—there were rocky creek beds, twisted spruce trees, dried snags, big rocks and a good deal of bog. There was also a good crop of high red top grass. When Dave finally came off, he was lucky enough to fall into the high grass. The mare ran back to the wagon. We stood around laughing and waiting for our cowboy to come up out of the grass. Then we realized that maybe he was hurt, so we went in search of him. He did finally get up, and the look on his face shut everyone up. He took the lead shank of the mare, crawled in the back of the wagon and rode there the remaining day and a half to Anahim. He also rode on the back of the wagon the two days home. On the way back the other Dave got smacked into a tree hard when the gelding ran away and hit the tree while going at a good speed. Dave tied a stiff lariat onto the horse's lower jaw for good leverage and rode him the rest of the way back to the ranch.

It was decided at the rodeo one year that they were going to have chariot races—it was the only year I ever knew them to have these races. Rick had a nice little quarter horse stud he'd taken to the rodeo that year for some reason. Woody Woodward, a colourful Chilcotin cowboy, then active in the amateur rodeo circuit, talked Rick into letting him take the stud into the race. The two-wheeled cart Woody came up with was pretty crude looking. The tires were truck tires and the drum was rusted and didn't look safe. The harness wasn't much better but at least the collar fit properly, and even had a pad. Woody was confident the horse would run, and that Rick and he would split the prize money. After the show was over for the day and most people had returned to their camps leaving the grounds semi-deserted except for the odd dog and a few drunks, Rick and Woody were going to have a trial run to prepare the horse for the next day's race. The stud was broken to ride and fairly well behaved and, considering he'd never been harnessed before or hooked to anything, he was pretty patient.

Rick stood by his head while Woody hooked up the traces and gathered up the lines and stepped into the drum. It took a few moments to get the horse started but finally they were off, and by gosh that horse could run! More from fright than anything else, I'm sure, what with the rattling and banging of the cart on the gravel, and Woody's yelling and whipping with the lines. They were making a real showing till they came into the first corner, which they cut too wide. It was all downhill after that.

One of the wheels of the cart caught a post on the railing. Woody somersaulted through the air; the horse broke through the railing and disappeared down through the camps in a cloud of dust. The cart, after a short flight, hit the ground in an assortment of pieces. Woody suffered a broken finger. Someone managed to catch the horse, unhurt but badly spooked. All Rick could say was "Oh, my good Lord."

It was in July after the stampede and we were all going down the north side of the Ilgachuz Mountains where the trail crosses the creek thirteen times. It was hot and the flies were out in droves, mosquitoes and horseflies driving the teams crazy. They wouldn't stand and were kicking at their bellies and shaking their heads, rubbing on one another and not paying attention to the trail, trying to wander about and falling in holes. Every time they passed a bushy tree they wanted to rub on it, and this was making it difficult to drive them. Lester Dorsey and Tom Mathews were with us, each with a team and wagon. Their wagons were empty, making it rougher to ride on the rocks. There was a lot of mud as well. The long tails of the horses were covered in mud that was added to by every pool of slop the teams waded through. Of course their tails swished constantly, throwing mud about and hitting the teamsters. I was riding saddle horse so was somewhat better off, but the flies were driving my saddle horse crazy too. I rode up alongside the wagon Tom was driving. Tom was somewhat cranky and that day was no exception, but he looked gloomier than ever. Thinking I would probably get a rise out of him, I put on my most cheerful face and asked him how he liked the road. Nearly shouting he replied, "This ain't no damn road, it's only a way to go!" Laughing, I rode on but there was a lot of truth in his answer.

The place was a madhouse that summer of 1965! There were planes and people coming and going every day. Between hunting the bears and trying to hay, we were kept busy. After haying all day, I would saddle up in the evening and ride around with the young crowd that was always present. Mom was busy cooking and feeding the crowd, but she seemed to enjoy it and was much more cheerful than she had been. Barry Wilwand probably spent two nights a week at our house, flying in after work and flying out early in the morning. He always had his plane full of people—usually girls —but not always. Barry also loved to wrestle so our evening entertainment would be a wrestling match between him and Rick in the front yard. On occasions Barry would bring out a TV and generator and we'd have movies. A first! Toby Cave found a water pump and enough hose to reach the house so we had running water of sorts. This was better than packing it all the way from the river. Now we would go start the pump and then fill all the water containers. Running water—another first! Of course this was good only through till it began to freeze—then we were back to the water pail.

The Malfaits returned that summer with another couple who had a son and daughter. The son, who was about sixteen, was on a wrestling team and felt he was quite good. After a few days of listening to his wrestling abilities, and thanks to Rick and his wrestling lessons, I grabbed the kid in a full nelson and threw him on the floor. He may have been in great shape, but then so was I! There was no way he was going to get away, and after fifteen minutes or so of rolling around on the floor, his elbows were skinned and his nose was bleeding; so then I let him go. We got along a lot better after that. Dad found it amusing, Mom only raised her eyebrows and his parents never said a word.

In early October, Yvonna and I decided to make a quick trip to Anahim for the mail, as we hadn't received any in a while. We took a pack horse, which would slow us some, but we needed a few things for the drive. I asked Dad for his watch, as I wanted to keep track of our travelling time. He reluctantly loaned me his pocket watch with a long lecture about how this watch had run longer than most watches he'd owned and don't lose it.

We didn't make good time. There was a skiff of snow and the ground was freezing, making it slippery for the shod horses. Darkness caught us at the lower end of the Corkscrew basin but we had no choice but to keep going, with me ahead leading the pack horse and Yvonna somewhere behind. I could hear her horse clicking on the rocks every once in a while. We were just approaching Three Crossings about six miles from the Lehmans' ranch where we planned to spend the night. And by now it was good and dark. I was relying on the horse to keep me on the trail, all the while trying to avoid the branches for fear of losing my glasses. I decided I had to see what time it was, as the time seemed to be passing so slowly, sitting on a horse in the dark. The watch didn't have luminous hands so I laid the reins across the horse's neck and lightly dallied the lead shank from the pack horse on the saddle horn. Removing both a Bic lighter and the watch from my pocket, I foolishly flicked the lighter to see the time. My saddle horse jumped out from underneath me and the pack horse reared back. I tumbled into the short brush and thick grass along the trail, losing both the watch and lighter. I knew I'd hear about this for months to come if I didn't find the watch.

Yvonna was asking me what happened. I told her to catch my horses, which were breaking branches as they moved off to my right along the creek. I then began to search for the watch. Crawling around on my hands and knees, feeling through the grass twigs and gravel, I managed to locate the lighter. I tried using the lighter to help the search but after a few seconds it would burn my fingers. Yvonna by then had caught the horses and tied them up. I gathered up some twigs and dried grass and started a fire so we were able to see a little. After searching some more, the watch was located and I'm sure I kissed it. I never did tell Dad, as he would have enjoyed telling everyone how stupid I'd been.

One weekend in winter Barry Wilwand arrived at the ranch with his ski-equipped plane, as he often did. He already had three girls on board but stopped to pick me up too, as there was a party at Anahim Lake. Well, I never turned down a party, so after I took a quick bath and changed my clothes, the five of us squeezed into his four-seater Stinson. Barry had parked as close as he could to the building. He turned the plane around and we headed east, skimming over the snow, through the drifts and across cattle trails, with full power on. The plane didn't want to lift off (probably due to the size of the load). Finally one of the skis hit a frozen pile of sod that was under the snow by an irrigation ditch and with a very loud bang, it bounced us up enough that we were airborne. With the force we had hit it, Barry figured we had probably knocked a ski off. We gained some altitude and began circling while Barry decided what to do. If the ski was gone, we had to head for Quesnel airport for emergency assistance if we were going to try to land on only one ski. He finally decided we were okay and turned the plane south into the beautiful sunset, all pinks and oranges. We began our climb to clear the Ilgachuz Mountains. Twenty-five minutes later we touched down on the ice of Anahim Lake and everyone was smiling when the skis supported the aircraft and we glided gently across the bay to the glowing lights in the windows of Wright's log house on the lakeshore.

In April Rick came to the Home Ranch riding a Honda dirt bike. This was the first dirt bike in the Blackwater, and it was a great novelty! It also drew a lot of attention. When Rick passed through the Alexises' place, two of the young Indian boys quickly saddled horses and raced behind the motorbike all the way to the ranch. Everyone with the exception of Dad and Ed learned to ride it or at least took one ride. Mom even had a go at it and thought it was fun. When Rob was home on spring break, he was constantly going somewhere on it. Dad thought we were all nuts and gave Rick a hard time about how useless dirt bikes were.

In May, Rick and I went to Anahim Lake for the spring cattlemen's meeting and dance. Actually, we went for the dance—we never did go to the meeting—and we had a good time.

On the way home to the ranch, we camped for the night at Tanswanket Creek at the foot of Woman Hill. In the morning, the team and the saddle horse were gone! One of the team was a horse that Rick had bought in Anahim Lake the year before, so we guessed it had started back towards Anahim, and the other two probably took off for the Blackwater. I took a bridle and halter and started for home, half-expecting to catch up to the two horses, which were on hobbles. Rick went off after the one that went to Anahim Lake.

Several hours later when I reached Irene Lake, I knew the horses must have broken their hobbles and were travelling faster than I was, but I was at the point of no return. Why go back to camp with no horses? So I kept going. I had taken some dried fruit, so I snacked on that and just continued on. Gumboots aren't really the best footwear for walking, and it was hot. My feet sweated and wrinkled up like prunes. I drank water from every clean mudhole that I came to and kept on walking. There were grizzly tracks along the trail and this left me pretty concerned. I sang and whistled as I walked along, hoping this would keep the bears aware of me and off the trail.

By 5 p.m. I had reached the Alexises'—this was a distance of about thirty-five miles, and I was dragging my feet. There was no one home at either the Squinases' or the Alexises', so I walked on down the trail to the crossing of the Blackwater River.

The river was bank to bank with spring runoff water. I sat on the bank fighting off a swarm of hungry mosquitoes and resting my throbbing feet. While I was sitting there, along came an old mare of Peter's. She was about ready to drop a foal, and she had ringbone in both her front feet so bad that it hindered her travel. But I knew she'd swim. She was easy to catch and I crawled onto her back and urged her into the river. Surprisingly, she went willingly and swam downstream to the opposite side and out on the shore. I was so grateful to her that I am sure I told her "thank you" a dozen times while she cropped on the fresh grass.

I took off my boots, poured out the water, wrung out my socks, tied the halter and bridle around my waist and continued on the last seven miles to home. After crossing the hay meadow, I had to cross the creek at the end of Tsilbekuz Lake. This was a spawning ground for the lake trout and also a fishing ground for the bears! With my heart thumping in my chest, and singing at the top of my lungs, I cautiously approached the creek, crossed and moved on with no sign of a bear—thank heaven!

I reached home about 8 p.m. and after a quick bite to eat I collapsed into my bed. The next morning I could barely move. My feet were swollen and my thighs were so sore it was a huge effort to put one foot ahead of the other. Dad took a team and returned to Tanswanket Creek, where he picked up Rick and the wagon. Me, I lay around and recuperated!

We ran horses at Sleepy Hollow and needed some at the ranch, so Kathy Lampert, who was staying with us for a few days, and Rick and I went off after them. The river had dropped, so we were able to cross and hunt the horses on the sidehills. We ran across a black bear there. Rick emptied his rifle at it but failed to kill it, just wounding it badly. Rick selected a solid club and went after the bear to finish the job while Kathy and I watched. Kathy's horse decided that this was a good time to buck her off! Rick was clubbing the bear, Kathy's horse was racing away with reins and stirrups flying, and my horse was snorting and running backwards while I tried to control it and hang onto Rick's horse at the same time!

The summer of 1966 was as busy as the previous summer. Barry Wilwand and Toby Cave flew in and out steadily, and Donnie Redden was often there with his plane as well. Mom spent a good deal of time in Quesnel, as she wasn't feeling well. She had begun to have fainting spells. The doctors couldn't seem to figure what was causing them, but it was clear that she needed a break from the constant cooking, cleaning and ranch work. Her duties fell on me when she was gone, but fortunately Marnie Cave spent a lot of time with us and she was excellent help. When we weren't in the kitchen, we were riding range trying to keep track of the cattle that the bears had scattered. We bought two weaner pigs that summer—the first in the Blackwater. Toby flew them in, tied up in gunnysacks. Ed took care of them and they grew quickly.

Rich Hobson passed away on August 9. Dad didn't find out till much later, but he understood that these things happen. Gone was his partner from the first hard years in the Blackwater country. Time was marching on.

Dad had a love for little horses. While he was at the cattle sale in

Quesnel in October 1966, he spotted a miniature Welsh pony stud for sale. He was a sorrel with some white on his face, weighed 230 pounds and was cute as a button. Dad wanted him, but was too embarrassed to bid on him. Guess it wasn't macho for a grown man with Dad's history to buy a miniature pony. So he talked me into bidding for him, and I got him for fifty dollars and fifty cents! Dad pretended very little interest, but his face glowed with excitement. He had Art Lavington haul him to Nazko, and Louie, as Dad called him, was tied behind the wagon for the trip home to the ranch.

Rob got a kick out of riding Louie. The only problem was that Louie was not popular amongst the other horses—they would kick at Louie. One day while Rob was riding him, Rob got kicked in the arm, which broke. Rick rode to Tsacha Lake Lodge and phoned Bill Lampert, who flew in and took Mom and Rob out for X-rays and a cast, then brought them back home the following day.

Louie was a pain in the butt. If he had been a large horse, he'd have been dangerous. Even at 230 pounds, he was major trouble. Dad had wanted to raise colts, so he built a ramp for the pony to breed the mares, but none of them ever produced a colt. When he was out with the other horses he fought with all of them. How he wasn't ever injured is beyond me. One time he had a large Clydesdale mare by the leg with his teeth and she had hold of him by the neck. Neither one would let go. They crashed around through the brush, squealing at the top of their lungs, which spooked the other horses. Dad thought it was really funny and stood on the sidelines laughing his head off at Louie's antics.

Another time Rick came through the large corral with the team and wagon and Louie ran up to the team, rearing up on his tiny hind legs. He bit one of the workhorses on the throat and wouldn't let go! The team spooked and tried to run, but Rick kept them in a circle and let loose with every swear word he had ever heard. Dad laughed while Louie was dragged along. Hearing the commotion, I went to investigate. I then got a stout club and got close enough to club the pony on his thick head and he finally let go. Dad laughed and laughed. I think Rick was pretty angry although he always controlled himself.

Louie was always interested in females, and it didn't have to be a mare. He would chase the sheep until he ran them down or they

escaped through the fence, scattering and bleating with their bells ringing, lambs darting every which way—it was constant chaos. The poor
milk cow would be lying down, contentedly chewing her cud, and Louie would race up and leap on her. She would scramble to her feet and
start running, with Louie nipping at her flank and squealing. All these
antics amused Dad until one day, when he was bent over in front of the
tack shed, Louie mounted him! That was the end of the stallion: the
next day he was gelded and order was restored to the ranch. But we had
lots of fun afterwards, teasing Dad about how he looked like a mare's
hind end. Dad did not enjoy being the butt of the joke.

I later sold Louie to the Vannoy family, who were then living at
Ivan's old place, for their kids. After Louie had been gone for several
months, he showed up one day as though he had never left. When Murray Vannoy came for him he told us they'd been having a picnic and
Louie decided to help himself to the bowl of salad. He received a rap on
the nose, after which he trotted off and was not seen again. They didn't
realize for several days that he must have made his way back to us.

Dad had received a letter from Ivan Demeniko, asking him to sell
off his cows, horses and equipment. Ivan had been ill for a few years and
now realized that he could never return to the loneliness of his ranch.
Dad and I went looking for his cattle. They'd been out all winter. We
found them near Geese Lake, in the spruce swamp just east of the lake.
There were probably twenty cows. No calves, as the bull had drowned
along with a number of Ivan's other cattle a couple of years before. It
was just as well: if a cow had been heavy with calf, it might not have
done as well.

We drove the cows to Peter Alexis's, corralled them there and then
fed them. The next day we took them on home to the ranch, where Dad
fed them till we could drive them in the fall along with our cattle to
market in Quesnel. The horses and his horse-drawn haying equipment,
sleigh, wagon and a few other belongings were sold locally—mostly to
the Indians. Ivan had lived a very simple life with no luxuries; it had
been a lonely existence and ultimately an unhealthy one.

Ivan's place was sold to the Vannoy family from Montana. They
moved in during the summer with their four small children. They had
no radio, no magazines, no newspapers or books. Their children re-

ceived very little, if any, education. Murray, the father, made regular trips to Anahim Lake, but the family stayed home. They rarely visited or received visitors. Mom and Mrs. Vannoy exchanged letters when Mom sent Murray home with some home-canned preserves in glass jars for her. Mom would wrap the jars in extra newspaper for her to read, and Mrs.Vannoy wrote back and told Mom she really appreciated the contact with the outside world. They lived there a few years, then decided to move farther north to a wild hay meadow on Matthew Creek. They were moving their belongings on a wagon behind their small tractor to their new homestead when the tractor overturned on Murray, killing him. His widow and children returned to Montana.

While raking hay with the team and dump rake, I developed a callus on the palm of my hand from the rake handle. The longer I used the rake the worse it got, until one day it started to swell and a red streak started up my arm. I knew it was blood poisoning. Luckily Toby was visiting with the plane, and he flew me into town. During the trip I sat and watched my arm swell. It was only an hour's flight but the swelling and red streak was up past my elbow by the time we reached the emergency ward at the hospital.

Rob was serious about trapping, even as a young boy. He would order different scents for his traps out of the catalogue from Sidney I. Robinson in Alberta. Some of these scents were extremely rank. Being a bit of a prankster, he took one of the bottles, opened the lid enough for the strong smell to seep out, and set it in the back of a cupboard. As I recall we were just getting ready to sit down to a meal when slight whiffs of the stuff drifted about. Comments were made but we continued eating. Pretty soon it was unbearable, and we all lost our appetites and began looking for the source of the putrid smell. Rob could keep quiet no longer and admitted to his prank, which was very poorly received. The bottle was removed from the house, but it still took an hour before the air was breathable again.

The fall of 1967 was the first year that we didn't take a wagon on the cattle drive. Dad had decided that one pack horse was all we needed. We argued about it for days but he insisted. Rick shod one pack horse, as per Dad's orders. Then I decided we were going to take two pack horses, and I shod one of mine.

Kathy Lampert flew in and came with us on that drive; she was working for the Williams Lake newspaper and was assigned to write an article for them. Herb Carter also came along. We didn't have the comforts that we would have had with the wagon, but we survived, and with less stuff it was easier to pack up and get going in the morning.

The first snow machine races were held in Anahim Lake back in 1968. There were only three snow machines in that first race: my dad's Snow Cruiser, which had a top speed of 22 mph; Floyd Vaughan's twin-track Ski-Doo with a top speed of 25 mph; and Don Baxter's machine. I wasn't at the races but apparently everyone shared the machines and had a good time. My dad didn't like to share but he was put in a position where he couldn't say no. He felt he had to give a detailed explanation each time anyone rode his machine, even if they had ridden it earlier the same day. I think this was the same year that Rob went to Anahim with Dad on homemade skis, skiing behind on a rope for seventy-seven miles because Dad felt his machine would wear out faster if it carried two people.

The Snow Cruiser was a very large, heavy machine. When Dad took it to Anahim Lake the second time, he had to fight his way the whole trip to Lessard Lake, what with all the fresh snow and his own lack of experience. When he arrived at the Holtes' place, he was feeling okay but had some chest pains. Theresa wanted to take him to Anahim Lake with the tractor and sleigh, but Dad, being as stubborn as he was, insisted on driving the machine all the way to Clesspocket the next morning. When he got there, they took him to the nursing station for evaluation and then sent him to the hospital in Bella Coola.

On January 30 I received a call from Bella Coola. Dad had suffered a heart attack and was in the hospital. He was out of danger but would be there for some time. He wanted me to go to the ranch to do the rest of the winter freighting.

The use of snow machines in our country really began in 1968. Ken Karran bought one and came to the ranch, doubling with Bob Cohen over the Ilgachuz Mountains. Back then, these machines were heavy and cumbersome in the deep snow. By the time Ken and Bob reached the ranch, they were exhausted. Bob said it was pretty hard to push the machine when you were in snow up to your neck, pushing with your arms over your head. Don and Marilyn Baxter and Dave and Shirley Benoit rode the next two machines to reach the Blackwater about a week after Ken and Bob, again doubling. They too were exhausted. I believe they returned to Anahim around the mountain. But it was the beginning of a new era.

When snowmobiles began to get popular, being qualified as a real snowmobiler was described to me this way: "Put your hands in a pail of ice water till they're thoroughly chilled, then into a deep freeze, where you take a carburetor apart with only your Leatherman (a multi-tool) and a flashlight with its batteries nearly dead. If you can do this, you probably qualify as a snowmobiler."

CHAPTER 24

Freighting

I flew home from Quesnel after getting the phone call from Bella Coola, telling me my dad was in the hospital there. I promised him I'd do the winter freighting. When I first got back to the Home Ranch, I checked all the horses that were on winter range and weaned some of the thinner colts. I loaded the sleigh box as tight as I could with all the hay I could pack into the box, put my sleeping bag and some grub on top and left for Anahim Lake mid-morning. I stopped at Helen and Andrew Squinas's for tea for a couple of hours and then continued on to Irene Lake. The sleigh trail followed Ulgako Creek from Cottonwood on open brush flats. These are wild meadows, which are much more level than the summer trail in the timber. This route could be used only after freeze-up. The trail went across the middle of Geese Lake, a mud-bottomed lake about a half-mile across. This was also a very popular moose wintering ground. One time, I counted over fifty moose around the lake! I spotted a few on the frozen lake that day, but not many. There was a strong westerly wind blowing and this would make the moose nervous, but there were still a few dotting the landscape as they browsed in the low bush or lay in the snow. They would lie there, chewing their cud, and they'd swing their massive heads to watch as we trotted on by.

I arrived at Irene Lake about an hour before dark, took care of the team and then spent the night in the cabin with Liza and Doggan Leon. They were very concerned about Dad's health, as there was a strong friendship there that spanned thirty-five years. Liza also expressed her concern over me travelling alone. I assured her that I was okay and would be back in five days.

Before I left the next morning in a heavy snowstorm, I put enough hay into a small corral to feed the team on the return trip. From Irene Lake to Rainbow Lake the trail was all in the timber, with a lot of hills. The team slowed down going up the hills, but on the downhill and flats they trotted right along. The heavy snow muted all sounds and vision was poor, but the trail was well broken so the team had easy travelling.

At Rainbow Lake, I turned to the left and took a winter trail that ran along numerous small lakes and sidehills. This trail came out at Eldash, the Holtes' old homestead site. No one had been living there for some time. I found only the dilapidated remains of the cabin and some bits of fencing sticking up through the snow. From there the country opened up into a large swamp and brush meadows for miles. The open country ran right up to the western end of the Ilgachuz Mountains, offering a beautiful view on a clear day. To the right there was another spectacular view—Anahim Peak, and beyond it the Rainbow Mountains.

On a warm, clear day this was the prettiest part of the trip, but on a windy, cold day it could be miserable. The wind has miles to gather speed across the open country, blowing the snow so hard it stings your face. The team hated to face into the wind, and it was windy that day! Snow built up on their blinders and harness; their eyelashes even froze up with icicles. Along their backs some of the snow melted from their body heat and then turned to ice. There was another Holte place farther on, known as Muskeg Meadows. The Holtes still did some haying, and there was a cabin and corrals that were presently deserted. The creek was often open here, showing a shallow, rocky bottom, but today there was still enough ice to hold the team and sleigh. From here on to Lessard Lake there were islands of timber, which gave the free-grazing horses we passed shelter from the winds. The Holtes' horses spent the winter in these swamps, where the red top and slough grasses grew thick, providing good feed. They watched with interest as we passed. Some called to the team, but others never even acknowledged our presence — they just kept pawing away in the deep snow in search of the grasses buried underneath. I overnighted at Lessard Lake.

The third day with the team took me the remaining eighteen miles or so to Clesspocket Ranch. I left the team and sleigh there, caught a ride to town and spent the night. In the morning I put together my load of freight: block salt, chicken feed, and five-gallon tins of lamp gas, kerosene, grain, crushed oats for the team and whatever groceries Mom had on her list. I also made a stop at the post office to pick up a large box of mail and to send off whatever outgoing mail I had from home. Between doing all this, as well as visiting and arranging for someone to haul the supplies to Clesspocket Ranch, the whole day was gone.

On the fifth day I arranged my 1,500 pounds of freight and groceries in the sleigh, taking care to leave anything that would freeze handy to get at and take inside at night. I harnessed up and left for Lessard Lake. The team had enjoyed a day's rest and they were now headed home, so they travelled faster. We travelled mostly in the timber and then crossed a swamp that took us to the shore of Lessard Lake, and from there down the centre of the lake to the Holtes' place. Theresa had been in town, and she came back with me to feed her cattle.

I left the next morning under cloudy skies and mild winds. It was slow from Eldash on, as there were a lot of hills to climb. The team was slowing down by the time we reached Irene Lake. There was no one there when we arrived except hungry cattle and horses. I took care of my team first and then spent the rest of the daylight forking hay to the cattle and horses that followed me out into the wild meadow to the haystack. I forked hay down and scattered it in all directions, allowing them all to feed together.

I then started the fire in the cabin and took the water pail and the axe from the chopping block by the door to open the water holes for my own water and to water my team and Leon's stock as well. There was a creek that wound past the cabin and corrals.

After a late supper, I spread out my bedroll and went to sleep. This was probably the first night that I ever spent without someone else nearby. The owls began their hooting as the moon rose. It shone on the window of the cabin, hitting the floor near my bunk. The trees popped and cracked as the temperature continued to drop. I awoke later to the booming sound of the lake ice as it started to crack from the cold. The team were moving about in the corral. I got up and put some more blocks of wood in the heater. As I lay in my sleeping bag I recalled another time I had been here when the family was all home. It had been a cold night. No one had had the foresight to gather enough wood to get through the night. Someone got up in the night, dressed, went outdoors and started the chainsaw to cut some wood. Sliding the window open, they threw the wood onto the floor, then came in and filled the heater. Needless to say, by then everyone was wide awake!

When I awoke at daylight, the cabin was freezing cold. I quickly started the fire and set the kettle on to make tea, then went out and fed the last of the hay to the team. After tea and some bread and jam, I opened the water holes with the axe and walked to the haystack in the meadow, giving the cattle and horses a generous portion of feed, as it could be days before they were fed again or possibly not until I passed by for my second run. The horses would go pawing for food, but the cattle would be the ones to suffer. When cattle are left for long periods, they will become browsers and will eat brush and poplar bark, and they will follow the creeks eating on their banks where the snow has melted. The strong survive and the weak die. All the cattle in that country were very hardy.

By the time I had watered, fed and harnessed up my team it was snowing hard. I loaded up the groceries that I had taken into the cabin the night before and then covered them with blankets and tarped the whole load. We pulled out into the falling snow, and as the horses were well rested they wanted to trot right along. It was easy going all the way to Peter Alexis's. I stopped at the Squinases' cabin, unhooked the team and led them into the barn, where I forked some hay to them. I then went into the cabin where Helen had tea ready and supper on the stove.

After letting the team eat and rest for a couple of hours, I hooked up and left on the last leg of the journey—seven miles to the Home Ranch. I pulled in at home long after dark to see the lights shining from the windows and smoke curling from the chimney. The dog barked his welcome as he came bounding out to the sleigh, leaping into the air and wagging his tail. Ed came out and took the team to the barn while I unloaded the groceries and mail.

I rested the team for a week before I went again, and this trip was much the same as the first one. Dad was ready to come home, and he wanted his snow machine home too. He felt he wasn't quite up to driving it, so he took the team and I took the snow machine. The machine was a heavy, miserable thing, and of course I had no experience with one either. The snow was wet, the track kept sliding off the centre part of the sleigh trail, and I would get stuck! At least when I was moving I was faster than the team, so I had time to dig it out before the team caught up.

We went from Clesspocket to Muskeg Meadows the first day and stayed the night in the Holtes' cabin. Dad was exhausted—everything seemed to be an extreme effort for him. He was very pale and I was concerned about his health, as it had been only six weeks since his heart attack. I felt that he shouldn't be going back to the bush so soon. As we lay in our sleeping bags, I listened to his breathing and to the night birds. I finally fell asleep and woke to dead silence! I couldn't hear Dad. I jumped from my bunk and reached for his still form in the other bunk. I shook him, and was relieved to hear, "What, what, Jesus Christ! Go to sleep!"

We got home with no further problems, and a few days later I was on the trail again, back to Anahim Lake. It had begun to thaw a lot and the south-facing hills were free of snow. I had sharp-shod the team, and it was a good thing that I had. The swamps between Eldash and Muskeg Meadows were all ice. The team trotted along, the empty sleigh skidding first one way and then the other. I just barely made it to Clesspocket, as the snow had melted off the roads, leaving ice or bare ground.

There was no time to spend a day in Anahim Lake. This was a trip for fuel for the tractor. The box of the sleigh was filled with ten-gallon drums of diesel fuel. I was in a hurry to get home. The sun beat down, the creeks ran water on top of the ice and the team often broke through the trail and slipped off it. I did okay on the return trip till I hit the south-facing hills between Rainbow Lake and Irene Lake—they were more than my team could manage. The poor horses could drag the heavily loaded sleigh only so far up the bare hills. When they couldn't go any farther, I had them stand still. I would unload the sleigh, and then drive the team to the top of the hill, tying them up. Going back down I would roll each barrel up to the top and load it back into the sleigh! This had to be done three times. When I finally reached the Leons' cabin at Irene Lake, I was exhausted.

When I unhooked the team, the horses tried to rub their sweaty heads on my shoulders, nearly knocking me down. After caring for them, I went into the cabin and, once again, no one was home. I emptied the pockets of my jeans onto the floor, lay down on a bunk, pulled my sleeping bag over me, and fell asleep immediately.

Sometime during the night I heard some sounds and knew that something else was in the cabin, but I was too tired to come fully awake or to care. It was dawn when I finally awoke. Every muscle hurt and my stomach was telling me I had missed supper. When I looked about, I realized that the coins, pocket knife, lighter and cigarettes that I had dropped on the floor the previous night were gone! My watch wasn't taken. After searching about, I found a few cigarettes and some coins, but I never did find my little pocket knife or lighter. I knew then that the visitor had been a packrat.

I left as soon as I had eaten and harnessed the team. I wanted to catch as much of the little bit of frost that I could. I was able to avoid unloading the drums of fuel again by taking other trails that had been cut out around hills in previous years. I got home late that night. It was the end of using the sleigh that spring.

CHAPTER 25

The Last Cattle Drive

In June of 1969 an American by the name of Bob Anthony flew in and made Dad an offer to buy the Home Ranch. For five summers the bears had been killing cattle. A total of seventy-three carcasses had been found; how many we didn't find, we'll never know. Dad's heart attack made him think seriously about a different life. Mom's health was failing and her arthritis was getting worse. Life on the ranch was becoming more difficult for her all the time, and she was spending more and more time in Quesnel. I was spending a good six months of the year away from the ranch as well. Dad decided to accept the offer.

Ed Adams, who had become like family after spending nine years with us, had bought the Sleepy Hollow property, so he was somewhat secure. Dad and Rick went together and bought the property at Tsetzi Lake for a future hunting camp base and a fly-in fishing resort. (Rick and I had built a cabin beside the lake four summers before, so there was at least one cabin there.) The hunting camp would be run only from April till November. After that, Rick would go logging and Dad would go to Quesnel, where Mom wanted to live.

Floyd and Laura Vaughan and John and Mari Lou Blackwell had moved into the country about this time. They were west of the Home Ranch at Moose Lake and Rich Meadow, which had been one of the Frontier Cattle Company holdings at one time. Floyd had an airplane, so he and Laura were often visitors at the Home Ranch, and quite often

John was there as well. They had a Cat bulldozer, so Dad made plans with them to build an airstrip at Tsetzi Lake the following summer.

Towards fall, a CBC film crew contacted Dad about filming the cattle drive. Since this would be our last drive, it had to be done that fall. Dad loved the attention and posing for the camera. He was up early in the mornings, and he would wrangle the horses before sun-up when the ground was still white with frost and a person's breath was like steam on the cold, crispy morning. The fog was so thick in the early morning that it looked as though the horses were coming out of the clouds! Once that part of the footage was filmed, Rick was the one sent out early to do the wrangling.

I guess because the documentary was about Pan Phillips, everyone else stayed in the background and away from the cameras. Gayle had come along for the drive—this was her first—and Rob also accompanied us. I was the cook and chuckwagon driver. Mom stayed home, although they did give her a few minutes of footage. The producer was Mike Poole, the cameraman was Norm Rosen and the soundman was John Seale. The drive was aired on CBC television on a show called *This Land of Ours*.

The footage was eight hours, uncut. Mickey Dorsey saw it when she visited the CBC studio in Vancouver. She was given the opportunity to view the entire footage before they began cutting it down to approximately twenty-six minutes for the show that was finally aired on TV. What they ended up with was a short documentary, narrated by John Foster of the CBC. John says, as he saddles up a horse, "A soft life! Only Pan Phillips would call it that, and if you didn't know him any better you might believe it. But if you wanted the real story you'd have to saddle up a horse in Quesnel, BC, and ride west for two hundred miles. Pan Phillips will beat you at poker, tell you awful lies and drink your liquor, and then—if he really likes you—he might take you on a cattle drive, perhaps the last real drive in North America. Back in 1934 Pan Phillips and his partner, Rich Hobson, came north from Wyoming looking for grassland. They crossed the mountains into little-known country in the Chilcotin northern plateau, and here beside a meandering stream they built the Home Ranch." (Here they show an aerial shot of the ranch.)

The film then shows Dad in the early morning mist bringing in the horses for the day's work on the ranch. The horse bells are tinkling and Dad occasionally yells as the horses appear and fade away, going the wrong way—but this is for the camera. Dad swings his lasso as he rides by. There is a shot or two of Ed on the hayrack with the team, and also Rick is shown dumping a load of hay. Dad is on the tractor just briefly and Mom is in her garden cutting a cabbage for dinner. The narrator comments that she is raising a fine garden of vegetables to have with the moose and venison meat that are the mainstay of our daily diet.

There is a shot of Dad shoeing horses—he did do this at one time, but he had long since passed the chore on to the younger generation. He said it was a soft life, and if he could do it all again, "he'd do the same damn thing." So, if he spoke the truth to the camera, he was happy with his life the way it had been. Over the years I heard him say more than once that the country was easy for men, but hell on horses and women!

The CBC crew even gave my cat Jackie footage! She was sitting on the log fence, watching the horses run by. One of the best scenes was of Dad, Rick and Gayle riding east away from the corrals and the barn and facing into the camera. The Ilgachuz Mountains rise in the background looking like the Grand Tetons of Wyoming. They could never be called grand but here they are spectacular. The camera zooms in on a frost-covered saddle and the narrator mentions the early hour that the cowboys are in the saddle.

Young Rob rides after the cows and, like Dad, he is very photogenic. He is filmed catching rainbow trout in a pool at the end of Squirrel Lake and then walking back to camp along the sidehills with their beautiful autumn colours, swinging his mess of fish on a forked willow hook.

They filmed the time that the horses were "spooked in the night" and got away—the team and four saddle horses. Dad and I rode out, hunting for the horses. Rob went looking also and Gayle stayed in the camp. On the second day, I found the horses and we were able to move on.

There were some good scenes at the abandoned Indian village at Kluskus. Dad was filmed entering the Catholic church. The statues of Jesus and the Virgin Mary were still there, but there was a bird's nest on Joseph and Mary, and Joseph and Jesus were all covered with bird droppings! The camera also caught the graveyard with its hand-carved fences and little spirit houses and the old granite headstones.

One scene is of us all standing around the campfire with our collars turned up against the rain that was dripping off our hat brims from a fierce thunderstorm that was going through. The last shots were the cattle crossing the Coglistiko River west of Nazko. Most people we talked to enjoyed the film, and of course it brought another flood of fan mail!

But then there are the real stories behind the scenes. A lot of the filming was done before we left the Home Ranch. People don't usually notice the little things, like extra riders or different horses. I was an extremely difficult actress. I felt if you wanted the "real story," then it should be the real story! The producer and I clashed often, and I wouldn't do a lot of the scenes. There was nothing in it for me anyway, and it did make for a lot of extra work. Dad was in seventh heaven with the filming and always wanted to hold centre stage. So it may have looked like a happy annual picnic, but there was a lot of tension. I don't think that there was a scene that I smiled in.

Dad received the most camera time, but then again, he was the celebrity! He referred to the drive as the annual picnic and some of the things he said were: "A cowboy was a sheepherder with his brains knocked out." "There was no sickness in the country; if there was you died." He said he rode to Quesnel once in three days, but he was awfully thirsty. He said he had a woman once (he was referring to his second wife, Shorty) who he took to the Blackwater with a rope around her neck. She didn't stay long because their views were different. He was selling the ranch "because there was no one to carry on. Some of the kids liked it, but they couldn't get along with the old man." Then he'd laugh.

In the documentary they say the horses spooked during the night, but in actual fact it was mid-afternoon at Kluskus. The cattle had grazed and bedded down, the team was unharnessed and hobbled. All the saddle horses but two were hobbled, but they were still saddled. Two were tied in camp. Rob had a good supply of firecrackers burning a hole in his pocket, and he set them off all at once—just for a joke! All hell broke loose: cattle were on their feet and running, and the horses left camp at a great speed. Horses that are used to hobbles can travel for short distances at a very fast speed. Of course these horses were used to the hobbles so they soon disappeared from sight!

Then the main concern was the cattle, which by now were racing up the sidehills raising a great cloud of dust. No one paid much attention to which direction the horses headed. Dad and I leapt onto the two remaining horses, which were badly spooked. They were hard to mount running sideways but we hit the saddles and loped after the cattle. We crashed though the thick underbrush and downed poplars. Luckily the country opened up and we were able to head the cattle off and return them to the flat below camp. After some time they stopped panting and settled down to graze. We had a big problem: the other horses had to be found, but we couldn't leave the cattle. Rob was sent out on foot after the horses (he was not too popular in camp just then!). Gayle and I thought it was funny but Dad and the filming crew didn't find it funny at all. We were short four saddle horses and the team! Rob's horse had a rifle in the scabbard on the saddle and Dad ranted on about this. Dad was stressed with only two horses. He had to deal with a film crew, a herd of cattle, a grub wagon with no team and three children who giggled privately amongst themselves.

Darkness fell with the horses not having been found and still no one knowing for sure which direction they had gone. Rob with his tracking experience was pretty sure that they hadn't gone in the direction of home. With Squirrel Lake to the southwest and extremely steep hills to the northwest, there wasn't much area left in between to look and Rob had covered this area well, so we had to concentrate our search in an easterly direction.

At daybreak the following day Dad rode one of the saddle horses and, with Rob travelling on foot, they moved the cattle to Lashaway Chantyman's place, which was four miles farther on. There, they could be put behind a fence. I took the other horse and began searching along Kluskus Lake and the bench land above the lake. When Dad returned from moving the cattle, he went hunting horses. Rob went as well and he had already walked eight miles! We hunted the hills till dark.

Gayle cooked and entertained the CBC crew, who had a lot of time on their hands. This was probably when they filmed the statues in the church, out of utter boredom. There are only so many things that a person can do in camp!

The day passed and night came. I had ridden all day with no sign of the horses, and Dad had not found anything either—no tracks on the trails or along the lakes—places where hobbled horses should have gone for water and feed or if they were thinking about heading home. The next morning I rode the higher country between the Blackwater River and the lakes. It didn't seem likely that hobbled horses could have gone up such steep hills that were so full of deep ravines and a lot of downed spruce and poplar as thick stands of timber. The undergrowth was thick also, with lots of rose bushes and fireweed, but surprisingly a lot of feed as well. I found their tracks up there and followed them, climbing all the time. The tracks were difficult to follow, but I now knew where they were. I was about three-quarters of the way to the top of the Kluskus Hills when I met the horses coming down! They were still hobbled and the saddles were in place, including the rifle. It appeared that only one saddle blanket was missing. They had found plenty of feed but no water, and this is what had started them down through the jungle of windfall— they were thirsty!

I tied my saddle horse to a tree, removed the hobbles from all of them, tailed three together and turned three loose. Getting back on my horse, I headed back to camp. There was a lot of smiling when I arrived with the six missing horses! It didn't take us long to break camp, load up the wagon and move the few miles down to Lashaway Chantyman's. That day would have been our day for a layover, so we were still on schedule.

Several days later we were on the banks of the Coglistiko River for a lunch stop. The cattle grazed down the trail ahead of us, picking up what they could find to eat. The film crew decided to film the scenes needed for the horse-hunting back at Kluskus. Of course I did my best to make things difficult, stating that the country was different, I wasn't riding the same horse or wearing the same clothes—anything to avoid the camera. I got on my horse and lay back over the saddle with my head hanging down over the horse's rump. Norm took footage of that. Finally I rode down the hillside by the river while they filmed, just to keep them happy! Mike told me that when the credits were shown at the end of the documentary, he'd put my face there, upside down over the horse's rump! Well, that didn't happen. Dad's face appeared instead—better than a horse's ass!

When we reached the end of the drive it was a sad time. We realized that this was the last drive that we would do as a family. Even though Mom was not with us, Dad, Gayle, Rob and I were together on this last drive. Our lives would change forever the following May when the new owners took over the ranch. What I didn't know then was that I would spend the next thirty-four years living a very similar life only seven miles from where I was raised. But that's another story!

Glossary

Airplane Lake: Cluchuta Lake, called Airplane Lake because many airplanes land there.

Bullet lighter: A lighter made in the shape of a large-calibre bullet.

Bunting (to bunt): What a calf does when it bumps the cow's udder with its nose.

Cantle: The raised, curved part at the back of a horse's saddle.

Corduroy: Logs laid side by side in muskeg to form a path or road.

Derrick poles: Long poles fixed in an upright position to act as a crane, used to stack loose hay.

Doubletree: A piece of hardwood used to harness two horses to a wagon; in the centre is a hole for a pin to attach to the wagon tongue or sleigh tongue.

Galled: Sore, chafed.

Glassing (to glass): Scanning the surroundings with binoculars [in hunting].

Hames: Metal piece of the horse's harness that fits around the collar to which the traces are attached.

Ilgachuz Mountains: Also known as Elgatcho, Ugatcho, Algak Mountains.

Irene Lake: Also known as Island Lake or Tilgatgo Lake.

Nicker: Neigh or whinny.

Pack string: Several horses loaded with packs.

Punching: Logs that are split in half and laid on the stringers of a roof.

Rowel: A spiked revolving disk at the end of a spur.

Sharp shod: Shod with horseshoes with metal grips on the bottom to prevent slipping on ice.

Singletrees: Two pieces of hardwood attached to the doubletree to which the traces are attached with chains and hooks.

Snake fence: A fence made of stacked logs that zigzag and are notched.

Snub: To check the movement of a horse, especially with a rope wound around a post or saddle horn.

Stooks: Small piles of loose hay in a field.

Stringers: In the framework of a roof, the horizontal supports connecting the uprights.

Traces or tugs : Side straps by which a horse is attached to a wagon or sleigh; the traces connect the hames on the horse's neck collar to the singletree on the wagon.

Ulkatcho Reserve: Also known as Ulgatcho Reserve.

Wagon tongue: The pole by which a wagon (or sleigh) may be steered or held back.

Index